Promoting Active Citizenship

Karl Henrik Sivesind · Jo Saglie
Editors

Promoting Active Citizenship

Markets and Choice in Scandinavian Welfare

Editors
Karl Henrik Sivesind
Institute for Social Research
Oslo
Norway

Jo Saglie
Institute for Social Research
Oslo
Norway

ISBN 978-3-319-55380-1   ISBN 978-3-319-55381-8 (eBook)
DOI 10.1007/978-3-319-55381-8

Library of Congress Control Number: 2017943650

© The Editor(s) (if applicable) and The Author(s) 2017. This book is an open access publication.
Open Access This book is licensed under the terms of the Creative Commons Attribution 4.0 International License (http://creativecommons.org/licenses/by/4.0/), which permits use, sharing, adaptation, distribution and reproduction in any medium or format, as long as you give appropriate credit to the original author(s) and the source, provide a link to the Creative Commons license and indicate if changes were made.
The images or other third party material in this book are included in the book's Creative Commons license, unless indicated otherwise in a credit line to the material. If material is not included in the book's Creative Commons license and your intended use is not permitted by statutory regulation or exceeds the permitted use, you will need to obtain permission directly from the copyright holder.
The use of general descriptive names, registered names, trademarks, service marks, etc. in this publication does not imply, even in the absence of a specific statement, that such names are exempt from the relevant protective laws and regulations and therefore free for general use.
The publisher, the authors and the editors are safe to assume that the advice and information in this book are believed to be true and accurate at the date of publication. Neither the publisher nor the authors or the editors give a warranty, express or implied, with respect to the material contained herein or for any errors or omissions that may have been made. The publisher remains neutral with regard to jurisdictional claims in published maps and institutional affiliations.

Cover illustration: VIEW Pictures Ltd/Alamy Stock Photo

Printed on acid-free paper

This Palgrave Macmillan imprint is published by Springer Nature
The registered company is Springer International Publishing AG
The registered company address is: Gewerbestrasse 11, 6330 Cham, Switzerland

Preface

Who should operate our social services, and how are service contracts to be distributed and managed? These are among the most important social issues today. In Scandinavia, there is little disagreement that the public should pay for the most important services in education, health, and social services. However, there is considerable variation in how welfare is delivered and managed among the Scandinavian countries. Sweden has gone further in terms of the introduction of user choice and vouchers, reducing barriers to establishment of new service institutions, and allowing distribution of profits. This has created a strong growth incentive in the profit-oriented enterprises offering welfare services. Denmark, and to some extent Norway, have by comparison a stronger element of nonprofit providers.

In our opinion, the welfare mix is too important to be left to chance. The public, nonprofit and for-profit welfare providers each have advantages as well as disadvantages. The composition of the welfare mix should, therefore, be deliberately designed in order to maximise these advantages. There may be political disagreement about the goals of welfare policies, but we nevertheless need knowledge about the consequences of the welfare mix to get a fruitful political discussion.

This was the starting point for our research project *Outsourcing of Scandinavian Welfare Societies? Consequences of Private and Nonprofit Service Provision for Active Citizenship*—which led to the publication of this book. The project was funded by the Research Council of Norway's programme on *Welfare, Working Life and Migration* (VAM) and directed by Karl Henrik Sivesind at the Institute for Social Research (ISF) in Oslo, Norway. However, the project has been a truly Scandinavian comparative effort. An extensive data collection has been carried out in selected case municipalities in Denmark, Norway, and Sweden. We would like to thank Malene Thøgersen (Denmark), Håkon Solbu Trætteberg (Norway), and David Feltenius (Sweden) for their work with data collection and documentation. This work also constitutes the basis for Trætteberg's Ph.D. dissertation, *Does Welfare Mix Matter? Active Citizenship in Public, For-Profit and Nonprofit Schools and Nursing Homes in Scandinavia* (2016).

Many individuals and institutions have provided valuable help and comments during the process. We wish to thank the contributors to the book for all the work they have done in writing their chapters, as well as their valuable comments at project meetings. We would also like to thank Prof. Lars Skov Henriksen at the Department of Sociology and Social Work, Aalborg University, for his contributions to the coordination of the Danish part of the project.

We were lucky with the timing of this project. All the Scandinavian countries had to implement a new EU directive for public procurement in 2016. We therefore got many invitations to present findings about changes in the mix of welfare service providers and about why there are differences between the Scandinavian countries. The Enterprise Federation of Norway, *Virke*, with a department for nonprofit service providers, arranged a large conference in January 2016 together with Nordic sister organisations. A panel of Scandinavian Ministers and MPs responded to Sivesind's presentation of new findings from this project. Later there were meetings with the Red–Green government parties and then the opposition parties in Sweden; in August there were meetings with the Norwegian conservative government parties and their parliamentary support parties at a 'Perspective Conference'. We also met with experts writing public investigations about nonprofit welfare providers in

Norway (NOU 2016:12) and Sweden (SOU 2016:78), just to mention some examples. It was a great experience to see that our research could inform debates about issues high on the political agenda.

Earlier versions of several of the book chapters have been presented at international conferences, including the 24th Nordic Local Government Research Conference, Gothenburg, 26–28 November 2015, and the 12th ISTR (International Society for Third-Sector Research) Conference, Stockholm, 28 June–1 July 2016. We thank the participants at these and other conferences and seminars for valuable comments.

Finally, we would like to thank the Research Council of Norway for the funding of the project, and our home institution, the Institute for Social Research, Oslo, for hosting this project in the best possible way and for supporting the open access publication of this book.

Oslo, Norway   Karl Henrik Sivesind
December 2016   Jo Saglie

Contents

1 Does Out-Contracting of Welfare Services Promote
  Active Citizenship? 1
  Karl Henrik Sivesind and Håkon Solbu Trætteberg

2 The Changing Roles of For-Profit and Nonprofit
  Welfare Provision in Norway, Sweden, and Denmark 33
  Karl Henrik Sivesind

3 Education and Elderly Care in Denmark, Norway
  and Sweden: National Policies and Legal Frameworks
  for Private Providers 75
  Signe Bock Segaard and Jo Saglie

4 Towards a More Diversified Supply of Welfare Services?
  Marketisation and the Local Governing of Nursing
  Homes in Scandinavian Countries 117
  David Feltenius

5 Local Governing of Schools in Scandinavia—Between
   State, Market and Civil Society   159
   Malene Thøgersen

6 Active Citizenship in Scandinavian Schools
   and Nursing Homes   203
   Håkon Solbu Trætteberg

7 Does the Type of Service Provider Affect User
   Satisfaction? Public, For-Profit and Nonprofit
   Kindergartens, Schools and Nursing Homes
   in Norway   261
   *Tord Skogedal Lindén, Audun Fladmoe
   and Dag Arne Christensen*

8 The Future of the Scandinavian Welfare Model:
   User Choice, Parallel Governance Systems,
   and Active Citizenship   285
   Karl Henrik Sivesind, Håkon Solbu Trætteberg and Jo Saglie

Author Index   311

Subject Index   317

About the Editors

Karl Henrik Sivesind is Research Professor at the Institute for Social Research, Oslo, Norway. He is currently manager of the project 'Conditions and Impacts of Welfare Mix' funded by the Norwegian Research Council, and he is leader for Work Package 'Elaboration and Testing of Impact Indicators' on the project 'Third Sector Impact—The Contribution of the Third Sector to Europe's Socio-economic Development' funded by the EU's 7th Framework Programme. He has studied changes affecting civil society by analysing data from population surveys and local association surveys as a part of the activities of Centre for Research on Civil Society and Voluntary Sector in Oslo/Bergen. He has also been involved in several comparative research projects about the nonprofit sector and welfare services.

Jo Saglie is Research Professor at the Institute for Social Research, Oslo, Norway. His main research interests include party organisations and intra-party democracy, local elections and local democracy, as well as indigenous politics. His publications include the coedited volume *Indigenous Politics: Institutions, Representation, Mobilisation*; as well as articles in *Journal of Elections, Public Opinion & Parties*; *Local Government Studies*; *Regional and Federal Studies*; and *West European*

Politics, among others. He is currently directing the Norwegian Local Election Study and the Norwegian Sámi Parliament Election Study, and he participates in several research projects on Norwegian local government and politics.

List of Tables

Table 1.1	Characteristics of the selected municipalities	21
Table 1.2	Selected municipalities and institutional sectors of the non-public institutions	24
Table 2.1	Paid employment in the welfare services in Scandinavia, total and sector shares (%)	39
Table 2.2	Service areas included in ICNPO main categories	42
Table 2.3	Paid employment in the nonprofit, for-profit, and public sectors within education, health, and social services in Denmark 2008–2013, full-time equivalents and percent	44
Table 2.4	Shares of paid employees in the nonprofit, for-profit, and public sectors within education, health, and social services in Sweden 2007–2013	47
Table 2.5	Paid employment in the nonprofit, for-profit, and public sector within education, health and social services in Norway 2006–2013, full-time equivalent employment and percent	51
Table 2.6	Paid full-time equivalent employment in the nonprofit sector in the welfare field in Norway 2006–2013	52
Table 3.1	Ideal models of government in public welfare production	77
Table 5.1	Analytical framework	164
Table 5.2	Elements of control in the local governing of schools	177

Table 5.3	Elements of competition in the local governing of schools	184
Table 5.4	Elements of collaboration in local governing of schools	190
Table 6.1	Active citizenship, dimensions, and empirical indicators	211
Table 6.2	Active citizenship in the nursing home sector	224
Table 6.3	Active citizenship in the school sector	238
Table 6.4	Key variations in nursing homes and schools	240
Table 7.1	Share of public, nonprofit and for-profit providers (institutions)	267
Table 7.2	User satisfaction by public or private service providers: Kindergartens, primary and secondary schools, and nursing homes. Unstandardised coefficients (OLS)	273
Table 7.3	User satisfaction by public, for-profit and nonprofit service providers: Kindergartens, primary and lower secondary schools, and nursing homes. Unstandardised coefficients (OLS)	275

1

Does Out-Contracting of Welfare Services Promote Active Citizenship?

Karl Henrik Sivesind and Håkon Solbu Trætteberg

Introduction

In the 1980s, Swedish welfare researchers travelled the world to present the Scandinavian social democratic model at conferences. The model represented a 'modern' alternative to the market economy and socialism, combining generous benefits and economic equality with high labour force participation for both women and men. However, the downside quickly became apparent: high taxes and swelling public debt. The transfer value to other countries was in question since the trend inspired by Thatcherism and Reaganomics was to cut taxes and slash public budgets. Was the model at all sustainable with an ageing population? But even as an economic crisis hit Scandinavia in the early 1990s, the welfare model did not die—it was transformed.

K.H. Sivesind (✉) · H.S. Trætteberg
Institute for Social Research, Oslo, Norway
e-mail: k.h.sivesind@socialresearch.no

H.S. Trætteberg
e-mail: h.s.tratteberg@socialresearch.no

In the new millennium, the Scandinavian countries—Denmark, Sweden and Norway—seemed to be on their way to overcoming at least some of the inherent problems of their welfare model. In a special issue in 2013, *The Economist* even presented the Nordic countries as 'the next supermodel' because they had reduced public debt and spending as shares of GDP, simplified and lowered taxes, and built pension systems on a solid foundation that made automatic adjustments for longer life expectancy, while at the same time developing open, innovative and knowledge-intensive economies. Furthermore, the Scandinavian countries have high levels of happiness and well-being (Helliwell et al. 2016) and social trust (Ervasti et al. 2008; Rothstein 2003) and navigated the 2008 global financial crisis better than almost everyone else. Norway had oil income invested in a sovereign fund and no public debt, but the other Scandinavian countries did not have such advantages. According to *The Economist*, there are compelling reasons to pay attention to these small countries on the edge of Europe: '… they have reached the future first. They are grappling with problems that other countries too will have to deal with in due course, such as what to do when you have reached the limits of big government and how to organize society when almost all women work. And the Nordic countries are coming up with highly innovative solutions that reject the tired orthodoxies of left and right'. Of particular interest is the fact that the Swedish public school system now has vouchers and for-profit schools competing with public schools. 'When it comes to choice, Milton Friedman [the neoliberal American economist] would be more at home in Stockholm than in Washington, DC', claimed *The Economist*.

Changes in the Swedish welfare model are indeed profound. In the early 90s, Sweden probably had the highest proportion of public welfare service employment of any of the West European countries. The nonprofit share was just 2% (Lundström and Wijkström 1997; Sivesind and Selle 2010). This was a result of a huge political project to fight poverty and inequality by building the most modern welfare state in the world. Popular movements and voluntary organizations supported this venture, to a surprising degree also when it implied handing over their welfare service institutions to the state. The historian Lars Trägårdh claims Swedish people's home (*folkhemmet*) built on a social contract between what was perceived as a strong and good state and equal and autonomous individuals, liberating them from traditional, paternalistic and oppressive institutions—'the family, the neighborhood, the churches, the charity organizations' (2007, 27–28). But it was not all harmony, the large state was challenged from the conservative and communitarian critics, and even on the left-wing there was a concern that the citizens were becoming passive clients and that the state was unresponsive and bureaucratized. All groups argued for a stronger civil society (Trägårdh 2007).

Reforms intended to reduce the Swedish welfare state were implemented. First, from 1991 to 1994, the conservative government gave the country's municipalities the opportunity to introduce competition and choice models. The social democratic government, from 1994 to 2006, did little to slow down this development. With the centre-right coalition, from 2006 to 2014, the reforms gained momentum again, in particular with the passing of a law on public procurement (Public Procurement Act, LOU 2007: 1091) and user choice (Freedom of Choice Act, LOV 2008: 962). Political reforms intended to empower individuals with the opportunity to choose welfare providers were introduced in more and more service areas, in combination with a more liberal system for approving new service institutions and no restrictions on extracting profits.

However, the expanding quasi-market for welfare services ultimately strengthened the profit-oriented welfare sector rather than civil society. State-funded welfare contracts in Sweden attracted private investments and venture capital, even from abroad. The welfare reforms stimulated strong commercial growth with a transformative effect. For-profit companies increased their number of employees from 90,000 to 236,000 between 2000 and 2013 and became 2.5 times larger. Their share of welfare employees rose from 9 to 19%, while the nonprofit share remained extremely low, at 3%, and the public sector share decreased from 88 to 78% (see Chap. 2). If the goal was to shrink the large welfare state, then the process was successful. However, perhaps unintentionally, private expansion to a large extent resulted in institutions owned by a small number of welfare conglomerates, with some of their owners situated in tax havens. What happened to the small, independent service units owned by local, responsible entrepreneurs, cooperatives or idea-based, nonprofit organisations? Sweden, the global exemplar for moderation, turned their welfare system completely around, from maximising public provision to welcoming international for-profit welfare investors (Henrekson and Jordahl 2012). Reforms signalled by the new centre-left minority coalition government in 2014 focused on counteracting some of the negative side effects of marketising welfare rather than stopping profit extraction. A widespread assumption seems to be that economic incentives are a necessary part of the restructuration process and that in any event, it is very difficult to stop the transfer of profits. Owners may not extract profits from year to year, but instead generate a surplus by buying and selling institutions or shares in welfare service units, or by paying more than market price for services or property rented from other companies they own. However, Sweden never seriously attempted to stimulate the expansion of the smallest nonprofit welfare sector in the EU, with the exception of former Eastern Bloc countries (Salamon and Sokolowski 2016). Massive goodwill from all political parties and a Compact (*Överenskommelsen*) between the Swedish Government and idea-based social organisations and service providers inspired by the UK were not enough (Johansson and Johansson 2012).

The legal establishment of user choice as a universal value, which is currently being introduced step by step in the Swedish welfare system, is just one example of old principles being sacrificed in order to improve the Scandinavian welfare system. Market mechanisms are being used in new ways to create progress in the welfare state. This was not part of the Scandinavian model promoted by welfare researchers in the 1980s as 'politics against markets' (Esping-Andersen 1985). Now, quasi-markets and tools inspired by New Public Management (NPM) have been widely implemented in all Scandinavian countries, but in slightly different ways (Kristiansen 2016). Surprisingly, this does not mean that the core welfare goals have been replaced. The policy documents still highlight deep-rooted Scandinavian ideals, such as public funding and regulation of core welfare services, decentralisation of governance, equal access for all to high quality services and the adaptation of services to user needs and preferences. However, there is also a willingness to innovate in order to better reach these goals. It is not always easy to see how market-emulating forms of governance can be the most suitable means to reach these goals. Maybe we are witnessing a change of welfare goals by means of governance reforms? When the role of the state changes from securing the equivalent quality of services for all to providing opportunities for choice, the responsibility for the results of the social policy shifts to the users, who make choices for themselves (Newman and Tonkens 2011). The Scandinavian eagerness in welfare reform results in large, rapidly evolving differences between the countries and between the service areas. In effect, Scandinavia has emerged as a laboratory for different welfare reform experiments; a proving ground for solving problems that other countries will also encounter in the future. The main approach in this book is therefore to compare the consequences of different forms of governance in three countries with shared welfare goals such as equivalent service quality and active citizenship.

The changes in Scandinavian welfare services based on public funding will be analysed in this book mainly by comparing the countries, service areas, and for-profit, nonprofit and public sectors. Each chapter will focus on different levels in the governance structure: laws and regulations at the national level, governance in municipalities and service institutions in elderly care and schools, and, finally, the consequences experienced by the users of the services. Which combinations of governance structures, service sector providers and user choice give the best results when it comes to promoting active citizenship? To set the stage for the following chapters, we will present the key service areas of schools and nursing homes and some of the key dilemmas facing Scandinavian welfare societies today; we will also describe how these issues will be analysed in this volume. To understand why it matters who provides welfare services, we use the concept of *active citizenship* active citizenship, which is subsequently explained. We then delve into theories about the fundamental differences between the public, nonprofit and for-profit sectors. Since we examine publicly financed welfare services, the institutional sectors will vary depending on how the state governs each service; therefore, it is also necessary to evaluate the role of the most important governance tools. Lastly, we give a brief overview of the different chapters in the book.

Comparing Service Areas and Sectors

The special issue of *The Economist* that focused on Nordic countries was particularly concerned with the voucher system, which lets private schools compete with the public system. However, Sweden is emerging from an era marked by very strong public sector domination in its welfare provision and is, in fact, a latecomer among the Scandinavian countries when it comes to private alternatives and choice in education. In Denmark, 15% of students attend private schools in a user-choice system that has existed for 150 years. The free schools are nonprofit organisations that receive financial support from the government but have few legal restrictions on the educational content. Norway has a similar but less liberal system for nonprofit private schools. Only 7% of students in upper secondary education, and 3% in lower secondary and primary education, attend private schools. In order to obtain public funding, these schools must offer alternative pedagogies or ideologies which are not offered by the public school system. However, at the same time, the core curriculum must be equivalent to that of public schools. In Sweden, teaching in private and public schools is subject to the same laws.

In other words, all three countries offer a type of voucher system and the right to choose private schools, instead of the public default option offered to all. The main difference is that in Sweden, for-profit businesses are allowed to run schools, while on paper there is less room for distinctive alternatives to the public system as there is in the other Scandinavian countries. This is the kind of 'experiments' that makes a Scandinavian comparison so interesting. The development of a Swedish system where 'Friedman would be at home', as *The Economist* put it, begs the question of whether this system is compatible with the ideals of a Scandinavian welfare model. Swedish school results, for median pupils as well as low and high performing pupils, have deteriorated more than any other country in OECD's PISA enquiry. Moreover, the difference between high and low performing students has increased: a troubling trend in light of the legal and normative foundations of the Scandinavian welfare model (Böhlmark and Holmlund 2012). This raises the question of whether better opportunities to choose schools have resulted in the separation of high and low performing pupils; and if so, whether this has had negative consequences for school results in general and for equal access to high quality education for all in particular. The social background has a very strong influence on how selective parents are, as well as their children's school results, and this may be the reason for increasing social differences in the Swedish voucher system. Perhaps the liberal free schools of Denmark or the more unitary school system of Norway, with fewer but more distinctive alternatives, is better suited to Scandinavian welfare ideals Put another way, what are the best methods for promoting active citizenship: nonprofit alternatives catering to special interests and needs, or competition over shares in a more standardised school market? The importance of governance, the roles and shares of the public, nonprofit and for-profit sectors for distinctive service profiles and active citizenship in compulsory schools, will be examined by Thøgersen and Trætteberg in this book's empirical chapters.

To obtain a contrast with schools, we will compare them with elderly care nursing homes, a service area that is also the responsibility of municipalities in all three Scandinavian countries. In this area, municipalities can decide to contract services out to commercial or nonprofit institutions, and the public administration generally has a much stronger influence over the allocation of users to service providers. Sweden has an increasing number of for-profit institutions, while Denmark has a long tradition of self-owning institutions, which are, in practice, nonprofit foundations. Norway not only has the most dominant public sector but also some traditional nonprofit providers owned by voluntary or religious foundations or associations. Recently, however, the country's nonprofit share has decreased while the for-profit share has grown (Statistics Norway 2016). All Scandinavian countries are moving away from the traditional framework agreements with private service providers, which would have been automatically renewed, and towards open tenders and user choice. Still, most municipal administrations are working hard to promote an equivalent quality of services to all users at all types of institutions. The use of quasi-markets and NPM tools has greatly expanded since the 1980s (Meagher and Szebehely 2013), as it has in other service areas. The question is whether this has changed the situation of users in relation to the institutions and municipalities. Since governance structures and the space for distinctive services are more limited in nursing homes for elderly care than they are in schools, we will compare the service areas to explore the consequences for users and their representatives. We can learn from such differences, not just those between countries but those between service areas as well.

The Scandinavian countries have chosen different tools of governance for influencing the mix of public, nonprofit and for-profit provisions. In general, quasi-markets with different combinations of competition, public certification and NPM-steering have become more widespread. However, Sweden has chosen what Ascoli and Ranci (2002, 6–9) would call a 'demand-based model', with user choice and simplified rules for the establishment of private services that can receive public funding. Norway has to a larger extent a 'supply-side model', with competition for public contracts occurring both within the public system and between public, nonprofit and for-profit providers. Denmark has a well-established but more liberal model of user choice, where local nonprofit alternatives flourish. At the same time, in all of the Scandinavian countries, citizenship rights and participation in the welfare field have been reinforced legally and through new best practices and professional standards (Rostgaard 2015).

The Concept of Active Citizenship

The balance between governance and user influence is critical in the Scandinavian welfare model. Services are not only influenced by voters through the electoral channel. The public administration and the welfare services it runs should also be directly responsive to affected citizens (Andersen and Hoff 2001; Petersson et al. 1989). When market-emulating tools of government have been implemented broadly and the dominance of the public sector in the service provision has been reduced or challenged, it is important to understand how different governance tools and types of providers affect the responsiveness of the institutions.

Historically, the Scandinavian social democratic approach to welfare has been that public dominance in all aspects of service provision is necessary in order to insulate citizens from the harmful effects of market forces. The public provision of services thus became a method for the collective creation of a new, democratic welfare society (Blomqvist 2004, 430; Sejersted 2011, 120–121). Indeed, the goal was to create services of such high quality that they would gain the support of citizens from all walks of life. Rothstein (1994) labelled this 'the high quality standardised solution': where nearly equal welfare services were allocated to all citizens via bureaucratic planning. This was not just important for reducing poverty and social inequality but was also considered crucial for the legitimacy of a system of welfare services funded by taxpayers.

In addition, the gradual establishment of citizens' rights meant that individuals were no longer forced to appeal for core services, but could demand them with some degree of authority. The combination of democratic control of services and strong citizens' rights are central aspects of what has been called a Scandinavian form of citizenship (Andersen and Hoff 2001; Hernes 1988). The decentralisation of influence is an essential tool used to reach the ideals of advanced social rights and equality. An implication of the decentralisation of influence is that it places decisions about service provision as close as possible to individuals and thus gives them influence over their own situations (Andersen and Hoff 2001).

On the input side, i.e. in the electoral democracy, important services such as care and education are a governmental responsibility. However, 'welfare municipalities' are in charge of important services that affect people's lives (Kröger 1997; Kjølsrød 2005; Loughlin et al. 2011, 11). Decisions about these services are made by local policy makers, who are closely connected to citizens. On the output side of the democratic process, Scandinavian citizenship entails that citizens who use services also have the power and right to influence the implementation of policies. This is where active citizenship is pursued: either collectively through user boards or individually when relatives of nursing home users seek to obtain a certain approach to care or parents request special follow-ups from their children's school.

Active citizenship is an analytic concept we use to examine the amount of control that citizens have over their everyday lives as users of public services. Their level of control is based on their citizenship role—the distribution of rights and obligations. To control their lives as users of public services, citizens need to have influence. More influence means more control, but absolute control can hardly occur in real life. If obligations are forced upon citizens who receive services, then this is the opposite of influence and entails a lack of control.

In the research literature, active citizenship is a contested concept with no shared definition. Different scholars have emphasised the issue of obligations in divergent ways. One approach sees active citizenship as 'a broad range of activities that promote and sustain democracy' (Hoskins 2014, 14). These activities include political participation in formal politics, but also involve activities situated in the workplace, civil society and the private sphere (Hoskins and Mascherini 2009; Holford and van der Veen 2003). Furthermore, Newman and Tonkens (2011) emphasised increased obligations for users as an aspect of the agency of citizens, as they used the term active citizenship to explain why responsibilities for services are transferred from the state to the citizens. These obligations can take the form of care for oneself or for relatives; and in the quasi-market, citizens are expected to be market actors who influence the welfare sector by giving market incentives, like enter and exit, to providers.

For our specific purposes, we have developed a conception that enables us to evaluate whether the citizenship roles of users vary by type of service provider. In the chapter by Trætteberg, the operationalisation of active citizenship as it is used in the empirical analysis is further elaborated. Here, it is sufficient to present the definition and the main dimensions. Put briefly, the concept of active citizenship reflects three main actors involved in deciding the content of a public service when a citizen becomes a user: the user, the staff and the administrators and local politicians at the municipal level. The user can influence a public service by meeting with staff and institutional leaders or via changes obtained in interactions with leaders at the municipal level.

With this analytic concept, one can assess local political processes and governance of institutions as well as day-to-day interactions between users and staff members and collective forms of user control via user boards and related media. The concept of active citizenship thus brings attention to formal as well as informal ways of influencing services and, accordingly, the implementation of public policies. Active citizenship encompasses the activities users can engage in when assessing where to become users—at their institutions, in local policy processes and in their communities—in order to influence the service in question.

The active citizenship of users of public services is the ability citizens or their relatives have to actively control their own lives while being users of public services. Active control can be exercised prior to becoming a user or while being a user. Both choice and voice are important instruments for practicing active citizenship (Hirschman 1970). More specifically, in this book, three dimensions of active citizenship are used to analyse differences in the capacity for active citizenship for users—and their next of kin—of public, for-profit and nonprofit welfare services: *choice, empowerment* and *participation*.

With its three dimensions, active citizenship is an analytic perspective that enables us to measure aspects of users' experiences with welfare services. At the same time, it is an ideal type to which an empirical reality can be compared to see if high or low levels of active citizenship are observed along its three dimensions.

Fundamental Sector Differences

New tools in the governance of Scandinavian welfare may alter the relationship between the welfare states and their citizens as well as the composition of the welfare mix. By welfare mix, we refer to the division of public, nonprofit and for-profit providers in a service area. Often, the concept of the welfare mix also includes families or other informal providers, but this book focuses on publicly funded service institutions; and in Scandinavian welfare, this means that the focus is placed on professional providers. However, as we will see, families and relatives can be important contributors to these services as volunteers by exercising active citizenship together with or on behalf of the users. The importance of changes in the composition of the mix of welfare service providers depends on the substantive differences between different institutional sectors. Economic theories of nonprofit organisations try in principle to answer the question of why we need the third sector when we have a market and a state. In order to do this, these theories identify essential aspects of each of the institutional sectors and explain why and how they are different (Steinberg 2006; Salamon and Toepler 2015). These aspects are general, theoretical features of the institutional sectors and their relevance in a Scandinavian context varies according to how the states govern the providers in the different service areas. To understand the consequences of the use of particular governance tools and changes in the welfare mix, it is necessary to grasp the differences between institutional sectors at a general level.

A key expectation relates to creating a complete selection of service profiles for the population. Citizens are an increasingly diverse group with respect to culture, religion, ethnicity and so forth, and thus it is becoming increasingly difficult to create services tailored to individual citizens (Phillips and Smith 2011). Governments may lack the knowledge, capacity and coordinative ability to create a diverse enough system to cover the entire population. In addition, the public sector has a tendency to centre its attention on the median voter and majority groups in society and thus overlook the interests of marginal groups. For-profit providers offer services to the largest market segment, which is not so different from the public sector's emphasis on the median citizen. Consequently, there is a gap in services for minority populations: a gap the nonprofit sector is well suited to fill (Weisbrod 1978). By directing services toward smaller niches in the population, nonprofit compensate for the lack of breadth in public and for-profit providers' offerings in terms of quality, special needs, interests, methodology, ideology or beliefs (Smith and Grønbjerg 2006, 224; Clemens 2006). In Scandinavian countries, nonprofit welfare providers are funded by the state and are thus presumably vulnerable to the decisions of the majority. Yet, in the multi-party system, the minority groups catered to by at least some of the nonprofits are represented by parties who see nonprofits as their tool to provide services to their minority constituencies. In this way, nonprofits give breadth to the range of services while simultaneously being part of core services in some service areas.

In welfare services, great information asymmetry exists between providers and users. Users often have bad health, and the complexity of the services makes it impossible for one user to acquire the same expertise as professional providers. Therefore, the ability for users and society to trust providers is decisive (Hansmann 1980). The less information users have, the more important it is for them to be able to trust the service provider. This applies both to users and public regulators, as there are limited opportunities for monitoring the quality of this type of service (Evers et al. 1997). Weisbrod (1988) proposed distinguishing between quality indicators that are easy to observe and assess and those that are difficult to observe and assess. Different market participants have different incentives to prioritise the two different forms of quality. A profit-oriented provider typically has an incentive to achieve high measurable quality; but if doing so reduces profits, this same provider will have an incentive not to devote resources to having high unobservable quality (Hansmann 1987, 29). Nonprofit providers do not have the same disincentive to allocate resources to improve invisible quality (Salamon and Toepler 2015, 2168). In the Scandinavian context, Meagher and Szebehely (2013) have argued that tight regulation is a reason why increased plurality in the welfare mix in elderly care has led to limited differences in quality. As this volume demonstrates, however, conformity in quality limits the ability to achieve the supposed benefits of an expanded range of service content that would stem from plurality in the welfare mix. This demonstrates some of the difficult trade-offs authorities face when regulating the welfare mix.

The potential benefits of nonprofits when it comes to trust and broadening the scope of public services can help explain their functioning in the welfare mix. Yet, it is an all but universal Western phenomenon that the state shoulders the main responsibility for welfare but cooperates with nonprofit and for-profit providers in solving social and economic problems (Salamon and Toepler 2015, 2161). To understand the persistence of this phenomenon, Salamon (1987) developed the theory of interdependence. Its guiding principle is that each of the three sectors has strengths and weaknesses, with the strengths of one sector to some extent compensating for the weaknesses of another.

In spite of the supposed benefits of nonprofit provision, such providers also have some potential weaknesses that make them unsuitable as the only type of provider. Their central weakness is that they do not have sufficient growth capacity to produce all of the services people want. They do not have access to capital from investors, and they tend to focus on their care mission rather than on its expansion. Furthermore, the research literature holds that they are particularistic since they adapt their services to small groups and do not reach out to the whole population. Finally, they are accused of being paternalistic, providing services with a special vision for the community in mind rather than accommodating the visions of the users or of society at large (Salamon 1987).

For-profit providers complement the strengths and weaknesses of nonprofits. Their ability to quickly scale up to serve large portions of the population is highly valued by Scandinavian policy makers. This capacity has been particularly demonstrated in kindergartens in Norway as well as in many service areas in Sweden. Nevertheless, when left unmonitored, for-profits have potential weaknesses: They may produce too few of the services parts of the population needs. If the financing of providers is based on user payments, then their services may be priced at a level often too expensive for much of the population, thereby limiting access to them. In addition, as mentioned previously, they have public trust issues (Anheier 2005, 181–182).

The public sector aims to compensate for the failures of the for-profits. When for-profits do not provide enough of a service, the public sector can provide the service itself, as in the traditional Scandinavian model. To ensure affordable prices for the population, the government can pay for the service through voucher systems or subsidies. To remedy the lack of trust, public authorities can regulate the service and provide increased information flow to users (Steinberg 2006).

However, public authorities cannot fully compensate for the failures of the for-profits. The government tends to adapt the service it provides in-house to the median citizen. This makes the range of services inadequate for citizens who want a particular quality of service, or who, for various reasons, want a type of service content that differs from the majority's preferences. Furthermore, lack of trust is often based on key aspects of health and care services not being readily observable (Steinberg 2006). The government can thus encounter difficulties regulating something it does not know much about, rendering their efforts at best incomplete. These weaknesses of the state are addressed by nonprofits that cater to niche populations at the same time as their motivations provide different incentives from those of for-profits (Anheier 2005, 129–131).[1]

Consequently, the state pursues widespread cooperation with other providers in the welfare mix. Since the state cannot reach an optimal service level by providing all services in-house, and since nonprofit and for-profit providers are dependent on public financing and steering, the three sectors are interdependent. The theory of interdependence in the welfare provider mix has set the agenda for extensive research on the three institutional sectors and how they solve different tasks (Steinberg 2006). Much of the empirical work has been done thus far in an American context, where the relationship between the sectors is different from that of Scandinavia, in particular, when it comes to sources of funding. That said, the theory has a general scope, which suggests that the mechanisms it describes may also be active in a Scandinavian context.

Governance Through Contracting or User Choice

Because of the perceived differences between institutional sectors, most countries have policies to manage the composition of welfare service providers (Boris and Steuerle 2006; Lundbäck and Lundberg 2012). Yet, given that there are differences between public, for-profit and nonprofit providers, these differences are not static. Different contexts and conditions may increase or decrease differences.

How the Scandinavian context creates conditions that affect the prominence of these differences is a central theme in this book. This dynamic is based on the established literature, which holds that within a contractual regime with the public sector, nonpublic providers may lose much of their distinctiveness (Salamon and Toepler 2015, 2169; Toepler 2010; Salamon 2002). However, there is an important difference between supply-based and demand-based financing of nonpublic service providers (Ascoli and Ranci 2002, 6–9). Supply-based financing involves the privatisation of the provision of services. The idea is that the state wants to change how services are supplied to the public by transferring management responsibility from a public agency to a nonpublic entity. This form of financing makes small alterations in the relationship between citizens and providers, but enables the state to make demands of potential providers who are seeking to become suppliers of services.

Demand-based financing means that the state wants to change the demand structure of the provision by enabling citizens to act as market customers by selecting their own providers. The changes sought from this type of financing are thus intended to influence providers by making changes in the relationship between citizens and providers.

Supply-based privatisation of the provision of services has a tendency to weaken nonpublic distinctiveness. Particularly, relevant examples are public tenders. This form of provider privatisation contributes to their commercialisation and promotes innovation related to management and organisation, not to the actual content of the service (Goodin 2003, 390–391). Tenders whereby nonprofit and for-profit providers compete on equal terms may lead the nonprofit to adapt the for-profit operational logic in order to remain competitive (Haugh and Kitson 2007).

Demand-based financing takes place when the users themselves choose an institution. As long as the public sector funds the service provider, it will be dependent on approval from public agencies; once this has been obtained, it can compete to attract users. Within this regime, market mechanisms to some extent replace public regulation. Since users are able to opt in and out of different institutions, it is not necessary for the government to impose the same level of regulation as it does when all users are forced to use the same institutions. The idea is that institutions whose services are not good enough will be uncompetitive and will thus be eliminated from the quasi-market. In this way, only institutions with an acceptable level of services remain, as the market does the job that the state must do when market forces are not allowed to function. This gives the different providers the increased ability to develop distinct characteristics as long as these are in accordance with users' preferences (Ascoli and Ranci 2002). Whether this happens depends on the heterogeneity of citizens' demands and the diversity of providers. For example, a multi-religious population can include schools which cater to different religious groups, each with their own distinct approach to school operations. Supply diversity is thus an empirical question for each context.

Outline of the Book and Its Chapters

To answer the question about the importance of the use of market-emulating governance tools and changes in the mix of welfare service providers, we compare between countries; between nonprofit, for-profit and public sectors; and between schools and elderly care as different service and policy areas, each with different governance models. We focus on how different ways of organising services on different levels of the Scandinavian welfare system affect the users in order to reveal which factors may promote active citizenship. We have selected cases that will allow for comparison across the three analytic dimensions:

1. *Country*: Denmark, Sweden and Norway. Traditionally, within the Scandinavian model, Sweden and Norway have focused on strengthening the legal rights of citizens as users, while Denmark has in addition actively used nonprofit actors to enhance user choice as a tool for citizen empowerment (Andersen and Hoff 2001). Lately, there has been some convergence, as all countries have prioritised more user choice (Segaard 2015, and Chap. 3) despite more divergence in the composition of the welfare mix (Sivesind, this volume). Since 2000, Sweden has moved towards empowerment through marketisation, with a rapidly growing for-profit share in the welfare mix. In this way, one could say that the three Scandinavian countries currently have three different strategies when it comes to the promotion of active citizenship (Sivesind 2013, and Chap. 2). The three Scandinavian countries thus represent some interesting institutional differences regardless of similar welfare ideals. Methodologically, comparisons between the countries are useful for assessing under what circumstances the conclusions may have relevance.
2. *Institutional sector*: public, nonprofit and for-profit providers. Does it make a difference which of them provides services? It is still an open question whether traditional coordination by municipalities, reforms promoting user choice or marketisation is the best-suited means to achieve active citizenship.

3. *Service area: Schools and nursing homes.* These two service areas are suitable for comparison since, as pointed out in the introduction, each has a different position in the Scandinavian welfare model. To compare them in light of the welfare mix and active citizenship is thus useful for understanding how changes in the former could potentially have different implications in different areas of the welfare model. At the same time, they are both core areas of municipal welfare services with different positions in the current political debate. The school sector is experiencing a conflict whereby liberal ideas about the rights of parents to choose schools with different content or better quality and to opt out of bad schools are challenging adherence to the 'unitary school', in which equality and social integration are given emphasis (Arnesen and Lundahl 2006). In the nursing home sector, the debate has focused less on variation in the content of care and more on the most efficient means to obtain sufficient care capacity with acceptable quality. In addition, the structure of governance is different. In schools, there is considerable national regulation with regard to the content of services (Helgøy and Homme 2006; Rönnberg 2014); while for elderly care, more of the decisions regarding the content of care are left to the municipalities (Vabo 2012).

What makes the Scandinavian countries particularly suitable for this kind of analysis is that they have similar welfare models and ideals but have chosen different governance tools to create changes. The welfare systems in the three countries are moving in such different directions that it resembles a natural experiment. This means that there are lessons to be learnt for other countries that are in the process of reshaping their welfare services while giving high priority to an active role for service users.

In the next two chapters of this book, we look into developments in these countries, sectors and service areas at the *national level*. In Chap. 2, Karl Henrik Sivesind analyses changes in shares of welfare service employment between the for-profit, nonprofit and public sectors on a national level in the three countries. The data are gleaned from national statistical agencies, public policy documents and studies of particular services in each of the Scandinavian countries. In Chap. 3, Signe Bock

Segaard and Jo Saglie discuss the national legal and institutional framework within which local welfare services are provided: the relevant EU directives and their implementation, national policy instruments and national politics.

In Chaps. 4, 5 and 6, David Feltenius, Malene Thøgersen and Håkon Solbu Trætteberg analyse data from comparative case studies at the *municipal level*—where policies for schools and elderly care are implemented. Seven municipalities—three in Norway, two in Sweden and two in Denmark—were selected for matched case studies using similar data-gathering strategies and interview guides. The data come from three types of sources: interviews with users, staff and leaders at the institutions as well as the political and administrative leadership in the municipalities; local user surveys; and local strategic documents. In total, 27 institutions were studied in the seven municipalities. Within each municipality, two institutions were selected from each service area: one public and one nonpublic. For more information about the methodology used in these chapters, see the appendix to this chapter.

The chapters written by Feltenius and Thøgersen focus on governance in the municipalities and the service institutions in elderly care and schools, as well as the consequences for distinctive profiles and equivalent service quality. Chapter 4 by Feltenius analyses municipal governance of nursing homes, comparing the three Scandinavian countries in addition to in-house, public sector service providers and private service providers (nonprofit or for-profit) in the same municipalities. Chapter 5 by Thøgersen examines schools in a similar fashion. Chapter 6 by Trætteberg compares the two service areas, schools and nursing homes with regard to active citizenship. Trætteberg asks whether the manner in which services are governed and the institutional sector the service provider belongs to make a difference for users. Where do we find the most important differences: between the countries, between providers from different sectors or between the service areas? What are the causes for these differences?

In Chap. 7, Tord Skogedal Lindén, Audun Fladmoe and Dag Arne Christensen analyse Norwegian population surveys about user satisfaction in elderly care institutions, child care and primary schools in order to obtain a more generalisable view of the consequences for users of private and public service provisions. In the concluding chapter, Sivesind, Trætteberg and Saglie discuss the lessons that can be learnt from the 'natural experiments' in the welfare service provider mix, institutional contexts and governance tools in Scandinavian welfare services. These lessons may also be relevant for other countries facing similar social and economic challenges while pursuing goals of equal access to high quality services funded by the government.

Appendix: Methods and Data Collection

Comparative Case Studies

Since the same methodology and data are used in Chaps. 4, 5 and 6, a shared presentation follows. The data were collected in order to make comparisons across each of the analytic dimensions presented above. The institutions studied operate at the municipal level in each country under examination. The strategy was therefore based on selecting municipalities whereby pairs of public and nonpublic institutions could be compared within the same context.

Twenty-seven institutions were selected in seven municipalities: three municipalities in Norway, two in Sweden and two in Denmark. The most important criterion in the selection process was that the municipalities had providers from different institutional sectors in both nursing homes and schools. In order to obtain findings that were as robust as possible, we used a strategy incorporating a diverse selection of municipalities that was beneficial 'where different combinations of variables are assumed to have effects on an outcome' (Gerring 2008, 651). In this case, variations were assessed in terms of geographic location and the status of municipalities as either urban or rural. In addition, we considered the political leadership of each municipality and identified particular characteristics within the municipalities which were relevant to the study. Table 1.1 provides the main characteristics for each of the selected municipalities. Since municipalities cannot be selected in a way that standardises all relevant characteristics, there were some unavoidable idiosyncratic features of the municipalities under study that need to be

Table 1.1 Characteristics of the selected municipalities

Municipality	Total number of schools and nursing homes	Political affiliation (at the time of data collection)	Relevant characteristics
Denmark			
Faaborg-Midtfyn Population: 50,953 (2015)	13 public schools 15 nonprofit schools 10 public nursing homes 1 nonprofit nursing home	A social democratic majority was in power at the beginning of the data collection period. After the 2013 elections, a liberal-conservative (Venstre) majority came into power	Faaborg-Midtfyn is a rural municipality situated on the island of Funen. It stands out as a municipality with a large share of students attending nonprofit schools (29%)
Herning Population: 86,864 (2015)	31 public schools 8 nonprofit schools 10 public nursing homes 5 nonprofit nursing homes	Liberal-conservative (Venstre) throughout the data collection period	Herning is a small town located in Jutland whose borders encompass a large geographic area Herning has a large number of nonprofit nursing homes
Sweden			
Östersund Population: 59,485 (2012)	35 primary schools, 4 of which are private (2 for-profit, 2 nonprofit) 22 nursing homes, 15 of which are public and 7 of which are for-profit. Östersund has a municipal policy that 25% of nursing homes	Social democratic majority	Östersund consists of a small town and surrounding rural area that covers a large geographical region. It is located in northern Sweden

(continued)

Table 1.1 (continued)

Municipality	Total number of schools and nursing homes	Political affiliation (at the time of data collection)	Relevant characteristics
Sollentuna Population: 66,859 (2012)	should be run by non-public providers 36 primary schools, 17 of which are private (only 2 are nonprofit; the rest are for-profit). 27% of the students in private schools 10 nursing homes, 7 of which are for-profit and 3 of which are public. The public nursing homes are run by a publicly owned company that is intended to function as a private unit	The town's mayor is affiliated with the Conservative Party, leading a centre-right majority in the city council	Sollentuna is one of the municipalities in Sweden that has gone the furthest towards introducing market mechanisms in the care sector and adheres strictly to an ordering–performing model Sollentuna is a suburb of Stockholm, Sweden's capital city
Norway			
Asker Population: 60,106 (2016)	24 public schools 3 nonprofit schools 4 public nursing homes 1 for-profit nursing home	Conservative majority	Asker is a wealthy municipality in the suburbs of Oslo, Norway's capital city. Asker is one of the first Norwegian municipalities to have a for-profit nursing home

(continued)

Table 1.1 (continued)

Municipality	Total number of schools and nursing homes	Political affiliation (at the time of data collection)	Relevant characteristics
Steinkjer Population: 21,781 (2016)	12 public schools 1 nonprofit school 3 public nursing homes 1 nonprofit nursing home	Centre-left coalition	Steinkjer consists of a small town and surrounding rural area that covers a large geographic region. It is located in the Trøndelag region of central Norway
Løten Population: 7588 (2016)	5 public schools 1 nonprofit school 1 public nursing home that was not included in this study	Labour Party majority	Løten is a rural municipality with no variation in terms of the nursing home sector; therefore, only schools were investigated

reported. The column labelled 'Relevant characteristics' presents idiosyncratic information for each municipality.

Within each municipality, we applied the matching case design strategy (Dunning 2010, 289–290). We selected two institutions from each service area: one public and one nonpublic. These institutions are complex organisations comprising a number of attributes that can together produce a given outcome. Therefore, we tried to minimise diversity between the selected institutions in each of the municipalities. In order to achieve a control effect for such attributes to better grasp variations stemming from the service sector, we limited diversity in terms

Table 1.2 Selected municipalities and institutional sectors of the non-public institutions

Country	Municipality	Nursing home	School
Denmark	Faaborg-Midtfyn	Nonprofit and public	Nonprofit and public
	Herning	Nonprofit and public	Nonprofit and public
Sweden	Östersund	For-profit and public	For-profit, nonprofit and public
	Sollentuna	For-profit and public	For-profit and public
Norway	Asker	For-profit and public	Nonprofit and public
	Steinkjer	Nonprofit and public	Nonprofit and public
	Løten	N/A	Nonprofit and public

of size, the socioeconomic circumstances of users and geographic location. Obviously, in real life, no two institutions are sufficiently similar to achieve complete control, something we consider in the qualitative case analysis. Table 1.2 lists the municipalities and institutional sectors of the selected institutions.

Data Collection

The data were derived from three types of sources: (1) interviews with users, staff and leaders at the institutions as well as interviews with the political and administrative leadership of the municipalities; (2) local user surveys; and (3) local strategic documents. Before collecting the data, we developed a field guide that specified which sources of data were relevant. The field guide detailed what kinds of documents and local user surveys should be collected and analysed, as well as who to interview. It also contained interview guides that were used to conduct semi-structured interviews with all groups of interviewees. When appropriate, one could add extra questions in each country.

In all cases, the interviews were conducted with one or two administrative leaders in the municipalities and with one or two political leaders. Because of this, we were not always able to cover the whole range of political views, but we nonetheless tried to select key informants with the best insights about the institutions from the perspective of the municipality. In all cases, we interviewed the leader of the institutions in question. From the staff, we selected the safety representative or leader of the local union. This was done in order to avoid self-selection, i.e. that the leader of the institution could pick who our interviewees should be and was based on the expectation that these staff members would be more informed than the average colleague. To gauge user opinions, we formed focus groups with either part of the user boards or the user boards as a whole. We tried to take into account that these users, by virtue of their seat on the user board, potentially had more personal resources than the average user. It must also be pointed out that the user boards in nursing homes mostly consisted of the users' relatives, not the users themselves. The same situation occurred in the investigated schools, where parents constituted the majority of users on the user boards. In some instances, people who the case study revealed to have potentially interesting perspectives were also interviewed. For example, the leader of the council for the elderly in one municipality was interviewed, as was the leader of a municipal-level council for school parents in another municipality. In total, we conducted 35 interviews in Denmark, 21 in Sweden and 57 in Norway.

Local user surveys were conducted by the municipalities. They were designed differently for each municipality and some municipalities did not have them at all. They are therefore not useful for making comparisons between municipalities; but in some instances, they are useful for making comparisons *within* municipalities. The surveys were thus not only used for procuring background information prior to conducting interviews, but also served as an independent source of information about user views. This is the only data source for Chaps. 4–6 where the opinions of a large number of users are represented. The substantial survey material used in Chap. 7 thus complements the approach taken in Chaps. 4–6.

The local strategy and policy documents include documents covering municipal policies pertaining to the service areas or general approaches to user influence. In addition, we obtained the corresponding documents at the welfare institutions. Not all of the institutions had formal steering documents; but when they did, this information was used to triangulate interview data and user surveys. In the analysis, concurrence between different sources gave robustness to the observations, while divergence between different sources indicated that further investigation was needed, for example, by including specific questions about contested topics in the interviews.

Note

1. Studies from Norway have shown that, generally, volunteer organisations enjoy more trust in the population than their public sector or for-profit counterparts (Wollebæk et al. 2000, Fig. 2–11).

References

Andersen, Jørgen Goul, and Jens Villiam Hoff. 2001. *Democracy and citizenship in Scandinavia*. New York: Palgrave Macmillan.

Anheier, Helmut K. 2005. *Nonprofit organizations. Theory, management, policy*. Oxon: Routledge Milton Parks.

Arnesen, Anne-Lise, and Lisbeth Lundahl. 2006. Still social and democratic? Inclusive education policies in the Nordic welfare states. *Scandinavian Journal of Educational Research* 50 (3): 285–300.

Ascoli, Ugo, and Costanzo Ranci. 2002. The Context of new social policy in Europe. In *Dilemmas of the welfare mix. The new structure of welfare in an era of privatization*, eds. Ugo Ascoli and Costanzo Ranci, 1–24. New York: Kluwer Academic/Plenum Publishers.

Blomqvist, Paula. 2004. The choice revolution: Privatization of Swedish welfare services in the 1990s. *Social Policy & Administration* 38 (2): 139–155.

Böhlmark, Anders, and Helena Holmlund. 2012. *Lika möjligheter? Familjebakgrund och skolprestationer 1988–2010*. Institutet för arbetsmarknads—och utbildningspolitisk utvärdering (IFAU): Uppsala.

Boris, Elizabeth T., and C. Eugine Steuerle. 2006. *Nonprofits & government: Collaboration & conflict*. Washington, DC: Urban Institute Press.

Clemens, Elisabeth S. 2006. The constitution of citizens: Political theories of nonprofit organizations. In *The nonprofit sector: A research handbook*, eds.

Walter W. Powell and Richard Steinberg. New Haven, Conn.: Yale University Press.

Dunning, Thad. 2010. Design-based inference: Beyond the pitfalls of regression analysis? In *Rethinking social inquiry: Diverse tools, shared standards*, eds. David Collier and Henry E. Brady, 273–312. Lanham, Md: Rowman & Littlefield.

Ervasti, Heikki, Torben Fridberg, Mikael Hjerm, and Kristen Ringdal. 2008. *Nordic social attitudes in a European perspective*. Cheltenham: Edward Elgar.

Esping-Andersen, Gøsta. 1985. *Politics against markets. The social democratic road to power*. Princeton, NJ: Princeton University Press.

Evers, Adalbert, Riitta Haverinen, Kai Leichsenring, and Gerald Wistow. 1997. *Developing quality in personal social services. Concepts, cases and comments*. European Centre Vienna: Ashgate.

Gerring, John. 2008. Case selection for case-study analysis: Qualitative and quantitative techniques. In *The Oxford handbook of political methodology*, eds. Janet M. Box-Steffensmeier, Henry E. Brady, and David Collier, 645–684. Oxford: Oxford University Press.

Goodin, Robert E. 2003. Democratic accountability: The distinctiveness of the third sector. *European Journal of Sociology* 44 (03): 359–396.

Hansmann, Henry. 1980. The role of nonprofit enterprise. *Yale law journal* 89 (5): 835–901.

———. 1987. Economic theories of nonprofit organization. In *The Nonprofit Sector: A Research Handbook. The Independent Sector: A Research Handbook*, ed. Walter W. Powell, 27–42. New Haven: Yale University Press.

Haugh, Helen, and Michael Kitson. 2007. The third way and the third sector: New labour's economic policy and the social economy. *Cambridge journal of economics* 31 (6): 973–994.

Helgøy, Ingrid, and Anne Homme. 2006. Policy tools and institutional change: Comparing education policies in Norway, Sweden and England. *Journal of Public Policy* 26 (02): 141–165.

Helliwell, John F., Richard Layard, and Jeffrey D. Sachs. 2016. *World happiness report, update*, vol. I. New York: Sustainable Development Solutions Network.

Henrekson, Magnus, and Henrik Jordahl. 2012. Vinster och privatiseringar i landet Lagom. *Respons* 1 (2): 12–18.

Hernes, Helga M. 1988. Scandinavian citizenship. *Acta Sociologica* 31 (3): 199–215.

Hirschman, Albert O. 1970. *Exit, voice, and loyalty: Responses to decline in firms, organizations, and states*. Cambridge, MA: Harvard University Press.

Holford, John, and Ruud van der Veen. 2003. *Lifelong learning, governance and active citizenship in Europe*. Brussels: European Commission Project HPSE-CT-1999–00012.

Hoskins, Bryony L. 2014. Active citizenship. In *Encyclopedia of quality of life and well-being research*, ed. Alex C Michalos, 14–16. Springer Netherlands.

Hoskins, Bryony L., and Massimiliano Mascherini. 2009. Measuring active citizenship through the development of a composite indicator. *Social Indicators Research* 90 (3): 459–488. doi: 10.1007/s11205-008-9271-2.

Johansson, Håkan, and Mairon Johansson. 2012. From a 'Liberal' to a 'Social democratic' welfare state: The translation of the english compact into a Swedish context. *Nonprofit Policy Forum* 3 (2). doi:10.1515/2154-3348.1057.

Kjølsrød, Lise. 2005. En tjenesteintens velferdsstat. In *Det norske samfunn*, eds. Ivar Frønes and Lise Kjølsrød, 184–209. Oslo: Gyldendal akademisk.

Kristiansen, Mads Bøge. 2016. One scandinavian approach to management by objectives and results? *Scandinavian Journal of Public Administration* 20 (1): 45–70.

Kröger, Teppo. 1997. Local government in Scandinavia: Autonomous or integrated into the welfare state? In *Social care services: The key to the Scandinavian welfare model*, ed. Jorma Sipilä, 95–108. Avebury: Aldershot.

Loughlin, John, Frank Hendriks, and Aanders Lidström. 2011. Introduction. In *The Oxford handbook of local and regional democracy in Europe*, eds. John Loughlin, Frank Hendriks, and Aanders Lidström. Oxford: Oxford University Press.

Lundbäck, Mattias, and Anders Lundberg. 2012. *Varför är det så få idéburna organisationer i välfärden?*. Stockholm: Tillväxtverket.

Lundström, Tommy, and Filip Wijkström. 1997. *The nonprofit sector in Sweden, The Johns Hopkins nonprofit sector series*. Manchester: Manchester University Press.

Meagher, Gabrielle, and Marta Szebehely, eds. 2013. Four Nordic countries—four responses to the international trend of marketisation. In *Marketisation in Nordic eldercare: A research report on legislation, oversight, extent and consequences*, eds. Gabrielle Meagher and Marta Szebehely, Stockholm: Department of Social Work, Stockholm University.

Newman, Janet, and Evelien Tonkens. 2011. *Participation, responsibility and choice: Summoning the active citizen in western European welfare states*. Amsterdam: Amsterdam University Press.

Petersson, Olof, Anders Westholm, and Göran Blomberg. 1989. *Medborgarnas makt*. Stockholm: Carlssons.

Phillips, Susan D., and Steven Rathgeb Smith. 2011. Between governance and regulation. Evolving government—third sector relationships. In *Governance and regulation in the third sector: International perspectives*, eds. Susan D. Phillips and Steven Rathgeb Smith. New York: Routledge.

Rönnberg, Linda. 2014. Justifying the need for control. Motives for Swedish national school inspection during two governments. *Scandinavian Journal of Educational Research* 58 (4): 385–399.

Rostgaard, Tine. 2015. *Når fortiden er længere end fremtiden*. Stockholm Nordens Välfärdscenter.

Rothstein, Bo. 1994. *Vad bör staten göra*. Stockholm SNS Förlag.

Rothstein, Bo. 2003. Introduction: Social capital in Scandinavia. *Scandinavian Political Studies* 26 (1).

Salamon, Lester M. 1987. Of market failure, voluntary failure, and third-party government: Toward a theory of government-nonprofit relations in the modern welfare state. *Nonprofit and Voluntary Sector Quarterly* 16 (1–2): 29–49.

Salamon, Lester M. 2002. *The Tools of government: A guide to the new governance*. New York: Oxford University Press.

Salamon, Lester M, and Stefan Toepler. 2015. Government–Nonprofit cooperation: Anomaly or necessity? *VOLUNTAS: International Journal of Voluntary and Nonprofit Organizations* 26 (6): 2155–2177.

Salamon, Lester M., and S. Wojciech Sokolowski. 2016. The size and scope of the European third sector. Brussels: European Union FP7 (grant agreement 613034). Third Sector Impact.

Segaard, Signe Bock. 2015. *Skole og eldreomsorg i Skandinavia. Nasjonale føringer for ikke-offentlige aktører*. Oslo: Institutt for samfunnsforskning.

Sejersted, Francis. 2011. *The age of social democracy Norway and Sweden in the Twentieth Century*. Princeton: Princton University Press.

Sivesind, Karl Henrik. 2013. Ideella välfärdstjänster: en lösning på den skandinaviska modellens framtida utmaningar? In *Civilsamhället klämt mellan stat och kapital. Välfärd, mångfold, framtid*, eds. Lars Trägårdh, Per Selle, Lars Skov Henriksen and Hanna Hallin, 75–88. Stockholm: SNS Förlag.

Sivesind, Karl Henrik, and Per Selle. 2010. Civil society in the Nordic countries: Between displacement and vitality. In *Nordic associations in a European perspective*, eds. Risto Alapuro and Henrik Stenius, 89–120. Baden-Baden: Nomos Verlagsgesellschaft.

Smith, Steven Rathgeb, and Kristen A. Grønbjerg. 2006. Scope and theory of government-nonprofit relations. In *The nonprofit sector: A research handbook*, eds. Walter W. Powell and Richard Steinberg, 221–242. New Haven, Conn: Yale University Press.

Statistics Norway. 2016. Table: 09929: Institutions for the aged and disabled, by ownership. www.ssb.no/pleie.
Steinberg, Richard 2006. Economic theories of nonprofit organizations. In *The nonprofit sector: A research handbook*, eds. Walter W. Powell and Richard Steinberg, 117–139. New Haven, Conn: Yale University Press.
Toepler, Stefan. 2010. Government funding policies. In *Handbook of research on nonprofit economics and management*, eds. Bruce Seaman and Dennis R Young, 320–334. Cheltenham: Edward Elgar.
Trägårdh, Lars. 2007. The 'civil society' debate in Sweden: The welfare state challenged. In *State and civil society in Northern Europe. The Swedish model reconsidered*, ed. Lars Trägårdh, 9–36. New York: Berghahn Books.
Vabo, Signy Irene. 2012. Tiltakende statlig styring av kommunesektoren—også på eldreområdet? In *Det norske flernivådemokratiet*, eds. Marit Reitan, Jo Saglie, and Eivind Smith, 97–135. Oslo: Abstrakt.
Weisbrod, Burton Allen. 1978. *The voluntary nonprofit sector: An economic analysis*. Lexington, MA: Lexington Books.
Weisbrod, Burton Allen. 1988. *The nonprofit economy*. Mass: Harvard University Press.
Wollebæk, Dag, Per Selle, and Håkon Lorentzen. 2000. *Frivillig innsats: Sosial integrasjon, demokrati og økonomi*. Bergen: Fagbokforlaget.

Authors' Biography

Karl Henrik Sivesind is Research Professor at the Institute for Social Research, Oslo, Norway. He is currently manager of the project 'Conditions and Impacts of Welfare Mix' funded by the Norwegian Research Council, and he is leader for Work Package 'Elaboration and Testing of Impact Indicators' on the project 'Third Sector Impact—The Contribution of the Third Sector to Europe's Socio-economic Development' funded by the EU's 7th Framework Programme. He has studied changes affecting civil society by analysing data from population surveys and local association surveys as a part of the activities of Centre for Research on Civil Society and Voluntary Sector in Oslo/Bergen. He has also been involved in several comparative research projects about the nonprofit sector and welfare services.

Håkon Solbu Trætteberg is a senior research fellow at the Institute for Social Research, Oslo, Norway. His main research interest is publicly-funded welfare services in general and the importance of the welfare mix in particular. Trætteberg received his Ph.D. in 2016, partly on work presented in this book.

Open Access This chapter is licensed under the terms of the Creative Commons Attribution 4.0 International License (http://creativecommons.org/licenses/by/4.0/), which permits use, sharing, adaptation, distribution and reproduction in any medium or format, as long as you give appropriate credit to the original author(s) and the source, provide a link to the Creative Commons license and indicate if changes were made.

The images or other third party material in this chapter are included in the chapter's Creative Commons license, unless indicated otherwise in a credit line to the material. If material is not included in the chapter's Creative Commons license and your intended use is not permitted by statutory regulation or exceeds the permitted use, you will need to obtain permission directly from the copyright holder.

2

The Changing Roles of For-Profit and Nonprofit Welfare Provision in Norway, Sweden, and Denmark

Karl Henrik Sivesind

Introduction

It is not so obvious that there is a Scandinavian welfare model if we look at how the service provision is organized, as the data presented in this chapter will show. Common features can primarily be recognized as ideals concerning equal access for all to high-quality welfare services in core areas of education, health, and social services. In addition, in all Scandinavian countries, citizens have rights to participate in decision-making. Adaptation of services to individual needs, interests, and preferences has been reinforced legally and through new best practices and professional standards. Another common objective is to decentralize governance to the municipalities and to lower administrative levels in order to adapt policies to local needs.

An additional common feature is the broad implementation of new public management (NPM) tools, influenced by global trends since the

---

K.H. Sivesind (✉)
Institute for Social Research, Oslo, Norway
e-mail: k.h.sivesind@socialresearch.no

eighties. Market-emulating types of governance increasingly regulate relations between public contracting authorities and providers of welfare services from nonprofit, for-profit, and public sector. EU directives and stronger national regulation of public procurement are important reasons for this, as the next chapter by Segaard and Saglie will show. Still, there is very broad political agreement about continued public funding and regulation of core welfare services. All these intentions are clearly expressed in policy documents from all the Scandinavian countries.

Despite common welfare ideals and the similar changes in regulation to other EU countries, this chapter will show that there are large differences in the employment shares of the for-profit, nonprofit, and public welfare providers among the Scandinavian countries. Rather than a single model, the situation resembles a natural experiment since different modes of regulation are used in different countries and service areas in order to better reach the same welfare goals. This is partly a result of historical differences, but recent policy initiatives and administrative reforms have increased the diversity in governance structures.

NPM reforms are influenced by international trends sweeping through advanced welfare societies. Priorities have shifted from the state as a social provider for the people to the state as a promoter of global competitiveness, Taylor-Gooby claims (2008: 4). Hence, in Scandinavia, the income tax percentage has gone down, and the welfare costs as shares of GDP have decreased slightly, while at the same time countries such as France, Austria, Germany, and Belgium have been catching up. In that way, the Scandinavian countries have become more similar to other rich, Western European countries. As a consequence, to reduce the gap between stagnating public benefits and higher income levels, more people sign up for private pensions and insurances for illness and disability.

The social investment thinking has not only consequences for transfers and entitlements but also for reforming the welfare service provision in order to improve the quality of education and health services and getting people back into the labour market, expecting that this will pay off in the future. In order to stay globally competitive, it is also necessary to cut costs and increase efficiency in services that the government pays for. In Scandinavia, there is a widespread worry that the dominating public service provision has become bureaucratized and stale. Many therefore see increased private provision of the state-funded services as an instrument for improving capacity, but more importantly, for creating competition, freedom of choice, and ultimately innovation to advance also the public service provision. However, the discussion about public versus private service delivery often overlooks the potential for pioneering and distinctive roles of nonprofit providers that initiated most of the welfare services we have today (Sivesind 2008).

In short, policymakers are worried that the public welfare spending may not give the best results, and to find out they wanted to create competition. This is the background for a very broad implementation of new public management tools and quasi-markets in Scandinavia. It all started when local governments made an internal separation between contracting authorities and providers of services. This happened in the beginning of 1990s in Sweden (Erlandsson et al. 2013, 27) and late in the 1990s in Denmark and Norway (Vabø et al. 2013, 171). Since then, responsibilities for results have been increasingly decentralized from political councils to lower administrative levels and even to semi-autonomous agencies, for example, regional health authorities in Norway. Frame agreements between public purchasers and service providers that would almost automatically be renewed are being replaced by contract negotiations, open tenders, and user choice in combination with voucher systems with national agencies authorizing service providers. This latter model has been spreading rapidly to new service areas and governance levels in Sweden since the 1990s, and it is recently getting wider implementation in Norway and Denmark as well.

User choice, influence, and adaptation are backed by several recent policy documents from all the Scandinavian countries pointing out that the dominant public provision is no longer capable of meeting new challenges that endanger the welfare model's sustainability. This includes the emergence of new groups of young users, more old people with a need for different kinds of help, limited personnel resources, increased private prosperity, and more social and cultural heterogeneity (An example from Norway is *Report to the Storting* (White Paper) nr. 29 2012–2013). These changes make recipients of all kinds of services require adaptation to individual needs. Traditional, standardized welfare services are struggling to meet these challenges. 'To secure the future legitimacy and sustainability' of the model, these policy documents claim that it is necessary to promote active citizenship by empowering the users and their next of kin to influence the content of services and also to assume more responsibility for the services. All sectors of society must be involved, including the voluntary engagement of families, local communities, nonprofit organizations, and social enterprises. Already in the 1980s, a change in policy orientation from a welfare state to a welfare society was announced. This development must continue, according to the recent policy documents. Consequently, the division of labour between public, nonprofit, and for-profit providers, which is the topic of this chapter, is critical for the future of the welfare model.

Despite common welfare ideals and the similar changes in regulation as in many other European countries, differences in the mix of providers of publicly funded welfare services between the Scandinavian countries continue to evolve. This is partly a result of path dependencies. Denmark has the largest shares of nonprofit welfare provision in Scandinavia, but on a level below what has been called the Western-European welfare partnership countries, which include Germany, France, and Austria (Salamon et al. 2004; Salamon and Sokolowski 2016). Norway has a mixed model; there is a strong dominance of public welfare provision in some areas combined with a small share of nonprofit actors, but quasi-markets and open tendering in more areas have brought for-profits on the rise. However, in the 1990s, Sweden broke away from the past with strong public-sector dominance and opened up for rapid growth in profit-oriented private services. To complicate the picture further, different modes of regulation are used in different service areas in each country.

The next section shows changes in the employment shares of welfare service providers from the nonprofit, for-profit, and public sector in Scandinavia. This is followed by more detailed mapping of changes in the service areas education, health, and social services in each country. This will be related to changes in how public contracts are allocated to welfare service providers in the nonprofit, for-profit, and public sectors. The conclusion looks at path dependencies and policy initiatives that can explain why common welfare ideals and the implementation of similar NPM tools of government do not lead to convergence among the

Scandinavian countries. On the contrary, there are increasing differences in the shares of providers of publicly funded services. Furthermore, there is no convergence with other welfare models either, and certainly not in the Swedish case.

Divergence in Welfare Provider Mix among the Scandinavian Countries

In Scandinavia, core welfare services in health, social services, and education continue to receive public funding to a comparatively high degree, and the government has assumed a larger part of the responsibility from the families than in other parts of Europe. This is what is commonly called the Nordic model in welfare research (Ervasti et al. 2008). These state-funded services have a huge impact on the lives of most of the population. In the following, we will be looking at changes in the shares of these services that are provided by the nonprofit, for-profit, and public sectors. To do that, we need a common measure that is comparable between countries and different service areas. Data on output are not available for all welfare service areas, and they are difficult to operationalize in a coherent manner. For example, it is difficult to compare the number of nursing home beds with pupils in primary schools. Alternatively, if we use expenditures as a proxy for output, the results may show a too large public sector because it often pays for costly treatments and procedures in addition to expensive infrastructure and equipment. A simpler solution chosen here is to compare shares of paid full-time employment as a common measure for each sector's 'market share,' or, rather, workforce input. This should work reasonably well in welfare areas compared that are dominated by employment-intensive services. In Sweden, unfortunately, only data on the number of employees are available. Still, this gives valid measures of shares of the institutional sectors and changes within each country, assuming that the distribution of part-time and full-time employment does not change too much.

Table 2.1 shows paid employment in welfare services in the nonprofit, for-profit, and public sectors, covering the longest time spans for which comparable data are available. This started in the year 2000 in Sweden, 2008 in Denmark, and 2006 in Norway, and ended in 2013 for all three countries. Although for a limited number of years, this is the first time comparable data on broad changes in welfare provider mix from the Scandinavian countries can be presented. The data show employment shares of the public, for-profit, and nonprofit sector providers in publicly funded welfare in the service areas education, health, and social services. To facilitate comparison between countries with data covering different time spans, changes in 5-year averages have been shown in Table 2.1. This means how much of the total employment each sector has gained or lost over the whole available data period in average for 5 years.[1]

Table 2.1 shows that oil-rich Norway experienced a strong growth in the total welfare sector employment between 2006 and 2013 with as much as 12% increase in a 5-year average, in a period when other countries struggled with a financial crisis. In Sweden, the increase in the number of employees was 7% in a 5-year average between 2000 and 2012, whereas in Denmark there has been almost no change at all between 2004 and 2013. The data on employment in the different economic sectors come from the national statistical agencies (see sources and typologies in the appendix at the end of the chapter).

Table 2.1 shows furthermore that the nonprofit sector's share of paid employment in 2013 was 8% in Norway, 3% in Sweden, and 14% in Denmark. These shares have been quite stable for a long time. The changes in shares were 1% point or less in 5-year averages. In fact, documentation from the Johns Hopkins Comparative Nonprofit Sector Project shows that the nonprofit share in Norway has been stable on about 7.5% of the full-time welfare employment back to 2004 and 1997 (Sivesind 2008a; Sivesind et al. 2004). In Sweden, the nonprofit share of welfare employees was just 2% in 1992, peaked at 3.5% in the year 2000 (Lundström and Wijkström 1997; Sivesind and Selle 2010), and then decreased slightly to 3.2% in 2013. The growth was partly due to the fact that since 2000, the Church of Sweden is no longer under state governance. This added 24,000 church employees to the nonprofit sector in several areas, including welfare services. In addition to this, the number of employees increased in social services (9100), education (1600), and health (800) (Wijkström and Einarsson 2006, 59). In Denmark, the

Table 2.1 Paid employment in the welfare services in Scandinavia, total and sector shares (%)

Sector	Norway			Sweden			Denmark		
	2006	2013	5-year change[a]	2000	2013	5-year change[a]	2003	2013	5-year change[a]
Nonprofit	7.4	7.8	0.3	3.5	3.2	−0.1	15.1	13.8	−1.1
For-profit	11.5	13.4	1.2	8.7	19.2	3.8	6.5	7.1	0.5
Public	81.2	78.8	−1.5	87.8	77.6	−3.6	78.4	79.1	0.5
Total	528,400	632,800	12.3	1,033,597	1,230,412	6.8	590,419	614,479	0.3

[a]5-year average change in employment shares, percentage points. Sources See tables for each country below

nonprofit share was 16.5% in 2003, as shown in the data from the Hopkins project (Boje et al. 2006, Table 5.9), but then it decreased to 13.8 in 2013 (Boje 2017). A more detailed analysis in the section about Denmark below shows that this may be a result of particular reforms in the social service area rather than a trend, at least for now.

However, employment shares do not tell the whole story. Because of different trends in total welfare employment growth, the nonprofit sector in Norway has increased strongly in real numbers from 39,000 to 50,000 full-time employees from 2006 to 2013,[2] even though the share only increased by 0.3% points in a 5-year average. Even in Sweden, with 0.1% points decline in a 5-year average, there is a very small real increase from 36,000 to 39,000 employees from 2000 in 2013. In contrast, Denmark, with a more stable total welfare employment and a nonprofit sector decline of 1.1% points in a 5-year average, had a decrease in the number of nonprofit sector full-time employees from 93,000 to 85,000 from 2003 to 2013, respectively.

It is important to note that the nonprofit welfare shares in all Scandinavian countries are much smaller than in welfare partnership countries such as Austria, Germany, and France with well-established, partly church-based welfare services and nonprofit welfare employment shares between 20 and 25%. The UK, as an example of a more liberal model, has nonprofit welfare provision on the same high level, but the services are funded and organized in a different manner. In fact, the levels in Sweden and Norway are only comparable to Eastern European countries that still are marked by the communist era when the nonprofit sector was kept at a minimum (Salamon and Sokolowski 2016; Sivesind and Selle 2010).

There are large differences in the for-profit sector shares among the Scandinavian countries in the most recent data. In Sweden, the share of the welfare employees is 19%, while in Norway the share of welfare full-time employment is 13%, and in Denmark just 7%. There has been growth in for-profit employment shares in all three countries, but mostly in Sweden. In 5-year averages, there was a little more than 1% point growth in Norway and half a percentage point growth in Denmark, but almost 4% points growth in Sweden. This may seem like a small change, but it means that the for-profit sector in Sweden has doubled its share of the welfare employees from 9 to 18% from 2000 to 2013, and the number of employees has become more than 2.5 times larger, increasing from 90,000 to 236,000. This is a change rate that in the long term has the potential of transforming the welfare model in Sweden. In Norway, there has also been an increase in for-profit welfare from 61,000 full-time employees in 2006 to 84,500 in 2012. In Denmark, which has the smallest share of 7.1%, there has been a real growth from 38,000 to 44,000 full-time employees.

At the moment, the public-sector employment share is almost the same in all three Scandinavian countries, between 78 and 79% of the welfare employment. However, it is decreasing rapidly in Sweden with—3.6% points in a 5-year average and—1.5% points in Norway, but it is increasing by 0.5% points in Denmark. In Norway, the public sector is still growing in real numbers, from 429,000 full-time employees in 2006 to 500,000 in 2013. In Denmark, the public sector reached a maximum in 2010 with 549,000 full-time employees, and in Sweden it peaked in 2007 with 974,000 employees.[3]

Although the public-sector shares still may seem large in comparative perspective, they are decreasing in real numbers primarily as a result of for-profit growth. This adds a new feature to the 'social democratic model', previously characterized by high public welfare spending and a small nonprofit sector. The public sector was preferred as a service provider to ensure unitary standards and equal access for all (Anheier and Salamon 2006; Salamon and Anheier 1998). For-profit sector growth also sets the Scandinavian countries apart from the corporatist and liberal countries, which have much larger nonprofit sectors (Salamon et al. 2004).

To sum up, in Sweden, the public-sector employment has decreased in real numbers, and a decline has recently started in Denmark too. In Norway, with no need for austerity measures, all three sectors still grow in real numbers, although the public sector's share decreases slightly. In all three Scandinavian countries, the for-profit providers are increasing their shares of the welfare employment faster than the nonprofits. The gap between the sectors is growing fastest in Sweden, where the nonprofits remain very small while the for-profit share has doubled. This has resulted in a dramatic shift from the public sector to the for-profit sector in Sweden, and while the for-profit sectors grow in Norway and Denmark too, the changes in provider mix are more moderate. The changes in Sweden may have significant long-term consequences, because the tools of governance that have brought the public sector share down to the same level as the other Scandinavian countries are continuing to produce rapid growth in the for-profit sector but not in the nonprofit sector's share of employees.

The main focus of this chapter is on changes within 'education,' 'health,' and 'social services,' which include the sub-categories shown in Table 2.2. The data presentation thus follows as far as possible the International Classification of Non-Profit Institutions (ICNPO) (United Nations 2003). However, to match with national statistical categories that cannot be broken down, nursing homes (ICNPO 3 200) are moved from Health to Social Services, and Research (ICNPO 2 400), which is not typically regarded as one of the welfare services, is excluded from Education and Research (ICNPO 2). Table 2.2 shows sub-categories for the most important types of social services in Scandinavia, which, in addition to nursing homes and home-based care, are day-care for children, child and juvenile welfare, and substance abuse treatment. More specific details about sources and the typologies used in each country's statistics are presented in an appendix at the end of the chapter.

Table 2.2 Service areas included in ICNPO main categories

2 Education
2 100 Primary and secondary education
2 200 Higher education
2 300 Other education
3 Health
3 100 Hospitals and rehabilitation
3 300 Mental health care
3 400 Other health services
4 Social Services
3 200 Nursing homes
4 100 Social services, including day care for children, child and juvenile welfare, substance abuse treatment
Other social services including (4 200) emergency and relief

Note Adapted from International Classification of Non-Profit Institutions (United Nations 2003)

In the following sections, we look at changes in the composition of providers within the welfare service areas in each of the Scandinavian countries. We also look at relations between the governments and the for-profit and nonprofit sectors that may explain the different trends.

Denmark: Relatively Stable Welfare Provider Mix and a Large Nonprofit Welfare Share

Denmark has the largest nonprofit shares in Scandinavia because of a long tradition of the government engaging voluntary organizations and self-owning institutions in social service provision. This is because nonprofit organizations have been pioneers in the welfare service area, as shown in an analysis of state–voluntary sector relations through the last 150 years (Henriksen and Bundesen 2004). Although many tasks have later been taken over by the public sector, self-owning institutions still perform a large part of the welfare services—often in close cooperation with the public sector. The nonprofit sector has a quite strong position in primary and lower secondary schools, where its share of pupils increased from 10 to 15.3% between 1990 and 2011.[4] This recent growth is primarily a result of parents stepping in when the municipalities want to close schools with too few pupils, exercising their legal rights to establish schools with public funding. Free schools get state funding equivalent to 72% of the average costs for a pupil in the public schools. Above that, the schools can determine the level of fees paid by the parents. The traditional free schools are nonprofit institutions, but even a newer type of private schools operates on a nonprofit basis (see Chap. 3).

Table 2.3 shows that in education, the nonprofit sector had about 29% of the paid employment and increased from 53,000 to 55,000 full-time employees, while the public sector had 69% of the employment and an increase from 124,000 to 131,000 full-time employees. The for-profit educational institutions had a little more than 4,000 full-time employees, which is just 2% of the total employment in the service area. There were no changes in the employment shares in education, even though the total number of full-time employees increased from 181,000 to 190,000.

Table 2.3 Paid employment in the nonprofit, for-profit, and public sectors within education, health, and social services in Denmark 2008–2013, full-time equivalents and percent

Service area	2008		2013	
	Employment	%	Employment	%
Education (P)				
Nonprofit	52,823	29.1	54,736	28.7
For-profit	4,291	2.4	4,405	2.3
Public sector	124,153	68.5	131,255	68.9
Total	181,266	100.0	190,396	100.0
Health (QA)				
Nonprofit	1620	1.3	623	0.5
For-profit	21,268	16.5	23,116	16.7
Public sector	105,703	82.2	114,534	82.8
Total	128,590	100.0	138,273	100.0
Social services (QB)				
Nonprofit	34,700	12.4	29,651	10.4
For-profit	12,673	4.5	16,106	5.6
Public sector	233,190	83.1	240,053	84.0
Total	280,563	100.0	285,810	100.0
Welfare field in total				
Nonprofit	89,142	15.1	85,010	13.8
For-profit	38,232	6.5	43,627	7.1
Public sector	463,046	78.4	485,842	79.1
Total	**590,419**	**100.0**	**614,479**	**100.0**

Sources See appendix at the end of the chapter

In health, the nonprofit share has for a long time been very small in Denmark because there are no large hospitals or other health institutions (Sivesind 2008b; Helander and Sivesind 2001; Boje 2006; Boje et al. 2006, Table 5.9). Table 2.3 shows that the employment has further decreased from 1,600 to 600 full-time employees from 2008 to 2013, which means that the share has gone down from 1.3 to 0.5%. There are no important changes in the welfare mix; the for-profit and public sectors had about 17 and 82% each of the employment from 2008 to 2013.

In social services, there were more profound changes. Table 2.3 shows that the nonprofit employment decreased from 35,000 to 30,000, and the employment share went down from 12 to 10%. In contrast, the for-profits had a small increase from 4.5 to 5.6%, and the public sector share also increased slightly from 83 to 84%. The for-profit and public sectors had increases in full-time employees of 3500 and 7000, respectively.

In Denmark, the decrease in nonprofits was partly a result of a decrease in self-owning kindergartens from 23.5 to 20% from 2007 to 2011. Such self-owning daycare centers for preschool children must have an operating contract and be supervised by the municipality. Parent payments must be kept on the same level as similar public-sector services. A new type of private kindergartens may transfer profits to owners, in contrast to the self-owning institutions (see Chap. 3), but in practice most of them stick to the traditional nonprofit form. However, according to the definitions in UN's handbook for satellite accounts for non-profit institutions (United Nations 2003), they should be regarded as part of the for-profit sector, as long as there is no formal ban on profit distribution. Their share increased from 2.7 to 4.4%, while the public sector has been rather stable at about 75% (Thøgersen 2013).

In addition, the nonprofit employment share in social services decreased because the total number of institutions for elderly care decreased strongly as a result of a change towards home-based care, similar to the development in many other countries. However, in Denmark, this seems to have implied an increase in municipal and for-profit employment. Even though the share of self-owning, nonprofit institutions stayed between 20 and 22% from 2000 to 2010, the number of employees decreased because of the reduction in the total number of institutions. In addition, several self-owning social service institutions were taken over by the public sector during a local government reform in 2007 that reduced the number of municipalities from 275 to 98. Additionally, since 2007, it has been possible to establish a new type of 'independent' nursing home that does not need an operating contract with the municipalities, and that may transfer profit to owners (see Chap. 3). In 2012, they only had 7% of the people enrolled in nursing homes in Denmark, but further growth can be expected since this is a relatively new form of organization (Thøgersen 2013).

When it comes to homes for disabled persons, the share of the self-owning institutions has been stable at around 25% from 2008 to 2011. Among other institutions, such as shelters for battered women, hostels for the homeless, institutions for drug and alcohol addicts etc., about 50% are self-owning institutions. Before the responsibility was transferred from counties to municipalities in 2007, the share was stable at about 55% from 2000 to 2006 (Thøgersen 2013). However, this is a complex field with overlapping types of services and institutions and frequent structure changes, so the statistics do not present the full picture. All in all, this results in a decrease in users of nonprofit social services and thereby also a reduction in the number of full-time employees, while the for-profit and public sectors increase.

Sweden: Strong Growth in For-Profit Welfare

Among the Scandinavian countries, the biggest change in welfare provider mix has happened in Sweden, which in the beginning of the 1990s probably had the highest proportion of public welfare services among the advanced welfare states in the world. The reasons for this were brought up in the introduction to the book and will be further discussed at the end of this chapter. In the new millennium, there have been dramatic changes in the Swedish welfare provider mix, as we have seen in Table 2.1 above, which shows changes for the welfare services in total from 2000 to 2013. Table 2.4 shows that the changes vary between the service areas of education, health, and social service, but the data only cover 2007 to 2013 because there was a change in statistical categories before 2007. In the recent years, the nonprofit share has been small but stable in all three welfare service areas, with about 5% in education, just 1% in health, and 3% in social services. However, the for-profit services increased their share of employees rapidly with 4 percentage points to 14% in education, 3 percentage points to 19% in health, and as much as 8 percentage points to 25% in social services. This resulted in significant reductions in the public-sector shares, which went down from 86 to 81% in education, 84 to 80% in health, and as much as from 82 to 72% in social services from 2007 to 2013.

In education, the nonprofit and public sectors increased with a few thousand employees each, but the for-profits increased with 25,000 employees. In health the total number of employees declined with 12,000, mainly in the public sector, while the for-profits increased by

Table 2.4 Shares of paid employees in the nonprofit, for-profit, and public sectors within education, health, and social services in Sweden 2007–2013

Service area	2007		2013	
	Employment	%	Employment	%
Education (SNI 85)				
Nonprofit	22,284	4.9	24,660	5.1
For-profit	42,754	9.5	68,175	14.2
Public sector	385,757	85.6	388,547	80.7
Total	450,795	100.0	481,382	100.0
Health (SNI 86)				
Nonprofit	3,768	1.2	2,485	0.8
For-profit	46,168	14.8	56,456	18.7
Public sector	262,770	84.0	242,411	80.4
Total	312,706	100.0	301,352	100.0
Social services (SNI 87–88)				
Nonprofit	12,173	3.1	12,006	2.7
For-profit	58,691	14.8	111,788	25.0
Public sector	324,985	82.1	323,884	72.3
Total	395,849	100.0	447,678	100.0
Welfare field in total				
Nonprofit	38,225	3.3	39,151	3.2
For-profit	147,613	12.7	236,419	19.2
Public sector	973,512	84.0	954,842	77.6
Total	**1,159,350**	**100.0**	**1,230,412**	**100.0**

Sources See appendix at the end of the chapter

10,000 employees, However, in social services, the number of for-profit employees almost doubled whereas the other sectors remained stable. This means that almost all growth in Swedish welfare employees has happened in the for-profit sector, with the biggest increase in social services.

In what services more specifically have the changes in provider mix occurred? The proportion of pupils in private schools, which was around 2% when private school reform was implemented in 1992, has increased to 15% in compulsory schools and to 25% in upper secondary schools in 2014 (Swedish National Agency for Education 2016). As much as 64% of the private schools are limited companies (Vlachos 2011), and this share is increasing because there are few restrictions on the school owners' options to take out the surplus, which is quite unique for western welfare states.

Within care for elderly and disabled, the nonprofit share has been stable around 2–3% over the past 20 years, while the share of private services has increased from almost nothing to 15% (Erlandsson et al. 2013; Szebehely 2011). Within care for individuals and families, which includes care for children and juveniles and substance abuse treatment, the private share grew strongly in the 1980s and 1990s, but there have only been minor changes since the year 2000. In 2010, a little less than 10% were employed in nonprofit organizations and 35% in for-profit companies (Wiklund 2011). Within hospitals and inpatient medical care, the share of private employment in Sweden is small, as in the other Scandinavian countries. About 4% worked in 2009 in for-profit companies and 1% in nonprofit organizations and foundations. Within outpatient health and medical treatment, however, private companies have about one-third of the employees, and they have taken over an increasing share of the service area since 1995. Nonprofit organizations and religious communities and foundations are almost absent (Johansson 2011). The private share has, in comparative perspective, been quite low in this field in Sweden. In 1994, more than 90% of the doctors were employed by the public sector, most of them by county councils (Zweifel et al. 1998). The emerging private sector consists largely of single units or smaller companies, besides some national chains that are either co-operatives owned by employees (Praktikertjänst) or corporations (Capio and Carema). Many new private service providers emerged after 2010, when the County Councils were ordered to organize primary health services so that users could freely choose providers, in line with the law on freedom of choice (LOV 2008: 962). Most of the new health services are established in highly populated areas, as one would expect. Consequently, half a million people have a second provider within a 5-min drive from their residence, so the number of options has increased for many (Swedish Competition Authority 2010). Availability is important as one of the preconditions for real consumer choice. However, these kinds of concentration and distributional effects indicate that this is only the beginning of the structural transformations in Swedish welfare resulting from increased freedom of choice and free rights to establish private institutions. Larger social differences in access to welfare services may be a consequence if there are no regulations on establishment.

The opening up for private competition within the public welfare services in Sweden has strengthened the for-profit sector but not the so-called "ideal sector" with strong ties to civil society organizations. Government-funded welfare contracts in Sweden have attracted private investors and venture capital even from international funds. The institutional and legal changes promoting private competition to the public service provision have resulted in commercial stimuli strong enough to transform the welfare model in a few decades. This is quite an unusual achievement in the welfare area, which is often described as a retrenched policy field (Pierson 2001). The question is whether there are unintended consequences as well, such as a small nonprofit sector, high concentration in ownership, no clear improvement in efficiency, and quality problems, such as the school results may indicate (Hartman 2011).

Norway: A Stable Nonprofit Share of Welfare Employment

In Norway, there has been an intense debate on the privatization of welfare services. It has focused on public versus private services, while the nonprofit sector often has been left out of focus. Despite this, we have not seen such dramatic changes as in Sweden. The centre-right minority government in office from 2001 to 2005 wanted to make it easier to establish private schools in Norway. The red–green coalition government that followed immediately put on the brakes before the reform gave any results of importance for the welfare provider mix. This was in line with the red–green cooperation statement expressing the wish to give the voluntary sector good conditions for providing noncommercial services (Soria Moria-erklæringen 2005). Procurement regulations allowed nonprofit organizations to be selected for closed tenders or negotiations about service contracts. In some areas, as in child welfare, the red–green government's goal was to select nonprofit organizations rather than commercial firms when the public sector itself did not have sufficient capacity (Sivesind 2008a). However, many structural welfare reforms have led to a decentralization of responsibility for the contracting of welfare services to more autonomous agencies, and this makes it difficult to implement such political intentions. Examples of such semi-autonomous agencies are regional state-funded child welfare and family counselling services (*Bufetat*) and regional health authorities (*helseforetak*) governed in a similar way as a private company with a director appointed by a board. The conservative minority coalition government from October 2013 has looked for opportunities to open up more for for-profit actors and user choice in health and social services. However, a new law in 2015 for private primary schools and secondary schools still requires that all public funding is used for educational purposes and not for profit distribution. The nonprofit providers continue to be involved in publicly funded services in areas where they have been innovators, such as elderly care, substance abuse treatment, medical rehabilitation, and somatic and mental health care. This results in a mixed model of public, nonprofit, and for-profit provision, to a large extent based on a patchwork of ad hoc policies that have emerged over a long time in different localities and service areas. Table 2.5 shows that the for-profit employment shares have increased in all service areas, and the nonprofit sector has had small increases in shares too, while the public sector has decreased between 2006 and 2013. However, since the total welfare employment has expanded, all sectors have had real increases in all service areas. The growth in the for-profit sector is primarily due to expansion in social services from 30,000 to 46,000 full-time employees, including elderly care, day care for children, child and juvenile welfare, and substance abuse treatment. There is a corresponding loss in public sector employment shares, despite real growth from 176,000 to 213,000 full-time employees. In real numbers, the nonprofit employment increased strongly from about 39,000 to 49,000 full-time employees. Ironically, media have mainly focused on nonprofit institutions that have been closed down. However, this has been more than compensated by employment growth in other institutions, which shows that the nonprofit sector also can be flexible and entrepreneurial under the right circumstances. The following analysis focuses on in which type of services the changes have happened.

Table 2.5 Paid employment in the nonprofit, for-profit, and public sector within education, health and social services in Norway 2006–2013, full-time equivalent employment and percent

Service area	2006		2013	
	Employment	%	Employment	%
Education (2)				
Nonprofit	8,177	5.1	10,609	5.8
For-profit	7,123	4.5	9,991	5.5
Public sector	144,700	90.4	162,300	88.7
Total	160,000	100.0	182,900	100.0
Health (3)				
Nonprofit	7,642	5.5	9,122	5.7
For-profit	23,558	16.9	28,278	17.6
Public sector	108,500	77.7	123,300	76.7
Total	139,700	100.0	160,700	100.0
Social services (4)				
Nonprofit	23,198	10.1	29,881	10.3
For-profit	29,902	13.1	46,219	16.0
Public sector	175,600	76.8	213,100	73.7
Total	228,700	100.0	289,200	100.0
Welfare field in total				
Nonprofit	39,017	7.4	49,612	7.8
For-profit	60,583	11.5	84,488	13.4
Public sector	428,800	81.2	498,700	78.8
Total	**528,400**	**100.0**	**632,800**	**100.0**

Sources: See appendix at the end of the chapter

Statistics Norway does not publish employment data separately for the economic sectors and has not yet implemented the ESA2010 institutional sector codes as Statistics Denmark has done. Table 2.5 is therefore based on full-time employment data from the Satellite Account for Non-Profit Institutions and employment data for the public sector, seen in relation to national account data for the welfare services in total. However, Table 2.6 presents data only from Statistics Norway's Satellite Account for Non-Profit Institutions and shows the changes in employment within the nonprofit sector in Norway. Similar detailed data do not exist for the other sectors. The other Scandinavian countries are in the process of implementing such satellite accounts but have not yet published full reports.

Table 2.6 Paid full-time equivalent employment in the nonprofit sector in the welfare field in Norway 2006–2013

Type of service	2006	2013	Change 2006–2013
Education	**8,177**	**10,609**	**29.7 %**
Primary and secondary education	4,395	6,031	37.2 %
Higher education	1,736	2,136	23.0 %
Other education	2,046	2,442	19.4 %
Health	**7,642**	**9,122**	**19.4 %**
Hospitals, rehabilitation, mental health care and other health services	7,642	9,122	19.4 %
Social Services	**23,198**	**29,881**	**28,8 %**
Nursing homes[a]	4,765	5,543	16.3 %
Day care for children	12,161	14,724	21.1 %
Child and juvenile welfare	1,000	1,045	4.5 %
Substance abuse treatment	2,012	2,244	11.5 %
Other social services including emergency and relief	3,260	6,325	94.0 %
Total welfare employment	**39,017**	**49,612**	**27.2 %**
Nonprofit share of welfare employment [b]	*7.4 %*	*7.8 %*	

Source SSB Satellite account for non-profit organizations. Table 08520, FTE employment by activity (ICNPO)
Notes[a]'Nursing homes' belongs to the ICNPO-category health, but here it is moved to social services to match with Table 2.5, which is set up in line with SN2007, which is Statistics Norway's version of EU's NACE Rev.2.
[b]Welfare employment in all sectors from SSB National economy. Table 09174, FTE employment in Education, Health, and Social Work

The strongest growth within the nonprofit sector in Norway was in primary and secondary education. Table 2.6 shows that the number of full-time employees has increased from 4400 to 6000 from 2006 to 2013. This happened despite stricter requirements for the establishment of new schools from 2007 to 2015. In practice, only noncommercial and established educational alternatives such as Waldorf and Montessori schools were approved. In secondary schools, there has also been strong growth from 1700 to 2100 full-time employees, but still only 7% of students in upper secondary and 3% in compulsory education are in private, nonprofit schools in 2014/2015 (Norwegian Directorate for Education and Training 2015). As we will see in the next chapter of this book, in primary and secondary education, the relations between the public sector as funder and the private providers are regulated by service concessions and not by tendering under the Public Procurement Act. This means that there is an opening for private initiatives to establish new schools as long as they can get approval by the Directorate for Education. This has resulted in an increase in the number of primary and lower secondary schools from 165 to 209 and upper secondary schools from 83 to 94 between 2010 and 2014 (Norwegian Directorate for Education and Training 2015), despite lack of enthusiasm for private schools from the red–green government in position between 2005 and 2013. In many cases, this has been schools that the municipalities want to close down because of too few pupils. In 2014 and 2015, 27 and 28 new primary or secondary schools received approval from the Directorate for education under the new conservative government. This means an increase in the nonprofit sector since the law requires that all public funding has to be used directly for educational purposes, although some of the schools in fact are limited companies. However, some schools rent space in properties and buy services from companies with the same owners as the schools. The educational authorities have opened investigations when prices are significantly higher than the general market level. This shows that it takes vigilance to sustain a nonprofit model when for-profit companies are allowed to own schools.

The category 'Higher education' in Table 2.6, which, for example, includes the BI Norwegian Business School and diaconal colleges engaged in nursing education, expanded from 1700 to 2100 full-time employees, and 'Other education,' which includes folk high schools and other forms of adult education, had an employment growth from 2000 to 2400. This is on par with the growth of the welfare field in total. Nonprofit organizations in 'Education' in total had an employment growth from 8200 to 10,600 and constituted 5.3% of all employment in this area in Norway (Statistics Norway 2016a).

The main category 'Health' in Table 2.6 includes only 'Hospitals, rehabilitation, mental health care, and other health services',[5] which grew from 7600 to 9100 full-time employees. This includes not only several diaconal hospitals but also other forms of nonprofit psychiatric centers and rehabilitation institutions. A large part of this is services that are purchased by the regional state health authorities in Norway. The nonprofit somatic and mental health hospitals and clinics are well integrated into that system for allocation of service contracts, because of their large capacity and special competence. The contracting authorities have had the opportunity to reserve tenders and negotiations with the nonprofits, in line with an exception to the rules on public procurements introduced in 2004 (see Chap. 3). However, this has not been used here because the for-profits do not have the necessary kind of capacity. Rather, they are involved in laboratories, radiology, and minor surgery. A large part of the for-profits public funding comes from patients with certain diagnoses that may choose from a list of public and private providers.

In rehabilitation, the contracting authorities buy services in a single market because they find it difficult to distinguish between nonprofit and for-profit providers. All in all, there is little direct competition between nonprofit and for-profit providers in health. The challenge for the nonprofit sector is instead that the public sector may decide to expand its own activities (Bogen and Grønningsæter 2016). However, the nonprofit sector also has activities outside the public procurement system and continues to develop new services such as low-threshold health services for drug addicts and for migrants who lack documents. These kinds of humanitarian tasks are difficult for the state or private companies to be legally responsible for.

Within the main category 'Social services,' the growth in nonprofit employment was from 23,200 to almost 30,000 between 2006 and 2013, as Table 2.6 shows. 'Nursing homes' includes both home care and institution-based care, which is largely a municipal responsibility. Nonprofit employment here grew from 4800 to 5500. Many municipalities have only public service providers, but about 70–80 nonprofit nursing homes have long-term framework agreements. Very few have got an operating contract through competitive tendering. There are only about 20 for-profit nursing homes that are part of the municipalities' normal systems for user allocation, but in addition, some private institutions sell single places to municipalities (Vabø et al. 2013, 180–181).

In total for institutions for the aged and disabled, almost 90% of all beds are operated by the municipalities. The for-profits increased their share from 4% in 2009 to 7% in 2015, while the nonprofits decreased from 6 to 5% (Statistics Norway 2016d). The for-profit share is still surprisingly small when seen in relation to the intense political debates in the Norwegian election campaigns about 'out-contracting of grandma' (Vabø 2011). There has been much enthusiasm for increased competition and user choice, but an administrative separation between contracting agencies and service providers have primarily been used to improve cost and quality control. Only 4% of Norwegian municipalities had introduced user choice in elderly care in 2012 (NHO Service 2013). However, this includes the biggest cities, Bergen and Oslo, with many users. Within home-based care, the public share of the costs is 97%, while the rest is split between for-profit and nonprofit contractors (NHO 2015, 77). In the small area of practical user-steered assistance[6]—publicly funded personal services mainly for people with disabilities—the nonprofit organizations have a major part because the private services, to a large extent, are organized through a cooperative called ULOBA[7] (NHO 2015; NHO Service 2010).

The dominant area in social services is day care for children, with 12,000 full-time employees in 2006 and 14,700 full-time employees in 2013. However, this is a field where the for-profit companies had an even stronger growth from 12,000 to 20,000 full-time employees in the same period as a result of generous public funding arrangements designed to finally reach full coverage of the demand for day care. As a result, the nonprofit share decreased from 22 to 20%, while the for-profit share increased from 22 to 27% of total full-time employment in kindergartens from 2006 to 2013 (Statistics Norway 2016c). In child welfare, we find institutions and homes funded by the state's Children, Youth, and Family Service (Bufetat) with its 5 regional offices. The red–green coalition government wanted to reduce the use of commercial organizations in this field. This may be part of the reason for nonprofit employment growth from 1000 to 1200 full-time employees from 2006 to 2008 (not shown in Table 2.6), but in 2013 the employment was down to the same level as in 2006 again. Other data indicate that the for-profit full-time employment in public contracts increased by more than 50% from 2007 to 2015, while the nonprofit and public sectors were stable (Statistics Norway 2016b). One reason for this may be that some regions have changed from the traditional framework agreements to tenders, and in open competition the for-profits tend to have an advantage.

In substance abuse treatment, which for the most part is services that the state health authorities buy, the nonprofit employment grew from 2000 to 2200 full-time employees (Table 2.6). This despite the fact that here too there have been increasing demands on documentation and some nonprofit institutions have been shut down (Bogen and Grønningsæter 2016). However, the nonprofit employment still grows because they are an important part of the substance abuse treatment with specific competencies and have had up to 40% of the total capacity in some regions (Hatlebakk 2014).

The backdrop for these changes is a number of comprehensive welfare reforms have increased the use of open tendering and quasi-markets in Norway. In some areas, competition for contracts only applies to the operation of new institutions and services, or just between the private providers, while in a few areas there is competition between public, for-profit, and nonprofit actors. The reforms have created special challenges for the nonprofit organizations because open tenders demand a lot of resources, the contracts often have a short duration, and methodological and ideological alternatives may not be much of a competitive advantage, despite the fact that user choice and adaptation have been requested by the politicians. There is an apparent tendency for the for-profits to take market shares when there is an open competition with the nonprofits, such as we have seen in kindergartens, child and family protection, and nursing homes in a few municipalities. The sectors have different advantages. The voluntary actors have in particular stood for the distinctive alternatives, although they are not always good at communicating that to the outside world (Trætteberg and Sivesind 2015). The profit-oriented companies on their side emphasize cost control and user satisfaction and often have a more professional system for quality measurement and preparation of tender documents. This may be because they have access to competence and capital from welfare concerns owned by private investors. This makes them more able to expand in a competitive environment.

All in all, Norway has a mixed model; there is a strong dominance of public welfare provision in some areas, combined with a small share of nonprofit actors. However, increased use of quasi-markets and open tendering in some areas has brought for-profits to grow faster than the nonprofits, in particular in social services. This has resulted in a decrease in the public share of the growing welfare employment.

Nonprofit Stagnation and For-Profit Growth

The composition of welfare providers in publicly funded services in the Scandinavian countries is diverging. Sweden now has the largest for-profit share—and it is still growing. In Norway and Denmark, the for-profits also grow faster than the nonprofit providers. In Denmark, there has even been a slight decline in the nonprofit share, but it is still large by Scandinavian standards. These changes are mainly due to changes in social services. The nonprofit sector in Sweden remains small, although the policy is intended to promote alternatives to the public services. This is because the private growth is stimulated by commercial incentives, while there are no tools for regulating the balance between the public, for-profit, and nonprofit sectors.[8] The for-profits have better access to the economic resources necessary to establish new service institutions that then seek approval from the government agencies based on general criteria. After that, it is up to the users to choose providers. This freedom of choice adds an important quality dimension. However, the Swedish nonprofits, which lost much of their institutional foothold before 1990, have difficulty with raising capital to expand their services in this new regime (Swedish Government Inquiries SOU 2016:78). Consequently, they are unable to realize their potential for providing a broader offer of qualitatively distinctive alternatives that the economic nonprofit theories emphasize (Weisbrod 1977; Steinberg 2006).

There are also differences between the service areas in the three Scandinavian countries. In education, the nonprofits are able to keep their employment shares. However, in Sweden, the for-profits have had a very strong growth. In Norway and Denmark, the nonprofit schools are still the only alternative to the public school system due to requirements for public funding, as we will see in the next chapter.

In health, only Norway has a share of nonprofit service providers of any significance. This is because they, in particular in somatic and psychiatric institutions and substance abuse treatment, are well integrated into the public specialist health system (Bogen and Grønningsæter 2016). In Sweden, there has been a decrease in the public sector and a strong growth in the for-profit shares, which has brought them up to the same level as in Norway and Denmark. This growth will probably continue because there is free right to establish new health services, provided that they get public approval.

In social services, the for-profits have had a stronger growth than the other sectors in all Scandinavian countries. This is the most important reason for a change in total shares of welfare providers in Scandinavia from the public sector to the for-profit sector. This has to do with increasing use of market-emulating tools of governance, such as open tenders, short-term contracts and increasing competition between the sectors. Additionally in Denmark, there have been several reforms that have reduced the nonprofit employment in social services in the short term. Consequently, the nonprofit sector's share goes down while the public and for-profit shares increase. It is too early to say if this is a new trend because the changes in full-time employees are quite small.

In general, nonprofit service providers have not been put under the same competitive pressure in the social services in Denmark as in the other Scandinavian countries. This is because several Danish municipalities include self-owning institutions in an in-house system for allocation of users instead of open tendering. Furthermore, the nonprofit schools have a positive development in Norway and Denmark, while the for-profits grow rapidly in Sweden. The difference is that the service concessions do not allow distribution of profit in publicly funded schools in Norway and Denmark. The self-owning institutions and smaller companies still dominate in Denmark, while there is an increasing concentration of for-profit ownership in a few conglomerates in Sweden and Norway. This shows that the changes in the mix of welfare providers are influenced by the different tools of governance used by the Scandinavian countries.

Why is the Mix of Welfare Providers in the Scandinavian Countries Diverging?

The changes in mix of providers of services funded by the public sector are primarily a result of policies responding to the particular situation in each country 15–20 years ago. Denmark has for a long time politically wanted to provide good and stable conditions for nonprofit welfare provision but has recently allowed for-profit provision in most service areas; Sweden wanted to decrease the public sector dominance in welfare provision and has created commercial incentives that promote growth in for-profit private services; while Norway has preferred public provision as long as there is sufficient capacity, in particular in the most basic types of health services and social care. Nonprofit providers have been invited to closed negotiation and tenders in certain areas, while for-profit providers have been used to increase capacity primarily in kindergartens, child and family protection, and some other social services. This has resulted in diverging changes in employment shares between the nonprofit, for-profit, and public sectors in the welfare services among the Scandinavian countries. The differences are so large that one may ask if there still is such a thing as a Nordic welfare model.

This divergence is happening despite broad implementation of New Public Management tools of government in all the Scandinavian countries. Not many years ago, few considered quasi-markets as a suitable coordination mechanism within the Scandinavian welfare model. Now, the strong prevalence is striking. This is partly a consequence of EU's public procurement directive with formal requirements to open tenders for contracts over a threshold value.[9] This directive also applies to Norway, which is not an EU member, due to the EEA treaty. However, the national regulation of public procurement in the Scandinavian countries is in many ways stricter than the EU directive, which will be a topic in the next chapter.

Some have assumed that the spread of market-emulating governance would result in convergence between the welfare regimes (Henriksen et al. 2012). Looking at the mix of welfare service providers, however, there is rather divergence among the Scandinavian countries—and with other welfare regimes. Sweden still has less nonprofit welfare service provision than any of the western European countries, but this is now combined with a rapidly growing for-profit share. The liberal countries tend to have much larger nonprofit sectors, whereas in the welfare partnership countries, the third sector plays a much larger and more independent role as welfare provider (Anheier and Salamon 2006; Salamon et al. 2004; Sivesind and Selle 2009; Salamon and Sokolowski 2016). In addition, the government, and not the market or the employment-based social insurances, remains the main source of funding for core welfare services in all Scandinavian countries. Denmark has a nonprofit share on a level between the other Scandinavian countries and the welfare partnership model, but this is a result of self-owning institutions and free schools and not semi-public welfare associations with dominating roles in welfare provision as in the welfare partnership countries. In those service areas that have been opened up for private providers, Norway has gone further in allocating contracts by open tenders than the other Scandinavian countries, which has resulted in for-profit growth. However, in other areas, the nonprofit share has been protected by continuation of framework agreements, particularly in nursing homes, and by closed tenders and negotiations in areas like child and family protection. Still, there has been little focus on taking advantage of the nonprofit sector's potential distinctiveness among the contracting agencies (Trætteberg and Sivesind 2015). All in all, the diverging development trends between the Scandinavian countries are a result of policy responses to different compositions of welfare service providers in each country that had evolved before the NPM tools were implemented. However, welfare reforms were also motivated by different political ideologies.

This is not the place to go through the long historic development of variations of the social democratic welfare model among the Scandinavian countries, but Sweden's development of a welfare model has been characterized by a centralized and paternalistic corporatism. According to Tim Knudsen and Bo Rothstein (1994), this was a result of a system of estate representation that was gradually changed to a liberal society. In Denmark, in contrast, there was an abrupt shift from modern absolutism to a representative democracy in 1848–1849. The end of absolutism was brought about by liberal movements, based on both farmers and liberal bourgeoisie. These forces demanded that alternatives to the public schools should get financial support from the public sector, resulting in a pragmatic welfare liberalism (Knudsen and Rothstein 1994). This turned out to be a model where different social groups could create institutions promoting certain views of life, values, pedagogies, or activities.

The different welfare models in Sweden and Denmark can also be recognized in the development after WWII. Sweden focused on developing welfare services provided by the public sector in order to reduce social inequality, to a large extent with support of the civil society (Rothstein and Trägårdh 2007). In Denmark, there was broad political support also for alternatives to the public sector, and the self-owning institutions and free schools could continue to evolve independently of which political parties were in government. By the beginning of the 1990s, Sweden had an extremely large public welfare employment share. For Sweden, the expansion of the private welfare provision after 2000 could be seen as steps towards becoming a normal, western welfare society. In Denmark, changes seemed less urgent. The larger nonprofit sector represented more distinct alternatives for choice, and volunteering and civic engagement were politically promoted as antidotes to bureaucratization and passivity that could be the result of a self-contained public welfare system (Henriksen and Bundesen 2004).

In Norway, the nonprofit sector's role was smaller than in Denmark and more fragmented, and the public policy towards it was often particularistic and pragmatic. Long-term collaborative relationships between the public sector and the nonprofit providers evolved in services like elderly care, substance abuse treatment, and health care, often as the result of the strength of counter-cultural popular movements in the peripheral districts related to lay Christian communities, new Norwegian language, or temperance (Sivesind and Selle 2010; Rokkan 1967). In the 1980s, privatization of welfare services was put on the agenda by a conservative political surge, and there has recently been for-profit growth in particular in social services like kindergartens, child and family protection, and rehabilitation.

However, as we have seen, in elderly care the changes in the welfare provider mix have been small, despite fierce political debates (Vabø 2011). Even in large municipalities close to larger cities with a conservative majority, only one or two institutions for elderly care have typically been out-contracted to for-profit providers. This is done to establish a market price that is then used for benchmarking of similar public sector services. Because of good economic conditions and expanding welfare employment, there have been less urgent needs to cut costs by contracting out services. In many welfare areas, it has even been difficult to get enough qualified professionals in the public sector. Private employers with lower pay and inferior pension systems would have little to offer in such a tight labour market. In addition, there was a strong resistance against privatization fronted by the Norwegian Union of Municipal and General Employees (Fagforbundet), which is the largest union in The Norwegian Confederation of Trade Unions (LO Norway) with nearly 340,000 members. Instead of just arguing for status quo, they collaborated with other trade unions and the Norwegian Association of Local and Regional Authorities (KS) and political authorities to initiate several programs for improvement of services in the municipalities that ran subsequently from 1998 to 2015, in many cases with measurable success (Vabø et al. 2013, 185–188). In many municipalities, framework agreements with nonprofit providers have been prolonged, but in the cases where there has been open tender competition, the for-profit providers tend to prevail, if not in the first round, then in almost all cases in the second round of tendering (Herning 2015). In Sweden, the public sector was under stronger pressure to cut costs, and private service providers in elderly care could offer lower costs than services provided in-house by the municipalities (see Chap. 4 by Feltenius).

Like the other Scandinavian countries, Sweden implemented NPM and quasi-markets as tools of governance. However, in Sweden, additional steps were taken to create competition between the public and private welfare providers. A centre-right government from 1991 to 1994 opened up for competitive tendering and user choice in the municipalities. The social democratic governments from 1994 to 2006 did not reverse these reforms, and the for-profit employment share kept increasing. There was a debate within the social democratic party between the 'state-socialists,' who wanted to stop the for-profit welfare growth and the 'popular movement democrats,' who did not see public monopoly on service provision as a precondition for a social democratic welfare state (Trägårdh 2007). At the party congress in 2001, this controversy resulted in a compromise involving an enquiry about nonprofit institutions (Lindbom 2013) that in retrospect has been of little consequence.

From 2006 to 2014, the centre-right minority government went even further by strengthening general rights for user choice (Freedom of Choice Act, LOV 2008: 962), which includes funding through some kind of voucher systems, reduced barriers for establishment of new welfare services depending on approval by national public agencies, and no restrictions on transferring profit to owners. The intention was to reduce the public sector dominance by creating effective quasi-markets where the users can reject service providers they dislike, and with low barriers for establishment of new service providers. The goal was to create a dynamic where bad institutions would disappear and good institutions would take over. However, an unintended consequence has been that a very large share of the for-profit companies is owned by a few conglomerates with vested interests in health, education, and social services. Politicians also argue that stronger and more direct measures against low performing institutions are necessary in the public as well as the private sectors.

The venture capitalists may not be taking out revenue from the companies on a regular basis, even if they have legal right to do so. If they can develop services and expand the business, they can sell with a profit after some years. This opportunity to buy and sell shares has introduced an incentive to growth for private companies. However, it does not work on the nonprofit actors. Their main concern is developing distinct service profiles in terms of religion, ideology, or methods, and they may therefore not be interested in competing on a bid to take over a welfare institution with its employees, maybe only to lose it again after a 3-year period. It takes time to form services in line with the organization's main goals. Growth is not a goal in itself. Nonprofit welfare providers may also have a more local basis and therefore lack capital reserves to come back if they lose the contract to operate a particular institution. In the long run, the for-profit providers prevail, and this endangers provision of qualitatively different services that, according to some economic theories, are characteristic for the nonprofit sector (Weisbrod 1977), and such distinct alternatives to choose from may be important for the long-term support of government-funded welfare services. A study by Dahlberg et al. shows that in service areas with the implementation of user choice in combination with rights to establish new service units in Sweden, there seems to be faster growth in the for-profit sector than in areas with competitive tendering. When the law of freedom of choice is implemented through one political decision on the national level, as it was in primary health care in 2010, this speeds up the for-profit growth (Dahlberg et al. 2013, 226).

Service providers owned by welfare conglomerates are emerging as a new type of actor with their own interests, business partners, and strategic alliances in politics and public administrations, which in turn results in improvement in their own framework conditions. When politicians that are sceptical of privatization come to power at the national, county, or local level, they may have stopped the acceleration but seldom reversed previous reforms. Political goodwill for the nonprofits is not enough to increase their share of the welfare employees when they are regulated in the same way as the for-profits. The growth incentives continue to work on the for-profit sector and not on the nonprofit sector, and the long-term result will be a fundamental change of the Swedish welfare model.

In all the Scandinavian countries, the nonprofit welfare providers enjoy broad political support, and the governments have even signed compacts with the voluntary organizations providing health services and social care, inspired by a similar agreement made in the UK (Johansson and Johansson 2012). The intention is to establish shared principles and guidelines for effective and high-quality services and dialogue while securing predictability, autonomy, and distinctiveness for the voluntary organizations. In Denmark, the compact signed in 2001 is a rather general declaration of interests, and it is difficult to put the finger on concrete results. Still, the compact was renewed in 2013.[10] However, we see clear effects of long-term, broad political support, and a highly institutionalized relationship between the government and the nonprofit organizations. An example of this is that the municipalities are stimulated by the government to involve voluntary organizations on the social service field by special funding (§18-collaboration between the municipalities and voluntary social organizations).

In Norway, the compact is followed up by dialogue meetings between the Minister and representatives of organizations once or twice a year. Since it was signed in October 2012, there are examples of tenders and negotiations that are only open to nonprofit actors, and also of a new type of service contracts that do not have a fixed termination date. When we consider the Norwegian nonprofit sector's growth (Table 2.6), there seems to be an effect of the red–green coalition government's (2005–2013) willingness to prioritize nonprofit organizations when the public sector itself does not have sufficient capacity. The conservative coalition government from 2013 also supported the compact, but has been more in favour of sector neutral policies. The for-profit sector has had a stronger growth rate as a result of the strategy of several governments to increase capacity through generous funding arrangements in areas like kindergartens.

In Sweden, the nonprofit sector did not have a real foothold before the privatization process started in the 1990s and has been lagging behind. Even though the compact that was signed in 2008 has a very elaborate strategy for stimulating regional and local processes, this has not resulted in an increase in nonprofit employment shares. It is difficult to create growth when the sector is reduced to a minimum and lacks effective framework conditions for growth. In addition, the population has little previous experience with distinctive nonprofit sector services so it is difficult for the stakeholders to muster broad political support.

A general finding from this comparison of welfare service areas and institutional sectors in Scandinavia is that competitive tendering results in for-profit growth and nonprofit stagnation or decline. It is difficult to find one example of a welfare area in Sweden and Norway where this is not the case. In Denmark, such changes are not yet so easy to see in the statistics because of a stronger tradition for nonprofit sector services.

However, recent reforms may encourage increasing for-profit shares in Denmark too. By comparing the tools of governance used by the Scandinavian countries, it becomes clear that equal opportunities and political goodwill are not sufficient to develop a distinctive nonprofit sector with critical mass. It takes long-term contracts and restrictions on transfer of profits, a clear preference for the distinctive features of the nonprofit providers, or negotiations or tenders reserved for nonprofits.

For example, the nonprofit sectors in Norway and Denmark have in particular had a strong position in primary and secondary education, which is regulated by service concessions with nonprofit status as a condition for approval, and not by competitive tendering. Another example is in-house law that is used to promote self-owning institutions in kindergartens and elderly care in Denmark. This shows that a differentiated welfare provider mix depends on differentiated types of regulation. However, this is not often recognized in political debates about how to reduce the public sector dominance and to increase competition, where arguments about equal competition dominate. Changes in the welfare provider mix, and in particular the share that remains for the nonprofit sector, tend to be unintended consequences rather than clearly formulated political goals. Denmark has been an exception so far, but now privatization and competition are becoming goals in themselves, and new regulations open up for profit-oriented companies in more service areas.

NPM tools are used to regulate the relation between the government's contracting agencies and welfare service providers in the public, for-profit, and nonprofit sectors in all Scandinavian countries in similar ways as in many other European countries. As such, this does not result in diverging welfare models. The social democratic welfare ideals, funding model, and a certain share of nonprofit services can be sustained together with these tools of governance, as we have seen in Denmark and in some service areas also in Norway. However, Sweden has chosen to implement an additional set of policy instruments, including increasingly broad enactment of user choice and reduced restrictions on the establishment of new welfare institutions, combined with no limits on transfer of profits. This has set in motion rapid and broad expansion of the for-profit sector with a long-term regime-changing potential. A diversified welfare mix depends on diversified tools of governance, which includes reserved tendering and negotiations, service concessions, or in-house service contracts. This can be used to secure a certain nonprofit share in service areas where policymakers consider it to be particularly valuable. These different types of regulation and legal frameworks in the Scandinavian countries will be the topic of the next chapter.

Notes

1. This means the number of percentage points change divided by the total number of years and multiplied by five. For total welfare employment, percent change is divided by total number of years and multiplied by five. Five-year periods are chosen because 1 year change would result in very small numbers, and the focus here is on cumulative long-term changes.
2. The real employment numbers are shown in Tables 2.3, 2.4, and 2.5.
3. Maximum years are not shown in the Table.
4. The main source for the following presentation of changes in the Danish welfare mix is a report by Malene Thøgersen about self-owning institutions in Denmark (Thøgersen 2013).
5. 'Nursing homes' is moved to social services here to match with Table 2.5, which is set up in line with Statistics Norway's version of NACE.
6. «personlig brukerstyrt assistanse (PBA)».
7. ULOBA is a cooperative that is employer for the personal assistants for disabled persons who are stake owners.
8. A new Swedish Government Inquiry (SOU 2016: 78) suggests a replacement of the Freedom of Choice Act (LOV 2008: 962) that includes tools to promote the nonprofit providers and regulation of the level of profits, but it is doubtful if there is political support for this in the Parliament.
9. EU's public procurement directive 2004/18/EC, which was replaced with Directive 2014/24/EU http://eur-lex.europa.eu/legal-content/EN/TXT/?uri=CELEX%3A32014L0024.
10. http://www.frivilligcharter.dk/sites/default/files/attachments/Frivillighedscharter.pdf.

Appendix

The definition of *nonprofit organizations* is based on UN's *Handbook on Non-Profit Institutions in the System of National Accounts* (United Nations 2003). The most important criteria are that the organization is not subordinate to public structures of governance, although substantial parts of the income may come from the public sector. The organization does not distribute profit to owners, directors, members, or others, which means that it does not primarily have a commercial orientation. The surplus must be used in line with the main goals of the organization.

The Danish data for nonprofit, for-profit, and total employment of the welfare area cover P Education and Q Health and social services in DB07, which is Statistics Denmark's version of EU's NACE Rev. 2. The source is Statistics Denmark's statistics bank, table «LBESK32: Fuldtidsbeskæftigede lønmodtagere efter branche (DB07 19-grp), sektor og tid». This is the only source of full-time employment data, but it only covers the years 2008–2013. To differentiate between health and social services, we use ratios for a number of employees from the table «RASOFF34 Beskæftigede lønmodtagere efter branche (DB07), sektor og tid». The data for nonprofit employment are estimates for the ICNPO categories Education, Health, and Social Services (Boje 2017, Table 4.10) except for the modifications described in Table 2.2 above. The data for nonprofit employment are higher than in table LBESK32, and this difference is subtracted from the public sector employment. This is because LBESK32 uses sector coding from ESA2010. This implies that self-owning institutions with operating contracts with the public sector according to the 'in-house' regulations are included in the public sector. However, according to the *Handbook on Non-Profit Institutions in the System of National Accounts* (United Nations 2003), they should be part of the nonprofit sector. The calculation of employment in 2008 is based on the assumption that there has been a linear growth from 2003 to 2013, which are the two data points covered by the source (Boje 2017, Table 4.10).

The Norwegian data for nonprofit employment are from Statistics Norway's satellite account (Statistics Norway 2015) for the ICNPO categories Education, Health, and Social Services, except for the modifications described in Table 2.2 above. Table 2.5 is set up in line with SN2007, which is Statistics Norway's version of EU's NACE Rev.2. The for-profit employment data are the residual between the total employment and the public and the nonprofit sector. The Swedish data do not show full-time employment but the number of employed persons from the table «Antal sysselsatta fördelat på sektor inom vård, skola och omsorg» in Statistics Sweden's 'Officiella Statistik Serie Offentlig Economi OE 29 SM 1001 2014' and 'OE 29 SM 1501 2015'. The services are classified according to SNI2007, which is Statistics Sweden's version of EU's NACE Rev. 2.

References

Anheier, K. Helmut, and Lester M. Salamon. 2006. The nonprofit sector in comparative perspective. In *The nonprofit sector. A research handbook*, eds. Walter W. Powell and Richard Steinberg, 90–114. New Haven: Yale University Press.

Bogen, Hanne, and Arne Backer Grønningsæter. 2016. *En ideell forskjell? Om ideelle aktører i spesialisthelsetjenesten.* (Fafo-rapport 2016:30). Oslo: FAFO.

Boje, Thomas P. 2006. Den danske nonprofitsektor sammenlignet med andre europæiske lande. In *Frivillighed og nonprofit i Danmark. Omfang, organisation, økonomi og beskæftigelse*, eds. Thomas P. Boje and Bjarne Ibsen, 217–224. København: Socialforskningsinstituttet.

———. 2017. *Civilsamfund, medborgerskab og deltakelse.* København: Hans Reitzels Forlag.

Boje, Thomas P., Torben Fridberg, and Bjarne Ibsen. 2006. *Den frivillige sektor i Danmark. Omfang og betydning.* København: Socialforskningsinstituttet.

Dahlberg, Matz, Mikael Elinder, David Isaksson, Henrik Jordahl, Anders Lindblom, Ulrika Winblad, and Richard Öhrvall. 2013. Slutsatser. In *Välfärdstjänster i privat regi. Framväxt och drivkrafter*, ed. Henrik Jordahl, 221–230. Stockholm: SNS Förlag.

Erlandsson, Sara, Palle Storm, Anneli Strantz, Marta Szebehely, and Gunn-Britt Trydegård. 2013. Marketising trends in Swedish eldercare: Competition, choice and calls for stricter regulation. In *Marketisation in Nordic eldercare: A research report on legislation, oversight, extent and consequences*, eds. Gabrielle

Meagher and Marta Szebehely, 23–84. Stockholm: Department of Social Work, Stockholm University.

Hatlebakk, Ingrid Myrset. 2014. Rusbehandling—mye i privat regi. *Samfunnsspeilet* (2/2014). Oslo: Statistisk Sentralbyrå.

Heikki, Ervasti, Torben Fridberg, Mikael Hjerm, Olli Kangas, and Kristen Ringdal. 2008. The Nordic model. In *Nordic social attitudes in a European perspective*, eds. Heikki Ervasti, Torben Fridberg, Mikael Hjerm, and Kristen Ringdal, 1–21. Cheltenham: Edward Elgar.

Henriksen, Lars Skov, and Peter Bundesen. 2004. The moving frontier in Denmark: Voluntary-state relationships since 1850. *Journal of Social Policy* 33 (4): 601–621.

Henriksen, Lars Skov, Annette Zimmer, and Steven Rathgeb Smith. 2012. At the eve of convergence? Transformations of social service provision in Denmark, Germany, and the United States. *VOLUNTAS: International Journal of Voluntary and Nonprofit Organizations* 23 (2): 458–501.

Herning, Linn. 2015. *Velferdsprofitørene*. Oslo: Manifest forlag.

Johansson, Ola. 2011. *Tjäna eller tjäna?—om vård eller vinst. Privatisering av vård, omsorg, skola—vilka tar över?* Stockholm: Famna.

Johansson, Håkan, and Mairon Johansson. 2012. From a 'Liberal' to a 'Social democratic' welfare state: The translation of the English compact into a Swedish context. *Nonprofit Policy Forum* 3 (2). doi:10.1515/2154-3348.1057.

Knudsen, Tim, and Bo Rothstein. 1994. State building in Scandinavia. *Comparative Politics* 26 (2): 203–220. doi:10.2307/422268.

Laura, Hartman. 2011. *Konkurrensens konsekvenser. Vad händer med svensk välfärd?* Stockholm: SNS Förlag.

Lindbom, Anders. 2013. Socialdemokraterna och privat drift i välfärden: två idétraditioner. In *Välfärdstjänster i privat regi. Framväxt och drivkrafter*, ed. Henrik Jordahl. Stockholm: SNS Förlag.

Lundström, Tommy, and Filip Wijkström. 1997. *The nonprofit sector in Sweden, The Johns Hopkins nonprofit sector series*. Manchester: Manchester University Press.

NHO Service. 2015. *Statistikk og trender 2015*. Oslo.

———. 2010. *Omsorgstjenester. Bransjestatistikk 2011*. Oslo.

———. 2013. *Status for valgfrihet i eldreomsorgen i Skandinavia*. Oslo.

Norwegian Directorate for Education and Training. 2015. *Skolefakta—Elevar, lærarar, skolar*. Oslo.

Pierson, Paul. 2001. *The new politics of the welfare state*. Oxford: Oxford University Press.

Report to the Storting (White Paper) nr. 29. 2012–2013. *Future Care*. Oslo: Helse- og omsorgsdepartementet.
Rokkan, Stein. 1967. Geography, religion, and social class: Crosscutting cleavages in Norwegian politics. In *Party systems and voter alignments*, eds. Seymor M. Lipset and Stein Rokkan, 367–444. New York: The Free Press.
Rothstein, Bo, and Lars Trägårdh. 2007. The state and civil society in an historical perspective: The Swedish case. In *State and civil society in Northern Europe. The Swedish model reconsidered*, ed. Lars Trägårdh, 229–253. New York: Berghahn Books.
Salamon, Lester M., and Helmut K. Anheier. 1998. Social origins of civil society: Explaining the nonprofit sector cross-nationally. *VOLUNTAS: International Journal of Voluntary and Nonprofit Organizations* 9 (3): 213–248.
Salamon, Lester M., S. Wojciech Sokolowski, and Associates. 2004. *Global civil society: Dimensions of the nonprofit sector*, vol. II. Bloomfield, CT: Kumarian Press.
Salamon, Lester M., and S. Wojciech Sokolowski. 2016. *The size and scope of the European third sector*. Brussels: European Union FP7 (grant agreement 613034). Third Sector Impact.
Sivesind, Karl Henrik. 2008. *Halvveis til Soria Moria. Ikke-kommersielle velferdstjenester, politikkens blinde flekk?* Oslo: Institutt for samfunnsforskning.
———. 2008b. Nonprofit organisasjoner på velferdsfeltet i Norden. In *Det frivillige Danmark*, eds. Bjarne Ibsen, Thomas P. Boje, and Torben Fridberg, 161–178. Odense: Syddansk Universitetsforlag.
Sivesind, Karl Henrik, and Per Selle. 2009. Does public spending "crowd out" nonprofit welfare? *Comparative Social Research. A Research Annual* 26: 105–134. doi:10.1108/S0195-6310(2009)0000026009.
Sivesind, Karl Henrik, Håkon Lorentzen, Per Selle, Dag Wollebæk, S.Wojciech Sokolowski, and Lester M. Salamon. 2004. Norway. In *Global civil society: Dimensions of the nonprofit sector*, vol. II, eds. Lester M. Salamon, S. Wojciech Sokolowski, and Associates, 261–275. Bloomfield: Kumarian Press.
Soria Moria-erklæringen. 2005. *Plattform for regjeringssamarbeidet mellom Arbeiderpartiet, Sosialistisk Venstreparti og Senterpartiet 2005-09*. Oslo, October 13 2005.
Statistics Norway. 2015. Table 08520: Full-time equivalent persons, by activity (ICNPO). *Satellite account for non-profit institutions*. https://ssb.no/orgsat.
———. 2016a. National economy. *Table 09174, FTE employment in Education, Health and Social Work*. www.ssb.no/pleie.

―――. 2016b. *Table 07126: Children's institutions. Contractual man-years adjusted for long-term leaves, by region, age of the personnel and ownership of the institution.* www.ssb.no/statistikkbanken.

―――. 2016c. *Table 09339: Man-years in kindergartens, by ownership and employment position.* www.ssb.no/statistikkbanken.

―――. 2016d. *Table 09929: Institutions for the aged and disabled, by ownership.* www.ssb.no/pleie.

Steinberg, Richard. 2006. Economic theories of nonprofit organizations. In *The nonprofit sector. A research handbook*, eds. Walter W. Powell and Richard Steinberg, 117–139. New Haven: Yale University Press.

Swedish Competition Authority. 2010. *Uppföljning av vårdval i primärvården. Valfrihet, mångfald och etableringsförutsättningar. Slutrapport.* Stockholm: Konkurrensverket.

Swedish Government Inquiries SOU 2016:78. *Ordning och reda i välfärden.* Stockholm: Ministry of Finance.

Swedish National Agency for Education. 2016. *Skolor och elever i grundskolan läsåret 2015/16.* Stockholm.

Szebehely, Marta. 2011. Insatser för äldre och funktionshindrade i privat regi. In *Konkurrensens konsekvenser. Vad händer med svensk välfärd?*, ed. Laura Hartman, 215–257. Stockholm: SNS Förlag.

Taylor-Gooby, Peter. 2008. *Reframing Social Citizenship.* Oxford: Oxford University Press.

Thøgersen, Malene. 2013. *Selvejende institutioner i Danmark. Institutionernes udvikling, udbredelse og karakter på udvalgte samfundsområder.* Aalborg: Netværk for forskning i Civilsamfund og Frivillighed.

Trætteberg, Håkon Dalby, and Karl Henrik Sivesind. 2015. *Ideelle organisasjoners særtrekk og merverdi på helse- og omsorgsfeltet.* Oslo: Senter for forskning på sivilsamfunn og frivillig sektor.

Trägårdh, Lars. 2007. The 'civil society' debate in Sweden: The welfare state challenged. In *State and civil society in Northern Europe. The Swedish model reconsidered*, ed. Lars Trägårdh, 9–36. New York: Berghahn Books.

United Nations. 2003. *Handbook on nonprofit institutions in the system of national accounts.* New York: United Nations.

Vabø, Mia. 2011. Active citizenship in Norwegian elderly care. From Activation to consumer activism. In *Participation, responsibility and choice. Summoning the active citizen in Western European welfare states*, eds. Janet Newman and Evelien Tonkens, 87–105. Amsterdam: Amsterdam University Press.

Vabø, Mia, Karen Christensen, Frode Fadnes Jacobsen, and Håkon Dalby Trætteberg. 2013. Marketisation in Norwegian eldercare: Preconditions, trends and resistance. In *Marketisation in Nordic eldercare: A research report on legislation, oversight, extent and consequences*, eds. Gabrielle Meagher and Marta Szebehely, 163–202. Stockholm: Department of Social Work, Stockholm University.

Vlachos, Jonas. 2011. Friskolor i förändring. In *Konkurrensens konsekvenser. Vad händer med svensk välfärd?*, ed. Laura Hartman, 66–110. Stockholm: SNS Förlag.

Voitto, Helander, and Karl Henrik Sivesind. 2001. Frivilligsektorns betydelse i Norden. In *Frivillighedens udfordringer*, eds. Lars Skov Henriksen and Bjarne Ibsen, 49–66. Odense: Odense Universitetsforlag.

Weisbrod, Burton A. 1977. *The voluntary nonprofit sector, an economic analysis*. Lexington: D.C. Heath.

Wijkström, Filip, and Torbjörn Einarsson. 2006. *Från nationalstat til näringsliv. Det civila samhällets organisasjonsliv i förändring*. Stockholm: Ekonomiska Forskningsinstitutet, Handelshögskolan i Stockholm.

Wiklund, Stefan. 2011. Individ- och familjeomsorgens välfärdstjänster. In *Konkurrensens konsekvenser. Vad händer med svensk välfärd?*, ed. Laura Hartman, 111–145. Stockholm: SNS Förlag.

———. 2010. Civil society in the Nordic countries: Between displacement and vitality. In *Nordic associations in a European perspective*, eds. Risto Alapuro and Henrik Stenius, 89–120. Baden-Baden: Nomos Verlagsgesellschaft.

Zweifel, Peter, Carl Hampus Lyttkens, and Lars Söderström. 1998. *Regulation of health: Case studies of Sweden and Switzerland*, vol. 7, Developments in health economics and public policy. Boston: Kluwer.

Author Biography

Karl Henrik Sivesind is a research professor at the Institute for Social Research, Oslo, Norway. He is currently manager of the project 'Conditions and Impacts of Welfare Mix' funded by the Norwegian Research Council, and he is leader for Work Package 'Elaboration and Testing of Impact Indicators' on the project 'Third Sector Impact—The Contribution of the Third Sector to Europe's Socio-economic Development' funded by the EU's 7th Framework Programme. He has studied changes affecting civil society by analysing data from population surveys and local association surveys as a part of the activities of Centre for Research on Civil Society and Voluntary Sector in Oslo/Bergen. He has also been involved in several comparative research projects about the nonprofit sector and welfare services.

Open Access This chapter is licensed under the terms of the Creative Commons Attribution 4.0 International License (http://creativecommons.org/licenses/by/4.0/), which permits use, sharing, adaptation, distribution and reproduction in any medium or format, as long as you give appropriate credit to the original author(s) and the source, provide a link to the Creative Commons license and indicate if changes were made.

The images or other third party material in this chapter are included in the chapter's Creative Commons license, unless indicated otherwise in a credit line to the material. If material is not included in the chapter's Creative Commons license and your intended use is not permitted by statutory regulation or exceeds the permitted use, you will need to obtain permission directly from the copyright holder.

3

Education and Elderly Care in Denmark, Norway and Sweden: National Policies and Legal Frameworks for Private Providers

Signe Bock Segaard and Jo Saglie

Introduction

As a starting point for the case studies of the following chapters, this chapter presents the national context for municipal welfare services: primary and lower secondary education, and institution-based elderly care. We aim to shed light on the national political, legal and institutional framework within which local welfare services are provided, and how different frameworks may have consequences for the welfare mix.

To what extent is the national context in Denmark, Norway and Sweden different? In the literature on 'welfare regimes', there is considerable agreement that the three countries can be placed within the 'Nordic model' (Ervasti et al. 2008, 5). This points to several similarities in the organisation of the welfare state. Welfare services are, to a great

---

S.B. Segaard (✉) · J. Saglie
Institute for Social Research, Oslo, Norway
e-mail: sbs@socialresearch.no

J. Saglie
e-mail: jo.saglie@socialresearch.no

© The Author(s) 2017
K.H. Sivesind and J. Saglie (eds.), *Promoting Active Citizenship*,
DOI 10.1007/978-3-319-55381-8_3

extent, publicly financed and provided on the basis of universal rights, and the municipalities play a crucial role in the implementation of these services. That is also to say that private providers of publicly financed welfare services operate within a context characterised by mainly public providers. Furthermore, during recent decades, promoting active citizenship in public service has been and still is an overall aim in all three Scandinavian countries. This has implied a stronger emphasis on more user involvement and empowerment as well as on developing a broader range of services and creating genuine user choice between alternative service providers. However, and as we will show in this chapter, the tools of government for promoting this aim have been different in the three countries. Another common element is that public-sector procurement is regulated by an EU Directive that all three countries have implemented, even though the implementation has to some extent taken place in different ways and at different points in time (Segaard 2015). On the one hand, an international perspective makes it clear that the Scandinavian welfare states share many features—which separate them from other countries. On the other hand, there are also considerable differences between the Scandinavian countries themselves, and these differences have become more pronounced during recent decades. As the previous chapter shows, the differences apply to the mix of public, nonprofit and for-profit services within education and elderly care. While the extent of private *nonprofit* providers is relatively large in Denmark, *for-profit* service providers play a more significant role in Sweden. In Norway, the roles of both of these types of private actors are in fact comparatively modest. However, in an international context, the sizes of the nonprofit and for-profit sectors in the Scandinavian countries are still relatively small.

The starting point is thus that some fundamental differences in the organisation of welfare services exist between the three countries, in spite of the overall similarities. This chapter aims to explore one possible explanation for this: the national policy, legal and institutional framework for private service providers. In exploring this, we develop and use three government models as a framework for comparison of the national policies on private—both nonprofit and for-profit—actors in service production. We make a distinction between direct, indirect and disconnected government. The underlying question is whether variations in such national government models can explain the observed differences in the national 'welfare mix' of public, nonprofit and for-profit services within both education and elderly care. Regardless of the answer, the next question is naturally whether some underlying factors affect differences in national policy models as well as differences in the actual welfare mix. There is no room for a comprehensive discussion of such factors in this chapter, but politics as a driving factor will be briefly discussed in the concluding section.

Three Government Models

As an analytical framework to explore and capture national welfare policy and legislation for private providers of publicly financed elderly care and education, we develop three ideal government models of how publicly funded welfare services might be organised: (1) direct government, (2) indirect government and (3) disconnected government. The models, summarised in Table 3.1, reflect different policies for public–private collaboration on public welfare production and thereby represent different approaches to the welfare mix on a more general level. The policies might manifest in contracts and institutional systems for approval and supervision, for example. The way supervision is organised (self-evaluation or control by national authorities, general or detailed criteria) is significant for understanding the freedom of discretion that each actor has.

Table 3.1 Ideal models of government in public welfare production

	Actors	Discretion
Direct government		
Pure public organisation	Public	Public
Contracting	Public/Private	Public
Indirect government		
Collaborative governance	Public/Private	Public/Private
Disconnected government		
Free market-based organisation	Private	Private
Philanthropy	Private	Private

The typology is developed by the authors based on Donahue and Zeckhauser (2006, 496ff).

Each of the government models reflects a specific solution for organisation and interaction between public and private actors—non-profit as well as for-profit—in the production of welfare services. The solutions are different with regard to where discretionary power over central aspects of service production is allocated.

We distinguish between three types of discretionary power. *Production discretion* involves the competence and possibility to specify the goals and means of the welfare service in question. *Payoff discretion* refers to the freedom to decide how the final outcome in monetary terms should be used and distributed by the private service provider. This also concerns the opportunity for the provider to transfer profits to owners and investors. Moreover, payoff discretion involves defining the end result: Should it be perceived as good or bad? The organisation of supervision and control may be significant in this respect. The service provider will have a larger extent of payoff discretion if supervision is based on self-evaluation with general evaluation criteria, compared with supervision carried out by a national authority and based on detailed criteria. Finally, *preference discretion* refers to the normative view and understanding of the welfare service and the mission behind it. Preferences and underlying values may be related to pedagogy, professional ethics, beliefs, philosophy or religious faith. Discretion in service production therefore involves a kind of freedom to define the public interest behind the service provision (Donahue and Zeckhauser 2006, 514).

Looking at how discretion is approached in the three government models, the public sector is assumed to have full discretionary power in the *direct government* model, regardless of whether a purely public organisation or contracting is chosen. In the latter case, the public principal commissions the work and governs through monopoly of discretion with regard to production, payoff and preferences. The monopoly will manifest in the contract, which will appear as a means for control and performance measuring (Phillips and Smith 2011). In this context, 'contracting' does not refer to the existence of a written contract, but rather interaction between the authorities and a private actor which is solely based on the simple delegation of tasks without any freedom of discretion.

In the *disconnected government* model, freedom of discretion is assumed to be fully handed over to the nonpublic service provider through the free market or pure philanthropy. The model of the free market assumes that government and organisation of welfare services take place through users' freedom of choice and competition between private service providers. The difference between free market and pure philanthropy is not related to discretion, but to the kind of private actors involved. In pure philanthropy, private actors are nonprofit, whereas a pure market model includes only for-profit actors. In real life, however, the picture is more mixed.

The *indirect government* category in the model comprises collaborative governance.[1] This refers to collaboration between a public principal and a private—for-profit or nonprofit—service provider characterised by self-regulation within a specific political and institutional framework (Sørensen and Torfing 2008, 10). Moreover, with regard to discretion, we consider collaborative governance to be '[t]he murky middle ground, in which both parties exercise discretion' (Donahue and Zeckhauser 2006, 514). The empirical question is how and to what extent discretion is divided when it comes to 'defining not only the means by which a goal is achieved but the details of the goal itself' (Donahue and Zeckhauser 2006, 497). In line with Donahue and Zeckhauser, we underline two considerations that are important for how discretion is shared between actors. First, a consideration of democracy requires that 'a large share of discretion must rest with a player who is answerable to the public at large' (2006, 509). At the same time, both the public principal and the nonpublic provider must have some share of discretion—otherwise, the relationship would not be collaborative (2006, 509).

The literature on governance points to 'relational contracting' as a distinguishing feature of collaborative governance:

> [a]lthough contracts may continue to be important policy tools, they would be more than a means of control over the purchase of service (...). The focus on strengthening relationships should be evidenced by more relational contracting which puts an emphasis on working toward common goals, promoting communication and flexibility, and developing trust. (Phillips and Smith 2011, 5)

Public–private interaction based on the idea of collaborative governance is often praised for its flexibility and capacity; but, as Donahue and Zeckhauser (2006, 497) stated, 'at the price of more ambiguous lines of authority and far greater strategic complexity'.

Table 3.1 presents the models of government in welfare production as ideal types. This is appropriate as an analytic framework when the intention is to identify similarities and differences; however, we are aware that it does not necessarily represent the whole empirical reality. The pure models may be combined with each other to create a more complex regime of government in welfare production. For instance, such a layered government may combine the idea of free user choice with elements from the (in)direct model when the authorities, through pure public organisation, contracting or collaboration with more than one service provider, facilitate the free choice of the user. Here, layered government implies organising the welfare mix through two steps: first, the selection of providers by the authority and then, in the next step, selection by individual users.

Our approach to and understanding of the welfare mix is (partly) based on the assumption that government models are chosen and developed over time in light of political visions and ideologies. This understanding is in accordance with Phillips and Smith's (2011) explanation of why private service providers—nonprofit as well as for-profit—have become more involved in public welfare production. They remind us that it is not the type of welfare state that explains the development towards more or less relational governance and involvement by the third sector, but rather political visions and the ability to collaborate (2011, 23–24):

> ...a vision of the role of the third sector that sees it as more than a social safety net or delivery agent of services, but that advances the value of the sector for democracy and citizenship and/or economic development. The vision then needs to be driven by strong political leadership. A connection to democratization or economic development is evident in all cases in which major reform has occurred (...). However, it is also clear that such a reform project has to be mutual and that neither government nor the third sector can drive it alone.

The remainder of this chapter comprises three sections. Each section discusses factors at the national level that may affect the use of nonpublic actors in local service production within primary and lower secondary education, and institution-based elderly care. We limit the analysis to the state as of mid-2015. *First*, in the following section, we briefly outline the EU Public Procurement Directive (Directive 2004/18/EC) that has been in effect the last decade and how national legislation in the three countries is related to it. To fully understand the national framework, it is necessary to take into account that EU policies set limits for the national legal framework. Norway, Denmark and Sweden are obliged to implement EU directives. Regarding outsourcing of welfare services, the EU Public Procurement Directive is especially relevant. *Second*, we address national policies on schools and elderly care. Within each country, national policy standards are set by means of various policy documents—legislation, instructions, guidelines, etc. Based on the analysis of these national policy documents, we compare and discuss national policies which direct how contracts are awarded and coordinated within these municipal welfare services. *Finally*, in the concluding section, we summarise our findings and discuss underlying political factors that may explain national policies as well as the welfare mix.

The EU Public Procurement Directive and Its Implementation at the National Level

In the Scandinavian countries, the use of public contracts with private service, work and supply providers is generally regulated by national legislation and instructions, but also by EU directives. Even though Norway is not a member of the EU, it is bound by EU directives through the EEA agreement (European Economic Area). *The EU Directive on the coordination of procedures for the award of public works contracts, public supply contracts and public service contracts* (Directive 2004/18/EC) has in the last decade served as an important backdrop for national policies on the use of nonpublic actors in the production of welfare services, when these services are produced on the basis of contracts between municipalities and providers. It is this directive that is the focus of this section.

The Directive (with attachments) specifies the process and procedures for public procurements based on written agreements between a contracting public authority at the state, regional or local level and an economic operator.[2] The overall principles for the award of public contracts are that the processes must be based on transparency and equal and non-discriminatory treatment of all operators.[3] One implication of these criteria is that a prior information notice with information about the 'buyer profile' must be published and that the information must not only be given to selected operators (see Chapter VI of the Directive). Moreover, the Directive stresses the standardisation of processes and the specification of clear requirements and expectations in the contracts. However, the Directive also defines several categories for public procurement procedures, each with different implications for which kind of economic operators may submit a tender. The document distinguishes between *open procedures*, *restricted procedures* and *negotiated procedures* (Article 1(11)):[4]

(a) 'Open procedures' means those procedures whereby any interested economic operator may submit a tender.
(b) 'Restricted procedures' means those procedures in which any economic operator may request to participate and whereby only those economic operators invited by the contracting authority may submit a tender.
(c) 'Negotiated procedures' means those procedures whereby the contracting authorities consult the economic operators of their choice and negotiate the terms of contract with one or more of these.

In addition to these procedures, the Directive defines a procedure entitled *competitive dialogue* (Article 1(11)(c)) that is meant to be used when a public contract is 'particularly complex'. This implies that the contracting authority is unable to specify the technical, legal or financial conditions and requirements without dialogue with the candidates admitted to that procedure.

Whether the Public Procurement Directive comes into operation depends on the value of the contract (cf. the threshold amounts defined in the Directive) and the type of contract. Regarding the latter, the Directive defines some specific exceptions. These exceptions include service concessions (see Chapter 2, Sect. 3, Article 17) which are of specific relevance for welfare services. A service concession implies that (CURIA n. d.)[5]:

> ...the consideration for the provision of services consists in the right to exploit the service, either alone, or together with payment.

> ...the service supplier takes the risk of operating the services in question (...) In order to find that there is a service concession, it is necessary to establish whether the agreed method of remuneration takes the form of the right of the service provider to exploit the service and entails it taking the risk of operating the service in question. While that risk may, at the outset, be very limited, it is necessary for classification as a service concession that the contracting authority transfers to the concession holder all or, at least, a significant share of the risk which it faces.

As the quotation states, the decisive criteria are that the service provider (concession holder) (also) runs a real risk by operating the right of the service in question. In other words, a service concession holder administers the right to provide a service to users.

National Implementation of the EU Public Procurement Directive

Basically, contract-based public procurement is regulated by a common EU Directive in Norway, Denmark and Sweden. However, while implementing the Directive, each Scandinavian country has left its own distinctive mark on the regulation of public procurement within its own borders. Here we will describe some of the country-specific conditions at the national legal level that have implications for the two welfare services, institution-based elderly care and primary and lower secondary education, and more specifically, the scope for nonprofit service providers.

The EU Directive on public procurement was implemented in Norwegian legislation through the Public Procurement Act in 1992 (Norwegian: *Lov om offentlige anskaffelser m.v.*). This act and its regulations have been revised several times since then (Ødegård 2006, Segaard 2015).[6] In addition, some other kinds of public procurements outside the scope of the Directive have been regulated in Norway for years. This is the case for service concessions (Udbudsrådet 2012, 19-20), procurement with lower threshold amounts than those defined by the EU, and 'B' (non-priority) services. Non-priority services include, for example, health and social services. In general, it is stated that all public procurements must fulfil the requirements of non-discrimination, transparency and predictability according to §5 in LOV-1999-07-16-69 (The Norwegian Government 2006). The Norwegian government emphasises that it is always possible to negotiate with the providers. In this way, national regulations are considered more flexible than the Directive (Konkurransepolitisk avdeling 2008).

Regarding opportunities for nonprofit organisations to provide welfare services within the health and social sector, the Norwegian government implemented an exception to the rules on public procurements in 2004 (FAD 2013). This exception went out of force when Norway implemented new rules on public procurements in June 2016 (Directive 2014/24/EU). At the time of writing, the majority in the Norwegian Parliament still want to support the nonprofit sector and be able to give priority to nonprofit service providers within the health and social sector. However, it is uncertain how this will be carried out. The Norwegian government is in the process of clarifying whether it is possible to maintain the exception through a so-called 'adaptation text' (DIFI 2014; Sejersted 2014). Nevertheless, the exception was important for the regulation of the welfare mix in Norway because it meant that national and local authorities could choose between negotiating with nonprofit organisations and following the ordinary rules for public procurements (Konkurransepolitisk avdeling 2005). Moreover, the exception implied that the contracting authority did not need to follow Part II of the regulation, including the requirement for national tender announcements in the Norwegian national notification online database for public procurement. It was thus possible to exclude contracts with nonprofit providers from the requirement for competitive tendering (Konkurransepolitisk avdeling 2008). However, it was also stressed that the contracting authority ought to pursue competition between nonprofit organisations (Konkurransepolitisk avdeling 2008). The background for this exception was that competitive tendering— where nonprofit actors must compete on equal terms with for-profit actors —was seen to contradict the overall aim of promoting societal engagement and collaboration with nonprofit organisations (FAD 2013, 99; see also Konkurransepolitisk avdeling 2005). Since 2007, the regulations have explicitly stated that in the case of public procurement of health and social services from nonprofit organisations, it is up to the contracting authority to assess whether the whole legislation on public procurement should be followed (Part I–III) or the exception should be used (FAD 2006, 2013). In other words, it is possible to give special treatment to nonprofit health and social service providers in Norway.

The Norwegian regulation of public procurement does not provide a precise definition of 'nonprofit organisation', but it does describe some of its characteristics (FAD 2013, 99ff). Nonprofit organisations are distinguished by volunteering and charitable work; they carry out tasks for society on behalf of public authorities, and their profit, if any, is used for their charitable work. Nonprofit organisations will often, but not necessarily, be organised as foundations (FAD 2006, 87; see also FAD 2013, 99ff).

Denmark implemented the EU Directive through a so-called Executive Order; in other words, a set of rules that expands and supplements an act (Udbudsportalen 2014a; Udbudsrådet 2012). The first Executive Order that implemented the EU Directive on public procurement came into effect on July 1, 1993 (BEK nr 415 af 22/06/1993), while the Executive Order in force in 2015 was implemented in 2011 (BEK nr 712 af 15/06/2011). Moreover, public procurements in Denmark are regulated by the Procurement Act (Danish: *Tilbudsloven*).[7] This act comes into effect when the contract value is between 500.000 DKR and the threshold amounts as defined at the EU level. This means that Denmark—like Norway—has expanded the scope of public procurement regulations compared to the minimum requirements defined in the EU Directive. Until 2013, non-priority services, including health and social services, were encompassed by the Procurement Act, but this is no longer the case.[8]

Regarding possible exceptions to the EU Directive, the argument based on the so-called 'in-house case law' is emphasised in Danish policy documents. For example, the Konkurrencestyrelsen (2010, 2) stated that 'the tasks carried out by self-owning institutions can be characterised as services executed in-house, and are therefore not subject to public procurement regulations' (our translation). Here, 'tasks' refer to a situation where a self-owning institution provides a welfare service (e.g., institution-based elderly care) on behalf of a municipality and the following two criteria are fulfilled (Udbudsportalen 2015, our translation):

- The criterion of contracting entity: The institution mainly carries out tasks for the municipality. If the institution carries out tasks for others, it must be of marginal extent only.
- The criterion of control: The municipality exercises control over the institution, which is similar to the control it exercises over its own departments. This may imply control over budget matters, commercial investments, strategies, etc.

In Sweden, the EU Directive on public procurement was implemented in national legislation in 1995.[9] Konkurrensverket, which is the inspection authority, stresses that following Swedish regulations on public procurements ensures that EU regulations are fulfilled as well (Konkurrensverket 2014). The relevant Swedish legislation builds mainly on the EU Directive 2004/18/EG. Regarding possible exceptions to the rules on public procurements, Swedish authorities, as with the Danish, refer to the in-house case law—the criterion of contracting entity and the criterion of control—and legal practice from the Court of Justice of the European Union (see Udbudsrådet 2012, 18; The Swedish Riksdag 2012).

Looking at the threshold amounts that determine whether a public procurement is the subject of national legislation, the thresholds are similar in Denmark and Norway but somewhat lower in Sweden (Udbudsrådet 2012, Fig. 2.1). The national threshold amounts defined in the national regulations of all three Scandinavian countries are lower than the threshold amount defined in the EU Directive.

Finally, it should be noted that an exception to the rules on public procurements for nonprofit actors parallel to the one in place in Norway does not exist in either Sweden or Denmark (Kronbøl 2015). Moreover, only Norwegian national legislation includes regulations on service concessions (Udbudsrådet 2012, 19–20). However, it is possible for Danish and Swedish authorities (e.g., in a municipality) to sign a contract with a nonprofit service provider without following the complete regulations for public procurements. The reason for this is the in-house case law (see Udbudsrådet 2012, 18; Konkurrencestyrelsen 2010; The Swedish Riksdag 2012).

The Importance of the EU Public Procurement Directive

Public welfare services are mainly a municipal task in Norway, Denmark and Sweden, and the municipalities have to some extent the power to decide how the services should be organised—with consequences for the welfare mix. Local autonomy and the principle of subsidiarity are traditionally appreciated in Scandinavian local government (Rose 2005, 57–60). However, the municipalities do not act in a vacuum, and the EU Public Procurement Directive affects local as well as national policy-making. The fact that municipalities have a certain amount of latitude is nevertheless important to stress.

The EU Directive itself does not exclude any of the three ideal models of government specified in Table 3.1: neither the direct, indirect or disconnected government model for organisation and interaction between public authorities and private service providers. One reason for this is that the Directive is primarily concerned with procedural principles for how contracts should be awarded and on what grounds. However, the descriptions of the different procedures for public procurement (Article 1, 11 (a)–(d)) gives the contracting authority the opportunity to restrict competition at an early stage and invite some, but not all, potential providers (economic operators) to submit a tender.

Moreover, it is also specified that the character of the service in question may weigh in favour of dialogue or negotiations with selected potential providers. In this kind of dialogue or negotiation, we consider it to be possible to influence the allocation of discretionary power, which is a key element of the government models in Table 3.1. To what extent dialogue or negotiations are relevant is an empirical question in each case. Finally, the Directive allows exceptions to the rules on public procurements and defines cases in which the Directive does not go into effect. If a public authority chooses to make use of the exceptions to the rules or organise its production of welfare services in a way that is outside the scope of the Directive, then that authority has a great opportunity to influence the welfare mix. In other words, we will emphasise that the common European policy for public procurements does not prevent different ways of organising welfare services in EU member states.

The national welfare mix is thus also a question of political choice, will and cultural traditions, and the EU Directive makes it possible to take these aspects into account. The openness to diversity is reflected in the national policies and legal framework for private providers in Scandinavia, as well as in the fact that the three countries to some degree use their freedom of action differently. In general, their national regulations are more restrictive than what the EU Directive requires; for instance, by setting lower threshold amounts for when open calls for tenders are required.

As mentioned above, after the implementation of new rules on public procurement, the Norwegian exception for nonprofit providers is no longer in force. We should nevertheless bear in mind that not only is a revised Directive on public procurement being implemented, but a new EU Directive on the award of concession contracts is being implemented as well (Directive 2014/23/EU).[10] According to the European Commission, it will be possible to exclude some forms of welfare services from the full application of this Directive, such as when public service production is organised though concession contracts (European Commission 2014). The Directive states:

[i]t is appropriate to exclude from the full application of this Directive only those services which have a limited cross-border dimension, such as certain social, health, or educational services. Those services are provided within a particular context that varies widely amongst Member States, due to different cultural traditions. (Directive 2014/23/EU, (53) page 10)

Furthermore, the new Directive on the award of concession contracts (Article 17) states that a concession that fulfils what we have previously described as the two criteria of the in-house case law (the criterion of contracting entity and the criterion of control) falls outside the scope of the Directive (see also paragraph 3.2 in SEC (2011) 1169 final). Moreover, the Directive allows EU member states to use discretion in the welfare mix:

> Given the importance of the cultural context and the sensitivity of those services, Member States should be given wide discretion to organize the choice of the service providers in the way they consider most appropriate. (Directive 2014/23/EU, (54) page 10)

The Norwegian authorities have raised the issue of the conditions for nonprofit actors—and the possibility of maintaining the exception to the rule for nonprofit actors—after the implementation of the revised Directive on public procurement. However, this appears to have been done without establishing whether alternative solutions for service production exist. The new Directive on concession contracts, the opportunity to set aside the regulations defined in the Directive, and common practice in Denmark and Sweden indicate that such alternatives do indeed exist. It appears that each individual country will still be able to use discretion in organising the welfare mix it considers the most appropriate, in light of its own cultural context.[11] These national policies are the subject of the following sections.

National Policies on School and Elderly Care[12]

Nonpublic Producers of Primary and Lower Secondary Education,[13]

In this section, we summarise the national private school policies of the three Scandinavian countries, drawing on the analytical government models from Table 3.1: direct, indirect and disconnected government. Based on detailed analysis of national policy documents such as legislation, instructions, and guidelines (see Segaard 2015), we aim to identify some central similarities and differences in the distribution and coordination of 'contracts' in primary and lower secondary education in Denmark, Sweden and Norway.

The public sector traditionally plays the leading role in education in Norway, Denmark and Sweden. A common feature is that the great majority of children in primary and lower secondary education attend a municipal school. There are, however, some variations between the three countries regarding the distribution of children between public and private schools. According to Eurostat (2012, 33), 95.6 percent of Norwegian school children attend a public school, whereas the corresponding figures for Denmark and Sweden are 86.5 and 89.4 percent, respectively. Norway thus has a lower share of children in private schools than in either Denmark or Sweden.

The problem with these figures is that official statistics often do not distinguish between different categories of private schools, such as between for-profit and nonprofit schools. As we shall see, this distinction is crucial when education policies in the three countries are compared. In Sweden, private primary and lower secondary schools that receive public funding can be run on a commercial basis. This is not allowed in Norway and Denmark. Private schools in Sweden are basically fully financed by the public sector, and the schools are not allowed to charge school fees. That is not the case in Denmark and Norway, where private schools are only partly funded by the state. Danish and Norwegian private schools may thus charge school fees—and are in fact expected to do so. In both countries, it is also required that public funding be used exclusively for educational purposes. Moreover, in Denmark, private schools are by law required to be run by nonprofit institutions. It is obviously appealing to be a for-profit operator in the Swedish primary education system, where schools are fully financed by the public sector, profits can be paid out to owners, and the authorities have in practice no right to examine the operator's accounts. In other words, Swedish for-profit school owners operate under much freer conditions in economic terms, but are somewhat more restricted in terms of educational content than in either Denmark or Norway.

In all three countries, primary and lower secondary schools fall under the jurisdiction of the municipalities, as the municipalities are obliged to offer education to all children in this age group. Nevertheless, private schooling of children in this age group is subject to an approval system at the national level. A state institution is responsible for approving private schools (the Norwegian Directorate for Education and Training, the Danish Ministry for Children, Education and Gender Equality, and the Swedish Schools Inspectorate). In primary and lower secondary education, nonpublic actors thus apply for the right to run schools, and a national public-sector body gives (or refuses) them this right. This can be regarded as a 'service concession' according to the EU Public Procurement Directive. As mentioned above, this means that the provider is given the right to provide services and runs a real risk in exploiting this right in practice. The argument is that the provider only receives a partial payment from the public-sector body, while the rest is paid by the users, who are free to choose whether they will use this service. Accordingly, we assume that private schools can be said to be outside of the scope of the EU Directive on public procurement.[14]

Contracts for private schools with public funding are awarded on the basis of a national authorisation system in all three countries, which ensures that the schools adhere to national regulations of the organisation and educational content. By means of this approval system, we consider national authorities to exercise indirect government by defining requirements and conditions for approval. Moreover, this approval can be revoked if inspections show that the schools have not adhered to these requirements and conditions. Accordingly, interaction between the authorities and private service providers is formalised in an agreement, with more or less detailed criteria for approval. This indicates the extent of formality (cf. Table 3.1).

The extent of national control and discretion given to each actor—both the authorities and the provider—vary substantially between the three countries. The focus of the regulations also differs. Danish private schools appear to enjoy more discretion regarding educational content as well as the values on which they are based. A central element of Danish school policy is that educational content should correspond to the basic values of the school, and that potential users must be informed of this. We suppose that the approval of Danish private schools is to a large extent performed on their own terms. This is evident because the regulations emphasise that the schools should be able to define their own teaching content and methods based on their own basic values and distinctive characters. In Norway, and perhaps even more in Sweden, the national authorities set forth detailed standards for education. Private schools must comply with the standards set for public-sector schools. In other words, we consider national requirements for the content and organisation of teaching to be less strict in Denmark than in Norway and Sweden. Whereas public-sector schools can be perceived as setting a *minimum standard* for primary and lower secondary education, in Denmark, public-sector schools in Sweden and Norway can be viewed as a *template* which private schools must follow. The fact that a single act governs both public and private schools in Sweden illustrates this point. In Norway and Denmark, private schools that receive public funding are regulated by a separate act.

In order to obtain a diverse educational system, Danish authorities also give private schools considerable leeway. Danish private schools can reject applicants, even if they have room to admit more pupils. In this way, we believe that a school can cultivate its own distinctive image. The primary and lower secondary school system as a whole can thus become more diverse. In contrast, Swedish and Norwegian private schools generally cannot reject applicants if they have room to admit them. This can be seen as a way to secure free choice for users. In practice, the democratic right of users to free choice can thus undermine distinctive alternatives to public schools and thereby reduce diversity within welfare services that the authorities in principle aim for. This is because the lack of opportunity to reject pupils also curtails the exercise of discretion on the part of the provider.

Although some differences exist, the users' right to free choice is a basic entitlement in Norwegian, Swedish and Danish primary and lower secondary education. In light of our analytical framework, this means that the indirect national government is supplemented by a form of disconnected government, because the market—the users, through their individual choices—takes part in shaping the educational system. However, the circumstances under which users can make an informed choice vary between the three countries, at least in terms of national regulations. Danish legislation and regulations, for instance, dictate that schools have a duty to inform users. The content of the information, as well as the channels through which information is conveyed, are fully outlined. Such regulations are largely absent in corresponding Norwegian and Swedish regulations.

Our opinion is that this statutory duty to inform users in Denmark highlights the importance of knowing which options to choose from and the consequences of each choice. Every choice certainly has consequences, especially with respect to the rights and obligations that pupils and their parents agree to accept. Denmark also stands out in this area. Parents of children in Danish private schools are given formal duties and the responsibility to participate in the running of the schools. A group of parents at a private school in question (called the 'circle of parents') is given a formal obligation to supervise the school. More generally, this aspect of what we call collaborative governance is evident in the Danish system for the supervision of private schools. Not only are the parents involved, but also the school itself can choose to assume an important role by means of self-evaluation. This is done on the basis of a template developed by a school association (a national organisation for private schools of a specific type, such as religious, German minority or Waldorf/Steiner education) and approved by the national Board of Supervision. The inclusion of parents and nonprofit organisations in supervising the schools is a striking example of how collaborative governance entails an aspect of self-regulation within a specific political and institutional framework at the national level (see Sørensen and Torfing 2008, 10). However, as Thøgersen points out in Chap. 5, there is little direct collaboration between nonprofit schools and the *municipalities* in which they are located. In other words, indirect government through collaborative governance seems to be limited to the relationship between the private service provider and national public authorities (e.g., through the national system for supervision). The Danish supervision system contrasts sharply with the Swedish system, where it is difficult to detect any form of collaborative governance. Swedish supervision is centralised and carried out by national authorities, and there is little involvement by users or parents. Users and parents may be involved in the Norwegian case, but they are not given any formal rights or obligations comparable to the Danish situation.

To conclude, the basic government model for nonpublic actors within primary and lower secondary education in all three countries appears to be indirect government. There are nevertheless substantial variations with regard to private service providers' freedom to use their own discretion; therefore, the influence of such providers also varies widely. There are also elements of market-based government, where choices made by users determine the composition of the welfare mix. In Denmark, the arrangements for the supervision system also display strong elements of collaborative governance. In this sense, we presume that the government regime can be described as layered. However, the final authority rests with the national authorities who establish the national standards for approval and have the power to revoke this approval.

Nonpublic Producers of Institution-Based Elderly Care[15]

In this section, we move on to policies on institution-based elderly care. Again, based on detailed analysis of national policy documents such as legislation, instructions, and guidelines and using the models from Table 3.1, we compare the three countries to show how contracts are awarded and coordinated in Denmark, Sweden and Norway.

There is a long tradition of public-sector elderly care in Scandinavian welfare states. The practice of elderly care has changed over time, for example, with regard to the balance between home-based and institution-based care. Likewise, attitudes towards the organisation of elderly care are gradually changing as well. For-profit providers of elderly care are no longer a distant possibility, but have become actual practice in many 'marketised' Scandinavian municipalities (Meagher and Szebehely 2012). Elderly care is a municipal responsibility, and each municipality decides how this task will be organised and carried out. The municipalities thus play a decisive role in shaping the welfare mix within elderly care (Ascoli and Ranci 2007). A nonpublic actor that wants to run a publicly financed nursing home is largely reliant on choices made by the municipality. This contrasts with schools, where municipalities have less influence over the welfare mix.

Unfortunately, comparable data on the welfare mix within elderly care in Scandinavia are scarce. Nevertheless, Marta Szebehely and Gabrielle Meagher (2012, 244-245) presented some estimates, and Karl Henrik Sivesind (2016; Chapter 2 in this book) described the changes in the welfare mix in Scandinavia based on different kinds of statistical data.[16] They all concluded that most care services are still provided by the public sector, but that there are some significant differences between each country: The nonprofit sector plays an important role in elderly care in Denmark and, to a minor extent, in Norway; whereas Sweden stands out as having a more extensive for-profit sector. In addition, in Sweden (and Finland), 'the growth of its share has been faster and large corporations have a stronger position', according to Szebehely and Meagher (2012, 242).

Individual municipalities usually enter into a contract with private service providers, but there are exceptions. In Denmark, a private care provider can bypass the municipality and obtain the right to provide institution-based care services through a national approval system for so-called 'independent nursing homes' (Danish: *friplejeboliger*). Under this system, a private provider of independent nursing homes acquires the right to offer a place to persons in need of nursing care. The provider must fulfil a number of predefined criteria in order to acquire this right. When the user's need for care is assessed and warranted by the municipality, he or she can opt for a place in an independent nursing home. The municipality is then required to enter into a contract with the private provider. Accordingly, a Danish municipality cannot single-handedly decide the welfare mix within its boundaries. This arrangement resembles what we find in the school sector: National authorities define the criteria for being approved as a provider. We therefore state that indirect government also exists in elderly care—in this case, a service concession contract. On the basis of in-house case law, Danish municipalities can also enter into agreements with self-owning institutions, which are outside the scope of the Procurement Act and the EU Public Procurement Directive. They can also launch open calls for tenders on institution-based elderly care.

In both Norway and Sweden, the municipalities themselves choose how institution-based elderly care within their borders will be organised (Vabo 2012). In Sweden, a municipality can choose between implementing LOV (The Freedom of Choice Act), using open calls for tenders according to the LOU (Public Procurement Act), or utilising the freedom of action provided by the in-house case law; a Swedish municipality can also choose a combination of these.[17] However, Swedish national guidelines nevertheless encourage the use of LOV.[18] In short, this means that users can freely choose between service providers approved by the municipality. The municipality must approve all providers that satisfy the requirements, which are formulated by the municipality itself. The money then follows the patient.

Norwegian national policy documents encourage open calls for tenders, but leave room for restricted competition between nonprofit providers. Norwegian municipalities can also implement free user choice, but this choice is restricted to those providers that have entered into a contract with the municipality on the basis of a framework agreement or the 'money follows the patient' principle.

National policies on the organisation of elderly care and municipal freedom of action are just some of the aspects of our models of government. Another aspect is each actor's *discretionary power* over the content of cooperation on elderly care. National authorities in all three countries express views on the requirements and conditions for entering into a contract. On the one hand, this includes formal procedures based on the EU Public Procurement Directive and adjacent national legislation. These are largely similar in the three countries. However, policy documents in Denmark—to a much greater extent than in the other two countries— stress that municipalities should find creative solutions. These documents emphasise that cooperation between public authorities and private providers can be organised according to a partnership model, rather than as a hierarchical customer–provider relationship (Udbudsportalen 2011, 16). We interpret this as a request for more collaborative governance.

On the other hand, national policies in all three countries also contain essential goals for elderly care. The emphasis on values such as self-determination, dignity and respect for the individual user, which supports the overall aim of active citizenship in welfare services through empowerment and the free choice of the user, constitutes a basic similarity between the three countries. There is nevertheless considerable variation when these values are translated into concrete regulations; that is to say, into 'tools of government'. The extent of discretionary power that rests with the provider clearly varies. In Sweden, so-called 'national evaluation' criteria include very detailed indicators, which are used as a starting point for national supervision of municipal care. National authorities also recommend that municipalities use these indicators in their supervision and specification of requirements for private providers.

All three countries have systems for the national supervision of institution-based care, covering all types of providers—public as well as private. The purpose is to ensure that care is carried out in accordance with legislation and other national regulations. This type of national supervision is supplemented by tasks that are assigned to municipalities and providers. The providers, for example, are required to have internal control systems.

The major difference between the countries is the role of the users and their relatives in supervision. Swedish national guidelines seem to devote less attention to these user groups as active citizens than do their Danish and Norwegian counterparts. National authorities in Sweden put much less emphasis on the institutionalised influence, participation and empowerment of users (e.g., user boards). Instead, Swedish guidelines tend to focus on informal day-to-day influence: for example, on the daily routines in nursing homes. Furthermore, there are no concrete recommendations on providing information to users, even though this topic has received considerable attention in many of the reports issued by Swedish national authorities. Only Danish municipalities and providers have a statutory obligation to inform potential users. Norwegian guidelines emphasise user involvement, but little is said about the information on which this involvement should be based. Norwegian municipalities are not obliged to provide easy access to relevant information in a way comparable to Danish requirements.

Generally speaking, we find that Scandinavian national authorities do not lay down clear regulations on the organisation of elderly care or the conditions for private providers. Thus, on the one hand, municipalities have considerable leeway in determining the welfare mix. On the other hand, national authorities express quite detailed expectations through legislation, regulations and supervision. In the case of Norway, Signy Vabo found that national steering of elderly care has increased over time. However, this steering focuses on processes instead of content or results. The increased steering is relatively 'soft' and does not interfere in any major way with municipal priorities (Vabo 2012, 122). This indicates a relatively large degree of discretion.

In light of the analytical models listed in Table 3.1, we assume several options to be available for the organisation of public–private collaboration on elderly care in the three countries. First, Danish and Swedish municipalities can practise direct government on the basis of in-house case law. Second, municipalities can practise indirect government through specifications in their call for tenders (all countries) and LOV announcements (Sweden). Third, Danish users (and Norwegian and Swedish users, if their municipalities allow it) can also exercise influence by choosing from among the approved providers.[19] In this respect, there is also an element of market-based organisation in the governing of elderly care.

In our discussion of the analytical framework, we pointed out that the use of different models of government within a single policy area can be described as *layered government*, meaning that the welfare mix is organised through several steps. In both Denmark and Sweden (but less so in Norway), the national authorities encourage municipalities to facilitate the free choice of users between pre-selected service providers. In this way, the idea of market-based organisation is combined with elements of direct or indirect government: The public sector facilitates consumer empowerment by means of contracts with or the approval of certain service providers. However, the organisation of areas of welfare service may also reflect *parallel government regimes*. That is to say, we find that national policy allows welfare mix to be organised in several distinct ways, implying that private service providers may have more than one alternative to become providers of publicly funded welfare services. This is seen in the Danish case, where private providers of independent nursing homes can be approved at the national level—bypassing the municipalities—and then enter the municipal welfare mix through user choice. This is also seen in Sweden, where it can be argued that the LOV has created parallel systems. Furthermore, private providers find yet another way into the municipal welfare mix in Denmark and Sweden: The municipality can enter into an agreement with a private provider based on the criterion of contracting entity and the criterion of control. This can be described as an extended form of in-house service production. Here, public authorities can supervise the private providers on equal terms with municipal providers.

Discussion: A Unified Scandinavian Model?

In this chapter, we have shown how national authorities in Denmark, Norway and Sweden approach the use of private providers—for-profit as well as nonprofit—in primary and lower secondary education, and in institution-based elderly care. All three countries stress elements of active citizenship, having designated a diverse spectrum of services, adaptations to the needs of the users, and user participation as central goals for their publicly financed welfare services. To reach these goals, they have looked for new ways to organise and direct the provision of welfare services. Alternatives to the traditional model, where the public sector both finances and provides the services, have been in demand. This served as the backdrop for our discussion of the interaction between the public sector and private welfare providers, especially the use of contracts. As a tool of government, contracts may reflect a direct, indirect or disconnected model of government.

The EU Public Procurement Directive is relevant in this context because it limits the latitude for national policymaking. All three countries have bound themselves to follow the Directive through EU membership (Denmark and Sweden) or the EEA agreement (Norway). Although standardisation is the general purpose, the Directive specifies several tendering procedures and types of contracts that fall outside of its scope. Accordingly, the Directive allows latitude for national policymaking. In conclusion, we find that the EU Directive does not itself decide whether welfare services will be provided through direct, indirect or disconnected government, nor does it unambiguously standardise the welfare mix across countries. However, even though the EU allows national latitude (Nyberg 2013; Directive 2014/23/EU, (53) page 10), it is clear that this latitude is approached and utilised differently in each Scandinavian country.

In both Sweden and Denmark, national policy documents define leeway for public authorities, which goes beyond the most detailed regulations of the EU Directive as well as national public procurement rules. This is done by using the in-house argument within elderly care, and by awarding contracts to approved providers within both schools and elderly care. Norway also has a system with approved private schools, but uses neither the in-house argument nor contracts to approved providers within elderly care. Instead, Norway has practised an exception to the public procurement regulations, which applies to contracts with non-profit providers of health and social services (including elderly care). However, although this nationally defined exception is important, it does not alter the general impression: Norwegian authorities largely consider the issue of private welfare providers a question of public procurement. Accordingly, the EU Directive establishes an important framework for the welfare service provision.

The overall impression is one of considerable similarity between Danish, Norwegian and Swedish national policies on the welfare mix, within both education and elderly care. As we have seen, the share of welfare services produced by private providers nevertheless varies considerably, and there are some differences that may contribute towards explaining this variation. The national frameworks for interaction between the public payer and the private provider vary substantially, especially concerning the distribution of discretionary power.

We conclude that all three countries fall under the indirect government model of Table 3.1 with regard to the school sector, where public authorities govern by means of predefined requirements for approving private schools, as well as by supervision. Private providers are neither governed directly nor free from any kind of control. Furthermore, there are elements of market-based organisation in the school sector, because users have the right to choose their schools. However, this choice is limited to publicly approved schools. The 'market' is thus a quasi-market, only partially disconnected from public steering.

Unlike the school sector, we find that the national policies for institution-based elderly care provide neither a unified Scandinavian model nor a single model within each country. Rather, the case of elderly care demonstrates that national policies can provide leeway for a combination of different models of government. Public procurement regulations and more or less detailed requirements for the content of the services are highlighted in policy documents in all three countries, but this is not the only type of indirect government that national policies allow. The municipalities themselves can largely choose their own tools of governance, but there are some differences between the countries.

In Denmark, the opportunity to enter into agreements with providers shows how public authorities can govern private providers directly, in a similar way as in-house providers. Furthermore, the Danish and Swedish cases clearly show how organisational and legal policy tools at the national level can facilitate disconnected government based on user choice. Strictly speaking, we regard this as a quasi-market-based organisation, since users can choose between approved institutions (as in the school sector). An important difference is that the Swedish users get a voucher—the money follows the care-needing elderly—while the Danish users can basically choose only between municipal nursing homes or nursing homes that have an agreement with the municipality. If a Danish user wants a place in an independent nursing home, the private provider of that nursing home has the right to refuse. Accordingly, private providers of independent nursing homes have the same discretionary power as Danish private schools. This will be discussed below.

Moreover, the Danish national system for the approval of independent nursing homes shows how government models within elderly care are not only layered, but also *parallel*. Sweden also has a parallel system, but unlike their Danish counterparts, Swedish municipalities are not at the mercy of a national approval system. Swedish municipalities decide for themselves whether to implement the LOV, which implies a local approval system and user choice.

When we refer to parallel models of government, we mean that private providers can enter into the welfare mix in different ways, and that the public sector can use different tools of government. This is not just a layered system, but a combination of parallel systems with different logics (such as competition, approval and internal organisation) and different regulation systems. We believe that parallel government models can be a key to diversity in welfare services. Through these parallel systems, it could be possible to encourage and support different purposes and actors in the production of welfare services. If a single model limits the possibility of promoting a certain welfare mix, a combination of models may prove more flexible.

We must, however, emphasise that a diverse welfare mix not only depends on the country's model of government, but also on the discretionary power of private actors. To what extent are they free to define the values and goals for their own welfare service production? If these values and goals are defined by narrow national standards, a diverse supply of services will be improbable. Consequently, it may also be difficult to achieve a central element of active citizenship: the possibility to choose between a broad range of different services. Phillips and Smith (2011, 22) maintained that national regulations may be an important incentive for cooperation with nonprofit organisations. However, nonprofit actors are often motivated by their ideals. They will hardly operate in a field which is regulated in detail if doing so means compromising their basic values.

Our account of the national frameworks within education and elderly care shows that the discretionary power given to private providers varies considerably. The greatest extent of discretionary power over non-economic issues is given to Danish service providers. There is no doubt that Danish national policies stand out by facilitating diversity, as they show more openness towards the (non-commercial) values of private providers. More concretely, Danish private providers are given more discretion with regard to their service production and its underlying values. The criteria for approving Danish private schools not only concerns quality and economy, but also whether the schools ensure that their values are communicated and upheld. Moreover, Danish providers of private schools and independent nursing homes can use more discretion in their selection of users; in other words, they can refuse admission. The differences between the countries are smaller with respect to elderly care, except that Sweden stands out with a more detailed control regime that indirectly restricts the discretionary power of the providers and encourages a for-profit perspective in the welfare mix. This is also the case within primary and lower secondary education,, where Swedish private owners—unlike their Danish and Norwegian counterparts—are allowed to make profits. With regard to payoff discretion, Swedish providers thus hold a unique position. The for-profit aspect is a more general trait of the Swedish welfare mix.

Concluding Remarks: The Role of Politics

There are thus both similarities and differences between the Scandinavian countries when it comes to national regulation of private providers within education and elderly care. Even though it may be debated whether the differences or similarities are the most conspicuous, there are certainly some distinctions and nuances that separate the models of welfare government in the three countries. Our analyses and discussion indicate that variations in these models may explain some—but not all—of the differences in the welfare mix. However, this leaves us with the question of why these government models differ. Politics may be an underlying factor that explains either the differences in the governance of welfare production or the differences in the actual welfare mix—or both.

One question is whether the party composition of national governments has affected national policies. This is clearly of importance in light of the changes that have taken place in Sweden. Reforms were initiated by the centre-right Bildt government (1991–1994), and further reforms, such as the User Choice Act, were implemented by the centre-right Reinfeldt government (2006–2014). Sweden is perhaps the foremost example of the impact of politics on the welfare mix—and the political will to change. During the 1990s, 'freedom of choice' and 'competition' were the leading slogans of Swedish politics. This led to several reforms, including in education and elderly care. Accordingly, Sweden went from being a welfare state where the public sector provided almost all welfare services, to a welfare society where the role of for-profit providers increased and the users themselves obtained the opportunity to affect the welfare mix through their choice of providers.

The impact of changing governments can also be seen in Norway: The centre-right Bondevik II government (2001–2005) made it easier to establish nonpublic schools which were neither religious nor pedagogical alternatives. This change was reversed by the centre-left Stoltenberg II government (2005–2013), while this policy once again was partly liberalised by the right-wing Solberg government (2013–). However, there is still no distribution of profits from state-funding in schools and the rigid requirements for approval have been maintained.

Although party politics matter, they cannot explain policy differences between Scandinavian countries. For example, the Norwegian Solberg government has not allowed owners to make profits from nonpublic schools. On the contrary, during the 2013 Norwegian election campaign, all parties described the Swedish situation as undesirable. The Norwegian Left accused the Right of wanting to introduce the Swedish policies in Norway, whereas the Norwegian Right emphasised the differences between themselves and their Swedish counterparts. Moreover, the Swedish policy shift is not just a matter of changing governments. Hicks (2015), for example, emphasised continuity between the social democratic and centre-right governments with regard to school policy: The reforms that led to an increasing for-profit sector were to a large extent accepted by the social democrats.

The Danish case also illustrates how party politics can be of limited importance. Since 2001, right-wing parties have been in government most of the time (2001–2011 and 2015–). However, there has been no major marketisation reform. The Danish case thus highlights the importance of national historical traditions. The country has a long-standing tradition of independent nonprofit schools, which influences the current political discourse. This tradition dates back to the middle of the 1800s, building on the work and philosophy of N.F.S Grundtvig. Today, there is a wide ideological range of nonprofit alternatives in Denmark—from left-wing alternative movements to Christians and liberals. Each of these groups has political allies, and this leads to cross-party consensus on the importance of the nonprofit sector.

Although the nonprofit sector is much smaller in Norway than in Denmark, elements of this situation are found in Norway as well. In the Norwegian case, the pivotal position of the Christian People's Party and the Liberal Party appears to be important. These parties have traditionally been sceptical of the marketisation of education and elderly care; their priority has been to protect nonprofit institutions from the effects of marketisation. In Sweden, in contrast, such barriers to the development of for-profit alternatives appear to be absent.

In short, there is a strong element of path dependency which limits the options that have been discussed and thereby also alternative developmental trajectories. This observation is in accordance with the predominant literature on welfare states, in which one main argument has been that 'history and politics matter' (Arts and Gelissen 2010, 570). The historical development—described by Sivesind in Chapter 2—can to some extent explain the policies today. Where nonprofit alternatives were weak initially, the discourse on alternatives, user choice, etc., now tends to focus on state versus market—as we have seen in Sweden. When a nonprofit sector of some size exists, it tends to mobilise its political supporters and thereby displace the left–right discourse, as we have seen in Denmark.

Notes

1. We use the term 'collaborative governance' as synonymous with related concepts, such as 'governance network'.
2. Article 1 in Directive 2004/18/EC.
3. Article 2 in Directive 2004/18/EC.
4. A fourth category is *design contests*, but it is not relevant for primary education and institution-based elderly care (Article 1(11)(e)).

5. In Article 1(4), a service concession is described as 'a contract of the same type as a public service contract except for the fact that the consideration for the provision of services consists either solely in the right to exploit the service or in this right together with payment'.
6. The act and regulations in force as per 2014 is the act from 1999 (LOV-1999-07-16-69) and the regulations (FOR-2006-04-07-402) that came into force in January 2007 (FAD 2013:9).
7. LBK nr 1410 af 07/12/2007 with changes made through LOV nr 618 af 14/06/2011 § 2 and LOV nr 1234 af 18/12/2012 § 1.
8. According to changes made through the law, LOV nr 1234 af 18/12/2012 § 1, 'the contracting authorities no longer have ... a duty to follow the regulation of the Procurement Act for announcement of the Annex II B-services independent of the contract value. However, the contracting authorities are still committed to follow some of the regulations in the EU Directive if the contract value is higher than the threshold amounts defined for EU tenders' (Udbudsportalen 2014b, our translation). For more information, please see Konkurrence-og Forbrugerstyrelsen (2013).
9. Sweden implemented the EU Directive for the first time through a 1995 revision of the 1992 Public Procurement Act (Swedish: *Lag om offentlig upphandling–LOU*) (see SFS 1995:704, SFS 1992, 1528). The act in force per 2014 is *Lag om offentlig upphandling* (SFS 2007, 1091) from 2008. Some amendments to the act have later been made, which correspond to changes made in Denmark and Norway.
10. The European Commission explains the main differences between a concession and a public contract, and the reasons for having separate legislation, in this way (European Commission 2014, 3): 'Concessions have specific features compared to public contracts which justify a special and more flexible set of rules for their award. Concessions are typically high-value, complex and long-term contracts which require appropriate flexibility during the award procedure to ensure the best possible outcome. Specific legislation for concessions helps distinguish between the rules applicable to concessions and the more detailed ones applicable to public contracts and therefore makes them simpler to use'.
11. In the MEMO 14/19 (page 3), the European Commission concludes that '[n]o public authorities in each Member State retain the possibility to define and enforce public service obligations and to organise the provision of services of general interest. By imposing public service

3 Education and Elderly Care in Denmark, Norway ...   107

obligations, public authorities remain free to define the characteristics of the service to be provided, including any conditions regarding the quality of the service, in order to pursue their public policy objectives'.
12. This section is based on our detailed analyses of the national policies on schools and elderly care in Norway, Denmark and Sweden (Segaard 2015).
13. The field of private schools is regulated by national legislation, e.g. *Friskoleloven* in Denmark (LBK nr 917 af 13/08/2014), *Skollag* in Sweden (SFS 2010: 800), and *Privatskoleloven* in Norway (Utdanningsdirektoratet (2014), as well as several supplementary policy documents (regulations, instructions, guidelines, etc.) Please see Segaard (2015) for further references to such policy documents.
14. Even though Swedish private schools are basically fully financed, the school owner bears the economic risk. This is because the funding depends on the number of pupils, not what it actually costs to run the school. The school owner is given the right to run a school when it is approved, but it is not guaranteed that the school will attract a sufficient number of pupils.
15. The field of private institution-based elderly care is regulated by national legislation and regulations: in Sweden, e.g. *Lag om offentlig upphandling* (LOU 2007:1091) and *Lag om valfrihetssystem* (LOV 2008:962); in Norway, e.g. *Helsetilsynsloven* (LOV-1984-03-30-15), *Helse- og omsorgstjenesteloven* (LOV-2011-06-24-30), *Forskrift for sykehjem og boform for heldøgns omsorg og pleie* (FOR-1988-11-14-932) and *Internkontrollforskriften* (FOR-1996-12-06-1127); and in Denmark, e.g. *Friplejeboligloven* (LBK nr 897 af 17/08/2011) and *Serviceloven* (LBK nr 1023 af 23/09/2014), as well as several supplementary policy documents (instructions, guidelines etc.). Please see Segaard (2015) for further references to such policy documents.
16. For details, please also see Szebehely (2011), Thøgersen (2013) and Statistics Norway (2015).
17. A national system for registration of social service providers in general and providers of institution-based elderly care in particular exists in Sweden, but it is not comparable to the Danish national authorisation system.
18. Unlike the municipalities, Swedish counties are required to implement LOV (Upphandlingsmyndigheten 2015).
19. Unlike the Swedish case, Danish users are not given a voucher which could be used to choose any provider.

References

Arts, Wil A., and John Gelissen. 2010. Models of the welfare state. In *The Oxford Handbook of the Welfare State*, eds. Francis G. Castles, Stephan Leibfried, Jand Lewis, Herbert Obinger, and Christopher Pierson, 569–583. Oxford: Oxford University Press.

Ascoli, Ugo, and Costanzo Ranci (eds.). 2007. *Dilemmas of the Welfare Mix: The New Structure of Welfare in an Era of Privatization*. New York: Kluwer.

BEK nr 415 af 22/06/1993. Bekendtgørelse om samordning af fremgangsmåderne ved indgåelse af kontrakter om offentlige indkøb af tjenesteydelser i De Europæiske Fællesskaber (Tjenesteydelsesbekendtgørelsen). https://www.retsinformation.dk/Forms/R0710.aspx?id=64623&exp=1. Accessed 4 Nov 2015.

BEK nr 712 af 15/06/2011. Bekendtgørelse om fremgangsmåderne ved indgåelse af offentlige vareindkøbskontrakter, offentlige tjenesteydelseskontrakter og offentlige bygge- og anlægskontrakter. https://www.retsinformation.dk/forms/r0710.aspx?id=137281&exp=1. Accessed 4 Nov 2015.

CURIA (not dated). Case C-274/09. http://curia.europa.eu/juris/document/document_print.jsf;jsessionid=9ea7d0f130d56f74bc2654fa42a6ba87a7b896d7c1ed.e34KaxiLc3eQc40LaxqMbN4Oc38Oe0?doclang=EN&text=&pageIndex=0&part=1&mode=DOC&docid=124672&occ=first&dir=&cid=180472. Accessed 9 Nov 2015.

Difi. 2014. Likevel unntak for ideelle under nye EU-regler? http://www.anskaffelser.no/nyhet/2014-06-11/likevel-unntak-ideelle-under-nye-eu-regler. Accessed 15 Oct 2014.

Directive 2004/18/EC. Rules on public works contracts, public supply contracts and public service contracts, applicable until 2016. http://eur-lex.europa.eu/legal-content/EN/TXT/PDF/?uri=CELEX:32004L0018&from=EN. Accessed 25 Aug 2015.

Directive 2014/23/EU. Directive 2014/23/EU of the European Parliament and of the Council of 26 February 2014 on the award of concession contracts. http://eur-lex.europa.eu/legal-content/EN/TXT/?uri=celex:32014L0023. Accessed 26 Oct 2015.

Directive 2014/24/EU. Directive 2014/24/EU of the European Parliament and of the Council of 26 February 2014 on public procurement and repealing Directive 2004/18/EC. http://eur-lex.europa.eu/legal-content/DA/LSU/?uri=CELEX:32014L0024. Accessed 26 Oct 2015.

Donahue, John D., and Richard J. Zeckhauser. 2006. Public-Private Collaboration. In *The Oxford Handbook of Public Policy*, eds. Michal Moran, Martin Rein, and Robert E. Goodin, 496–525. Oxford: Oxford University Press.

Ervasti, Heikki, Torben Fridberg, Mikael Hjerm, Olli Kangas, and Kristen Ringdal. 2008. The Nordic Model. In *Nordic Social Attitudes in a European Perspective*, eds. Heikki Ervasti, Torben Fridberg, Mikael Hjerm, and Kristen Ringdal, 1–21. Cheltenham: Edward Elgar.

European Commission. 2014. Directive of the European Parliament and of the Council on the award of Concession Contracts – Frequently Asked Questions. MEMO/14/19. Brussels. http://europa.eu/rapid/press-release_MEMO-14-19_en.htm. Accessed 4 Nov 2015.

Eurostat. 2012. Key Data on Education in Europe 2012. Brussels: Education, Audiovisual and Culture Executive Agency. http://ec.europa.eu/eurostat/documents/3217494/5741409/978-92-9201-242-7-EN.PDF/d0dcb0da-5c52-4b33-becb-027f05e1651f. Accessed 24 June 2015.

FOR-1988-11-14-932. Forskrift for sykehjem og boform for heldøgns omsorg og pleie. Last changed 01.07.2013. https://lovdata.no/dokument/SF/forskrift/1988-11-14-932. Accessed 11 Mar 2015.

FOR-1996-12-06-1127. Forskrift om systematisk helse-, miljø- og sikkerhetsarbeid i virksomheter (Internkontrollforskriften). Last changed 01.07.2013. https://lovdata.no/dokument/SF/forskrift/1996-12-06-1127. Accessed 11 Mar 2015.

FOR-2006-04-07-402. Forskrift om offentlige anskaffelser. http://lovdata.no/dokument/SF/forskrift/2006-04-07-402. Accessed 23 Apr 2015.

Fornyings- og administrasjonsdepartementet (FAD). 2006. Veileder til reglene om offentlige anskaffelser. http://www.regjeringen.no/upload/kilde/fad/bro/2006/0006/ddd/pdfv/299663-veileder_reglene_offentlige_anskaffelser_rev.pdf. Accessed 13 May 2014.

Fornyings- og administrasjonsdepartementet (FAD). 2013. Veileder til reglene om offentlige anskaffelser. http://www.regjeringen.no/upload/FAD/Vedlegg/Konkurransepolitikk/Anskaffelsesveilderer_2013.pdf. Accessed 8 May 2014.

Hicks, Timothy. 2015. Inequality, marketisation and the left: Schools policy in England and Sweden. *European Journal of Political Research* 54 (2): 326–342.

Konkurransepolitisk avdeling. 2005. Forskrift om offentlige anskaffelser og ideelle organisasjoner. (Letter addressed to Vogt and Wiig Trondheim AS – Advokatfirma dated 14.04.2005). http://www.regjeringen.no/upload/kilde/mod/red/2004/0001/ddd/pdfv/243678-vogt_og_wiig.pdf. Accessed 13 May 2014.

Konkurransepolitisk avdeling. 2008. Anskaffelsesregelverket ved kjøp av barnevernstjenester fra private aktører. (Letter addressed to Ministry of Children and Equality dated 21.01.2008). http://www.regjeringen.no/upload/FAD/Vedlegg/Konkurransepolitikk/Anskaffelser/Fortolkningsuttalelse_ansk_barnevern.pdf. Accessed 23 Apr 2015.

Konkurrence- og Forbrugerstyrelsen. 2013. Køb af B-tjenesteydelser. Vejledning. Valby: Konkurrence- og Forbrugerstyrelsen. http://www.kfst.dk/~/media/KFST/Offentlig%20konkurrence/Regler%20og%20vejledninger/Vejledninger/Vejledning%20om%20koeb%20af%20Btjenesteydelser%203%20september%202013%20FINAL.pdf. Accessed 25 Aug 2014.

Konkurrencestyrelsen. 2010. In-house begrebets betydning for kommunal aftaleindgåelse med selvejende institutioner. http://www.udbudsportalen.dk/ImageVaultFiles/id_41818/cf_202/Vejledende_udtalelse_om_In-house_begrebets_betydni.PDF. Accessed 17 Mar 2015.

Konkurrensverket. 2014. Upphandlingsreglerna – en introduktion. http://www.konkurrensverket.se/globalassets/publikationer/informationsmaterial/upphandlingsreglerna–en-introduktion.pdf. Accessed 20 Apr 2015.

Kronbøl, Trine. 2015. Phone call with Signe Bock Segaard 16.03.2015. Kronbøl works at the Udbudsportalen.

LBK nr 1023 af 23/09/2014. Bekendtgørelse af lov om social service (Serviceloven). https://www.retsinformation.dk/Forms/R0710.aspx?id=164215. Accessed 18 Aug 2016.

LBK nr 1410 af 07/12/2007. Bekendtgørelse af lov om indhentning af tilbud på visse offentlige og offentligt støttede kontrakter. https://www.retsinformation.dk/forms/r0710.aspx?id=113858. Accessed 26 Oct 2015.

LBK nr 897 af 17/08/2011. Bekendtgørelse af lov om friplejeboliger (Friplejeboligloven). https://www.retsinformation.dk/Forms/R0710.aspx?id=136448. Accessed 19 Mar 2015.

LBK nr 917 af 13/08/2014. Friskoleloven. https://www.retsinformation.dk/forms/r0710.aspx?id=164404. Accessed 19 Nov 2014.

LOU 2007:1091. Lag om offentlig upphandling. http://www.riksdagen.se/sv/Dokument-Lagar/Lagar/Svenskforfattningssamling/_sfs-2007-1091/. Accessed 8 Apr 2015.

LOV 2008:962. Lag om valfrihetssystem. http://www.riksdagen.se/sv/Dokument-Lagar/Lagar/Svenskforfattningssamling/Lag-2008962-om-valfrihetssy_sfs-2008-962/. Accessed 8 Apr 2015.

LOV nr 1234 af 18/12/2012. Lov om ændring af lov om indhentning af tilbud på visse offentlige og offentligt støttede kontrakter og lov om kommuners udførelse af opgaver for andre offentlige myndigheder og kommuners og regioners deltagelse i selskaber. https://www.retsinformation.dk/forms/r0710.aspx?id=144417. Accessed 26 Oct 2015.

LOV nr 618 af 14/06/2011. Lov om ændring af lov om håndhævelse af udbudsreglerne m.v. og lov om indhentning af tilbud på visse offentlige og offentligt støttede kontrakter. https://www.retsinformation.dk/forms/r0710.aspx?id=137689. Accessed 26 Oct 2015.

LOV-1984-03-30-15. Lov om statlig tilsyn med helse- og omsorgstjenesten m. m. (helsetilsynsloven). Last changed 1 July 2014. https://lovdata.no/dokument/NL/lov/1984-03-30-15. Accessed 12 Mar 2015.

LOV-1999-07-16-69. Lov om offentlige anskaffelser (anskaffelsesloven). https://lovdata.no/dokument/NL/lov/1999-07-16-69. Accessed 26 Oct 2015.

LOV-2011-06-24-30. Helse- og omsorgstjenesteloven.

Meagher, Gabrielle, and Marta Szebehely (eds.). 2012. *Marketisation in Nordic eldercare: a research report on legislation, oversight, extent and consequences*. Stockholm: Stockholm University.

Nyberg, Linda. 2013. Vad får staten göra? – EU:s statsstödsregler och svensk förvaltningspolitik. In *När förvaltning blir business*, eds. Linda Rönnberg, Urban Strandberg, Elin Wihlborg, and Ulrika Winblad, 187–206. Linköping: Linköping University Press.

Ødegård, Anne Mette. 2006. *Offentlig innkjøp som regulator*. Oslo: Fafo Østforum. http://www.fafo.no/Oestforum/Kunnskapsbase/Publikasjoner/Oestforum_publikasjoner/art_offanskaff_amo.pdf Accessed 8 May 2014.

Phillips, Susan D., and Steven Rathgeb Smith. 2011. Between Governance and Regulation. Evolving Government—Third Sector Relationships. In *Governance and Regulation in the Third Sector. International Perspectives*, eds. Susan D. Phillips, and Steven Rathgeb Smith, 1–36. New York: Routledge.

Rose, Lawrence E. 2005. Demokratiteori – forventninger og virkelighet. In *Det kommunale laboratorium: Teoretiske perspektiver på lokal politikk og organisering*, 2nd ed, eds. Harald Baldersheim, and Lawrence E. Rose, 53–86. Bergen: Fagbokforlaget.

SEC(2011) 1169 final. Commission staff working paper concerning the application of EU public procurement law to relations between contracting authorities ('public-public cooperation'). Brussels: European Commission.

http://ec.europa.eu/internal_market/publicprocurement/docs/public_ public_cooperation/sec2011_1169_en.pdf. Accessed 27 Oct 2015.

Segaard, Signe Bock. 2015. *Skole og eldreomsorg i Skandinavia. Nasjonale føringer for ikke-offentlige aktører*. Report 2015:07. Oslo: Institute for Social Research.

Sejersted, Fredrik. 2014. Rettslig vurdering av om unntaket for kjøp av helse- og sosialtjenester fra ideelle organisasjoner kan videreføres. https://www.regjeringen.no/no/aktuelt/Sejersted-rapporten-klar/id765116/. Accessed 25 June 2015.

SFS 1992:1528. Lag om offentlig upphandling. http://www.riksdagen.se/sv/Dokument-Lagar/Lagar/Svenskforfattningssamling/Lag-19921528-om-offentlig-u_sfs-1992-1528/. Accessed 26 Oct 2015.

SFS 1995:704. Lag om ändring i lagen (1992:1528) om offentlig upphandling. http://www.lagboken.se/Views/Pages/GetFile.ashx?portalId=56&cat=24593&docId=357029&propId=5. Accessed 26 Oct 2015.

SFS 2007:1091. Lag om offentlig upphandling (LOU). http://www.riksdagen.se/sv/Dokument-Lagar/Lagar/Svenskforfattningssamling/_sfs-2007-1091/. Accessed 8 Apr 2015.

SFS 2010:800. Skollag 2010:800. Svensk författningssamling. http://www.riksdagen.se/sv/Dokument-Lagar/Lagar/Svenskforfattningssamling/Skollag-2010800_sfs-2010-800/?bet=2010:800. Accessed 12 Feb 2015.

Sivesind, Karl Henrik. 2016. Endring av fordelingen mellom ideelle, kommersielle og offentlige velferdstjenester i Skandinavia. In *Mot en ny skandinavisk velferdsmodell?*, ed. Karl Henrik Sivesind, 66–73. Report 2016:01. Oslo: Institute for Social Research.

Sørensen, Eva, and Jacob Torfing. 2008. Introduction: Governance Network Research: Towards a Second Generation. In *Theories of Democratic Network Governance*, eds. Eva Sørensen, and Jacob Torfing, 1–21. Hampshire: Palgrave Macmillan.

Statistics Norway. (SSB). 2015. Pleie og omsorgstjenester. http://www.ssb.no/pleie. Accessed 9 May 2016.

Szebehely, Marta, and Gabrielle Meagher. 2012. Four Nordic countries – four responses to the international trend of marketization. In *Marketisation in Nordic eldercare: a research report on legislation, oversight, extent and consequences*, eds. Gabrielle Meagher, and Marta Szebehely, 241–288. Stockholm: Stockholm University.

Szebehely, Marta. 2011. Insatser för äldre och funktionshindrade i privat regi. In *Konkurrensens konsekvenser. Vad händer med svensk välfärd?*, ed. Laura Hartman, 215–257. Stockholm: SNS Förlag.

The Norwegian Government. 2006. Gjennomgang av den særnorske delen av regelverket om offentlige anskaffelse – mandat for offentlig utredningsutvalg. http://www.regjeringen.no/upload/FAD/Vedlegg/Konkurransepolitikk/Anskaffelser/Anskaffelser_utvalg_mandat.pdf. Accessed 13 May 2014.
The Swedish Riksdag. 2012. Betänkande 2011/12:FiU42. Offentlig upphandling från eget företag. http://www.riksdagen.se/sv/Dokument-Lagar/Utskottens-dokument/Betankanden/Arenden/201112/FiU42/. Accessed 17 Mar 2015.
Thøgersen, Malene. 2013. Selvejende institutioner i Danmark. Institutionernes udvikling, udbredelse og karakter på udvalgte samfundsområder. Working paper 1, 2013. Aalborg: Netværk for forskning i Civilsamfund og Frivillighed. http://www.cifri.dk/Webnodes/da/Files/Arbejdsnotater/Selvejende+institutioner+-+01+2013.pdf. Accessed 9 May 2016.
Udbudsportalen. 2011. Vejledning i udbud af drift af plejecentre. February 2011. København: Udbudsportalen.
Udbudsportalen. 2014a. Det klassiske udbudsdirektiv. http://www.udbudsportalen.dk/Ret-og-regler/Direktiver-love-og-regler/Udbudsregler/Det-klassiske-udbudsdirektiv/. Accessed 25 Aug 2014.
Udbudsportalen. 2014b. Køb af B-tjenesteydelser. http://www.udbudsportalen.dk/Ret-og-regler/Direktiver-love-og-regler/Udbudsregler/Tilbudsloven-Danske-regler-for-udbud/Ophavelse-af-annonceringspligten-for-bilag-II-B-tjenesteydelser/. Accessed 25 Aug 2014.
Udbudsportalen. 2015. In-house begrebets betydning for kommunal aftaleindgåelse med selvejende institutioner. http://www.udbudsportalen.dk/Vejledninger/Oficielle-vejledninger-om-udbud/Konkurrencestyrelsens-vejledende-udtalelse-om-in-house-begrebets-betydning-for-kommunal-aftaleindgaelse-med-selvejende-institutioner/. Accessed 17 Mar 2015.
Udbudsrådet. 2012. Offentlig-privat samarbejde i Danmark og Sverige. Valby: Udbudsrådet. http://www.opiguide.dk/media/49156/Analyse_-_Offentlig-privat_samarbejde_i_Danmark_og_Sverige.pdf. Accessed 03 Sep 2015.
Upphandlingsmyndigheten. 2015. Om LOV. Valgfrihetswebben. https://www.valfrihetswebben.se/om-lov.aspx. Accessed 9 Dec 2015.
Utdanningsdirektoratet. 2014. Tolkning av privatskoleloven med forskrifter. http://www.udir.no/Regelverk/Private-skoler/Regelverk-for-private-skoler-/Tolkning-av-privatskoleloven-med-forskrifter/. Accessed on 6 Nov 2014.
Vabo, Signy Irene. 2012. Tiltakende statlig styring av kommunesektoren – også på eldreområdet? In *Det norske flernivådemokratiet*, eds. Marit Reitan, Jo Saglie, and Eivind Smith, 97–135. Oslo: Abstrakt forlag.

Authors' Biography

Signe Bock Segaard is a senior research fellow at the Institute for Social Research, Oslo, Norway. Her main research interests include public administration and politics, welfare policy, and third sector, local elections and local democracy, as well as political behaviour and communication. Her publications include a coedited volume on social capital in Norway, as well as articles in *Journal of Elections, Public Opinion & Parties*; *Nordicom Review*; *Information Polity*; and *Scandinavian Journal of Public Administration*, among others. She is currently project manager on the EU-funded research project 'The Contribution of the Third Sector to Europe's Socio-economic Development' and participates in several research projects on Norwegian local government and politics and welfare mix.

Jo Saglie is Research Professor at the Institute for Social Research, Oslo, Norway. His main research interests include party organisations and intra-party democracy, local elections and local democracy, as well as indigenous politics. His publications include the coedited volume *Indigenous Politics: Institutions, Representation, Mobilisation;* as well as articles in *Journal of Elections, Public Opinion & Parties*; *Local Government Studies*; *Regional and Federal Studies*; and *West European Politics*; among others. He is currently directing the Norwegian Local Election Study and the Norwegian Sámi Parliament Election Study, and he participates in several research projects on Norwegian local government and politics.

Open Access This chapter is licensed under the terms of the Creative Commons Attribution 4.0 International License (http://creativecommons.org/licenses/by/4.0/), which permits use, sharing, adaptation, distribution and reproduction in any medium or format, as long as you give appropriate credit to the original author(s) and the source, provide a link to the Creative Commons license and indicate if changes were made.

The images or other third party material in this chapter are included in the chapter's Creative Commons license, unless indicated otherwise in a credit line to the material. If material is not included in the chapter's Creative Commons license and your intended use is not permitted by statutory regulation or exceeds the permitted use, you will need to obtain permission directly from the copyright holder.

4

Towards a More Diversified Supply of Welfare Services? Marketisation and the Local Governing of Nursing Homes in Scandinavian Countries

David Feltenius

Introduction

Scandinavian countries are often believed to share a similar type of welfare state, one that is often referred to as the social democratic welfare model (Esping-Andersen 1990) or simply the Scandinavian model (Einhorn and Logue 2010). This type of welfare state is highly developed and covers an extensive range of social needs. Another common feature is that laws regulating social policy are universal in nature and target all citizens rather than specific groups (Anttonen 2002; Beland et al. 2014; Bergman and Strøm 2011; Burau and Vabo 2011). Accordingly, the model places a strong emphasis on equality in the sense that all citizens should be treated the same, regardless of where they live or their level of income (Kamp and Hvid 2012).

One of the dominant features of the development of the welfare state in Scandinavia in recent years can be summarised by the concept of

---

D. Feltenius (✉)
Department of Political Science, Umeå University, Umeå, Sweden
e-mail: David.Feltenius@pol.umu.se

© The Author(s) 2017
K.H. Sivesind and J. Saglie (eds.), *Promoting Active Citizenship*,
DOI 10.1007/978-3-319-55381-8_4

marketisation (Pierre 1995; Salamon 1993). This entails the establishment of a mix of different types of providers (public, nonprofit and for-profit) within welfare sectors, such as schools and elderly care (Ascoli and Ranci 2002; Blomqvist 2004; Feltenius and Wide 2015). Although this development has been similar across the Scandinavian countries, there are several differences in the sector that is our focus here; namely, nursing homes within the elderly care system.

The most evident difference is that a mix of different providers of nursing homes is more common at the local level in Sweden than it is in Denmark and Norway. In addition, Sweden has a larger share of for-profit providers and a more modest share of nonprofit providers than either Denmark or Norway (Dahler-Larsen 2015; Dølvik et al. 2015; Hartman 2011; Sivesind 2016).

The logic behind the establishment of this welfare mix is mainly to be found in the concept of new public management (NPM). There are many interpretations of what this concept actually stands for, but one key variable is governing through market-based mechanisms (Boston 2011; Dunleavy and Hood 1994; Ferlie 1996; Hood 1991; Pollitt 1995). Accordingly, the citizen is considered to be a customer in a market of different welfare providers. Allowing citizens to choose a certain provider over another in fields such as education, social services and health is believed to improve the quality of the welfare provision. This implies the exercise of 'active citizenship' through 'choice' of provider, whereby users can obtain services with a preferred profile. These concepts were presented in the first chapter of this book and will be further elaborated in Trætteberg's chapter, which compares consequences of different types of governance for the welfare service users' ability to control their own lives.

In order to establish alternatives among which citizens can choose, one might expect the growth of different profiles of nursing homes reflecting different types of providers.[1] It has also been argued that privatisation allows for a more diversified supply of services than what public providers can offer (Ascoli and Ranci 2002; Weisbrod 1988). For instance, it is believed that nonprofit providers have a greater capacity to offer innovative and specialised services (Mariani and Cavenago 2013; Osborne 1998; Osborne 2010; Salamon and Abramson 1982).

The argument that privatisation creates a more diversified supply of services is not universally accepted. In other types of care for the elderly —for example, home care services—it has been argued that there has been a 'decrease of choice despite the rhetoric of freedom of choice' (Dahl and Rasmussen 2012, 41). The cause of this paradox can be found in procedures of codification of care, which are a prerequisite for contracting out services. Codification of care refers to the specification of the amount of time devoted to, as well as the coding of, the performance of various tasks (Dahl and Rasmussen 2012, 41). In sum, this development implies greater local government steering, which leaves less room for the differentiation of services necessary to create different profiles of care.

Whether local government steering has in fact diminished, or whether the opposite is true, remains an open question, because very little is known about the local governing of nursing homes within the context of marketisation. Previous studies, at least in Sweden, have focused mainly on national laws directed at marketisation and elderly care (Erlandsson et al. 2013; Szebehely 2011). Considerably less attention has been devoted to the question of how municipalities handle their relationships with different types of welfare providers and what consequences this has for the profiling of welfare services. The work presented here seeks to address this topic.

Accordingly, the purpose of this chapter is to compare and explain similarities and differences in the service provision of nursing homes managed by different types of providers (public, for-profit and nonprofit) in six municipalities in Scandinavia. The primary focus of the comparisons is different types of providers. However, we will also explore differences between Scandinavian countries. The following research questions guided the study: Are there any differences between public and private (nonprofit or for-profit) providers with regard to developing a distinct profile of services? Are there any differences between the Scandinavian countries in this respect? To what extent can similarities and differences be explained by local governments' use of governing instruments? What are those instruments, and are they applied differently to public and private providers of care for the elderly? What is the rationale behind the use, or non-use, of those instruments?

The argument of this chapter is that, contrary to what might be expected, there are no major differences between nursing homes managed by different types of providers. The similarity exhibited by different providers is a result of the fact that local authorities retain control of financing and regulation. In general, the regulations are detailed and make no distinctions between providers. This is evident from our empirical study of six Scandinavian municipalities. In these municipalities, interviews were conducted with politicians, administrators, managers and personnel at nursing homes. In some of the nursing homes, interviews were also conducted with residents. In addition, written documentation from nursing homes and public authorities (e.g., policy documents and evaluations) was examined.

This chapter is structured as follows. In section two, the theoretical framework of NPM is developed and a brief description of the research design is presented. In the third section, a brief discussion of care for the elderly in Scandinavian countries is presented. Sections four through six present the main empirical findings for Sweden, Norway and Denmark. In each section, the nursing homes and their activities are introduced, along with a presentation of the governing strategies performed by the municipalities. In the seventh section, we compare different types of welfare providers and draw conclusions regarding the service profiles of nursing homes and how such facilities are governed. In the final section of the chapter, the most significant findings are summarised and important questions for further research are discussed.

Creating a Market for Elderly Care

Marketisation and New Public Management (NPM)

Facing numerous challenges from the late-1970s onwards, welfare states have responded in many ways. One of these responses, particularly evident during the 1990s, is welfare retrenchment i.e. cutbacks in welfare spending (Pierson 1994; Lindbom 2001). Another response has been to reorganise the welfare state using the market as a model i.e. marketisation (Petersen and Hjelmar 2013; Pierre 1995; Salamon 1993). A theoretical account of this development is represented in the concept of New Public Management (NPM) (Boston 2011; Dunleavy and Hood 1994; Ferlie 1996; Hood 1991; Pollitt 1995).

NPM is an umbrella concept that covers different features of the organisation of the public sector based on the model of the market. These features include explicit standards and measures of performance, greater emphasis on output controls, disaggregation of units in the public sector, a private-sector management style and a shift to greater competition in the public sector. The emphasis on competition implies a greater role for contracts and tendering procedures (Hood 1991).

'Contracting' means that the delivery of services is delegated to private providers, while public authorities are responsible for regulation and financing. The public authority's choice of provider is the result of a tendering process in which different actors compete with each other on price or quality (Elinder and Jordahl 2013; Stolt and Winblad 2009). However, it is seldom the case that public authorities contract out all services within a given welfare field. A more common approach is delivering some part or parts of a particular service themselves while contracting out other parts. The result is a welfare mix of different providers, both public and private, which can be either for-profit or nonprofit.

The Welfare Mix and Its Rationale

The logic behind the establishment of this kind of welfare mix is that it allows for a more diversified supply of services in fields such as education, health and social welfare (Ascoli and Ranci 2002; Blomqvist and Rothstein 2000; Weisbrod 1988). Allowing for a more diversified supply is supposed to encourage the development of a broader catalogue of services compared to what public providers can offer on their own. It is believed that public service providers generally target the average citizen. The same is true for private, for-profit providers, who target the population that belongs to the largest segment of the market (Traetteberg and Sivesind 2015). However, this argument does not apply to nonprofit service providers. Quite the contrary, it has been argued that nonprofit providers have a greater capacity to offer innovative and specialised services (Mariani and Cavenago 2013; Osborne 1998; Osborne 2010; Salamon and Abramson 1982; Salamon 1987).

According to Lester M. Salamon, nonprofit service providers have several strengths, including a significant degree of flexibility in their operations. This results from the proximity of their governing boards to the field of action. Another major strength is the ability of nonprofit providers to offer greater diversity regarding the content of services. This is possible due to their small scale of operations, which allows them to tailor services to specific needs (Salamon 1987; Weisbrod 1977).

User Choice

One of the chief merits of a welfare mix is that citizens, who are referred to as 'customers', have alternatives from which to choose. Le Grand discussed the possibility of competition without choice and choice without competition (Le Grand 2007, 45). However, according to him, it is only when user choice is coupled with provider competition that the ends of a marketised welfare system are fully achieved. Le Grand considers this to be a case of governmental steering through 'the invisible hand'. Among the ends achieved by this type of steering are greater user autonomy, higher service quality and greater efficiency (Le Grand 2007).

Quality can be referred to in terms of both 'input' and 'output'. Input can be measured in relation to various parameters; for example, staff qualifications and expertise, class sizes in schools and the physical condition of buildings. The other aspect of quality, output, can be measured in terms of the results achieved by medical treatment or school attendance. Efficiency of welfare provision refers to achieving the highest quality and quantity from a given level of resources (Le Grand 2007).

However, it is important to note that the desired ends of 'choice' and 'marketisation' are not solely a matter of quality and efficiency. Another important end is the empowerment of citizens by making it possible for them to choose 'exit' in order to give them influence in welfare provision. Before marketisation, citizens could influence the provision of welfare foremost through 'voice', i.e. by expressing their opinions to decision-makers, either as individuals or as a collective body (Blomqvist and Rothstein 2000; Hirschman 1970).

Governing Through Contracts

Although customer choice is an important mechanism for achieving the aims of marketised welfare (i.e. improved quality and efficiency), it is far from the only one. Contracting out welfare services is a process regulated by national law and, in the field of elderly care, implemented by municipalities. A central feature of this process is that the municipalities stipulate the criteria that service providers must follow. This type of steering by municipalities is referred to as management by contract or governing through contracts (Almqvist 2001; Kamp and Hvid 2012, 40; Vabø 2007, 53; Walsh 1995).

The idea behind governing through contracts is that it makes it possible for public authorities to measure performance, which is a precondition for efficient service provision. In order to measure performance, the contract must be somewhat specific concerning the goals to be achieved (Vabø 2007, 54). However, it has been pointed out in the literature that writing contracts for services is a difficult task because it is hard to identify objective standards. This is especially true in the field of care, due to the fact that it concerns the well-being of the elderly. Drawing conclusions concerning deterioration and improvement in quality as well as efficiency is a complicated matter (Almqvist 2001; Erlinder and Jordahl 2013; Walsh 1995, 52–53). One solution to the problem is to focus more on the methods that providers should use. However, this solution represents a deviation from the ideal, which is that the purchaser sets the targets and providers compete over how to achieve them using their best and most effective solutions (Almqvist 2001).

The ability to measure performance also requires establishing and implementing procedures for audits and inspections. This is considered to be particularly important in environments that provide services like care, where the providers usually have more information than the purchasers. Inspections can be carried out in many ways; for example, by responding to public complaints, conducting unannounced visits and examining random samples of work (Walsh 1995). The performance of these tasks requires a new kind of competence and administration at the level of the purchasing authority. It has been argued that the need for this type of administration eclipses some of the efficiency gains achieved by contracting out.

Decreasing Choice—A Paradox

From the discussion above, it follows that there are different mechanisms for reaching overall goals through the use of marketisation. These mechanisms have been referred to in terms of user choice and governing through contracts. Whether the mechanisms are compatible or not has been a topic of lively discussion. One issue that has received a significant amount of attention is the idea that marketisation actually creates a market of different providers with their own special profiles. It has been argued that customers actually have less choice and receive fewer individualised services than before—a condition that has been referred to as the 'decrease of choice despite the rhetoric of freedom of choice' (Dahl and Rasmussen 2012, 41).

To understand this argument, we will return to the practice of governing through contracts, which requires the codification of care. Without this, it would be difficult or nearly impossible to both write and evaluate contracts. By codification of care, we mean the specification of the time devoted to and the coding of the performance of various tasks. Completing such codified tasks is facilitated by the use of modern technology in home care services; for example, personal digital assistants. The overall result of this process, according to Hanne Dahl and Bente Rasmussen, is a growing standardisation of care (Dahl and Rasmussen 2012).

Standardisation of care represents a paradox in relation to arguments concerning the 'welfare mix' and 'customer choice'. This paradox has been clearly described by Dahl and Rasmussen, who argued that, contrary to what one would expect of marketised welfare, 'customers have less choice and receive fewer individualised services than they did in the old model where they were allotted time rather than tasks' (Dahl and Rasmussen 2012, 41). In the old model, the professionals, i.e. care workers, had a stronger position and a greater degree of flexibility in carrying out their tasks. It is argued that this environment gave the elderly more choices and thus more individualised service (Dahl 2009; Dahl and Rasmussen 2012, 41).

Based on the theoretical argument articulated by Dahl and Rasmussen, one might expect there to be no differences between public and private nursing homes due to the growing standardisation of the services carried out. However, their argument is built primarily on research related to home care services in Denmark. Whether this argument is also relevant in the context of nursing homes is an open question. It may be that governing in this particular activity is softer, thus leaving providers with greater room for providing a variety of services.

The Empirical Study—A Brief Note

In order to discuss the validity of the theoretical account of marketisation and expectations with regard to the profile of welfare services, an empirical study has been conducted. The study covers different types of welfare providers (public, nonprofit and for-profit) and their relations with municipal administrations in six municipalities: two in Sweden (Sollentuna and Östersund), two in Norway (Asker and Steinkjer) and two in Denmark (Faaborg-Midtfyn and Herning). In Sweden, two public and two for-profit nursing homes were scrutinised in greater detail. In Norway, two public, one for-profit and one nonprofit were investigated. In Denmark, the research focused on two public and two nonprofit nursing homes. The empirical investigation was carried out in 2013–2014 and followed a similar scheme in all countries. Considering the limited number of cases investigated in each country, the study is obviously only explorative but it nevertheless provides a point of departure for further research.

The empirical study consisted primarily of interviews with civil servants in the municipal administrations, politicians responsible for elderly care policy, and site managers at the nursing homes.[2] A total of 20 interviews were conducted in Sweden, 19 (with 29 people) in Denmark and 26 (with 44 people) in Norway. The interviews were performed by different members of the research group. Each member was an expert on his or her country. A more elaborate presentation of how the empirical investigation was conducted can be found in the first chapter of this book and in the appendix covering the data collection and methods.

Managers at the municipal administrative unit responsible for care of the elderly are referred to as 'head managers of the administration'. Managers at the nursing homes are referred to as 'site managers'; it is also evident from the references in the text whether the unit is public, nonprofit or for-profit. Finally, interviews conducted with local politicians responsible for care of the elderly are simply referred to as 'politicians'.

In addition to the interviews, a variety of written documents were examined, including policy plans for care of the elderly, surveys, informational brochures about the nursing homes and party documents. This material was used to prepare for the interviews, as well as to triangulate information obtained from them. In the next section, the results of the investigation will be presented. We begin with a brief introduction of both the organisation of elderly care in Scandinavian countries and the municipalities chosen for this study.

Organisation of Elderly Care

Responsibility of the Municipality

In Scandinavian countries, care for the elderly is the responsibility of municipalities. In performing this task, municipalities are restricted by national laws only to a limited extent, because the relevant laws are 'framework laws' without detailed regulation. This is in accordance with the Scandinavian tradition of strong municipal self-rule (Gustafsson 1999, 52; Loughlin et al. 2011, 11). Municipal responsibility for care of the elderly includes both a financial and regulatory responsibility. It is the municipalities that interpret national laws and work out local guidelines for needs assessments. Thus, the decision to grant an elderly person home care services or a place at a nursing home is made by a care administrator following local guidelines for needs assessment.

The overall balance between home care services and nursing homes for the elderly is also a matter for the municipality to decide. In recent decades, in all three countries, municipalities have started to give priority to home care services rather than offering elderly people a place at a nursing home (Hermansen and Gautun 2011; Hjemmehjælpskommisionen 2013). A natural consequence of this strategy is that the threshold to secure a place in a nursing home has risen (Gjevjon and Romøren 2010). In 2005, about 80% of those living in Norwegian nursing homes suffered from dementia (Haugen and Engedal 2005). Nursing home users, therefore, are in relatively poor health and make up only a fraction of the elderly who receive municipal services.

Development of a Welfare Mix

In all three countries, municipalities also have the authority to decide whether care for the elderly should be marketised. The municipality can decide that all services should be performed in-house or by a mix of public, for-profit and nonprofit actors. Denmark deviates in this respect because a national law from 2007 makes it possible for both nonprofit and for-profit actors to establish nursing homes irrespective of the wishes of the municipality (LBK 897)—so-called 'independent' nursing homes.[3] Most of the independent nursing homes that have been created since the law came into effect are run on a nonprofit basis (Rambøll 2012, 15).

The most rapid development towards marketisation has taken place in Sweden's 290 municipalities (Jordahl and Öhrvall 2013). In 1999, 54 municipalities had private providers of nursing homes. This figure had risen to about 93 by 2016 (Socialstyrelsen 2004, 2017).[4] These are mainly for-profit companies because nonprofit organisations play a very limited role in Sweden (Erlandsson et al. 2013; Stolt and Winblad 2009).

In Denmark, nonprofit providers play a more important role than their for-profit counterparts, although the overall development of the privatisation of nursing homes has been modest (Bertelsen and Rostgaard 2013). The development of privatisation has also been modest in Norway, although most non-municipally operated nursing homes are run by for-profit care companies. According to figures from 2010, about

70 Norwegian nursing homes are managed by civil society organisations, such as foundations or voluntary organisations (Vabø et al. 2013).

In sum, it is evident from this section that the organisation of care for the elderly is similar in Scandinavian countries. It is the municipalities that have the overall responsibility for this task and can decide the type of welfare provider. In the next three sections, the results of the empirical investigation will be presented for each of the three countries. Each section begins with a presentation of the nursing homes that were investigated. This is followed by a deeper examination of the issue of how municipalities govern nursing homes for the elderly.

Sweden

Nursing Homes and Their Profiles

In both Swedish municipalities, the welfare mix consists of public and for-profit providers. In Östersund, most of the nursing homes are operated by the municipality's provider. The situation is the opposite in Sollentuna, which has only a few public nursing homes. These are run by Sollentuna Omsorg (SOLOM AB), which is owned by the municipality.

In both municipalities, private providers consist of nationwide, for-profit companies such as Vardaga, Attendo, Förenade Care and Aleris. In addition, there are smaller for-profit companies in both municipalities; for example, Vårdstyrkan AB and Strukturrutan. In Östersund, contracting out has been deliberately organised in a way that facilitates the participation of smaller companies.

Two nursing homes per municipality were scrutinised in detail: one private (in both municipalities, one of the homes owned by a nationwide company) and one public. The four nursing homes were similar in terms of the number of beds and clients. They were also similar with regard to the physical and mental (dementia) diagnoses of the clients. To determine whether there were differences among the nursing homes, interviews were conducted with site managers, politicians and administrators. In addition, relevant documents were examined; for example, informational brochures, websites and annual reports.

From the interviews, it appears that there is no clear profile among the investigated nursing homes. Instead, special competencies among the staff or the implementation of particular projects were mentioned. For instance, at one of the private homes, one nurse is a 'Silvia-nurse', a title one earns by attending a special training programme that emphasises care for elderly persons with dementia (Interview, site manager, private, 2014-02-05). Another example, from the other private nursing home, is a project involving putting pets in the care facility in order to promote well-being among the elderly (Interview, site manager, private, 2014-04-14).

Particular projects like these can also be found at the public nursing homes. For instance, cooperation with civil society was mentioned in the interviews. The local branch of the Red Cross visits nursing homes and offers activities for the elderly such as 'sing-alongs' or reading aloud (Interview, site manager, public, 2014-04-14). However, none of these projects are undertaken with the aim of giving the nursing home a distinct profile. In one of the public nursing homes, the site manager explained that the elderly are often in poor physical and/or mental health and are thus not vigorous enough to participate in different activities: 'You don't move here because you are interested in gardening or anything else' (Interview, site manager, public, 2014-02-14).

This statement reveals something important about the situation at nursing homes in Sweden today. Elderly persons are given places at nursing homes only when they are seriously ill and cannot manage on their own without assistance from home care providers. One manager claimed that once you move into a nursing home, it is probably the last place you will live in your life. This fact needs to be considered when discussing 'choice' and a 'diversified supply of services'.

Rather than referring to differences, site managers at nursing homes emphasise similarities. One of the similarities is working with a municipal programme about basic values within elderly care. This programme is the municipality's interpretation of the national basic values outlined in the Social Services Act. At each nursing home, regardless of provider, there is a member of staff who is responsible for implementation. In Östersund, the basic values have been interpreted as guarantees for the elderly. First, each elderly person is guaranteed a contact person responsible for ensuring that communication among the resident, relatives and staff functions satisfactorily. Second, an individual implementation plan must be drawn up, with information about how and when care is to be performed. Third, care must be provided at a time upon which the parties agree (Östersunds kommun 2014).

The individual implementation plan (i.e. care plan) is a central feature of care at all nursing homes.[5] Its purpose is to ensure that care is planned on the basis of the particular needs of the individual. Upon arrival, the elderly and their relatives meet with the nursing home staff. The staff provide information about daily routines and what to expect in terms of activities. The elderly and their relatives explain their expectations of the nursing home. The elderly resident is asked questions, such as 'What food do you like to eat for breakfast?' 'What clothes do you prefer?' 'Do you have different preferences on weekdays as opposed to weekends?' All the information is recorded in an implementation plan that is then accessible to the staff at the nursing home (Interview, site manager, public, 2014-04-14).

The aim of this procedure of drawing up individual plans is to provide an opportunity for the elderly to influence the care they receive and how it is performed. At one of the private nursing homes, the manager explained that this procedure represents an important development over time, in which the focus of user influence has shifted from 'users as a collective' to 'users as individuals' (Interview, site manager, private, 2014-04-14).

Given the similarities among the nursing homes we investigated, it is not surprising that elderly residents and/or their relatives rate the quality of care as equivalent. In Sollentuna, a quality survey was carried out in 2012. It measured a range of variables such as safety, social interaction, self-determination and integrity. An index comprised of all variables revealed only negligible differences between the two nursing homes we studied. The private home had a slightly better score (Sollentuna kommun 2012). In Östersund, however, the public provider received a slightly better score in a survey from 2013.

On a question concerning overall satisfaction, the public nursing home received an average value of 8.8 out of 10 (response rate, 63%) (Östersunds kommun 2013-06-13), while the private home received a value of 6.5 (response rate, 50%) (Östersunds kommun 2013-09-16). According to statements made in the survey's open-answer section, one possible explanation for this difference is that the private nursing home is located in an old building, while the municipal nursing home is located in a relatively new building.

Governing of Nursing Homes

It is evident from the interviews that the similarities among the nursing homes can primarily be explained by the way the municipality steers elderly care. While national guidelines and laws also play an important role in determining the services provided, the focus here is on municipal (local) governance of nursing homes. One governing instrument are long-term plans for elderly care. For instance, in 2006, the Östersund council adopted a plan with multiple goals, including accessibility, influence, culture and competence among staff (Östersunds kommun 2006). Sollentuna has a similar policy document containing key areas identified as subjects of special attention. Among them are elderly people's influence and independence, safety and active lifestyle (Vård-och omsorgsnämnden 2013).

Another type of governing instrument, or perhaps more of an underlying precondition, is the procedure for choosing a nursing home. Municipal care administrators decide whether an elderly person qualifies for a place at a nursing home. If so, he or she has the right to express a preference for a particular facility. However, this preference is not always easy to accommodate, because there are a limited number of rooms available at each nursing home. When a room becomes available, it is reported to the municipal administration, which passes the information on to the elderly person. Since people who are waiting for a space in a nursing home are generally in poor health, they typically accept the room that is offered, regardless of whether it is their first-choice (Interview, head manager, administration, 2013-12-13). That the system operates this way also impacts the incentives that providers of nursing homes have for developing different profiles. Since elderly persons are placed at a particular nursing home, the homes do not need to 'attract customers on a market'. In reality, the market is very limited (if not non-existent), since the ability of an elderly person to make an active choice is very restricted for both medical and capacity reasons.

Another type of instrument are contracts between the municipality and the nursing homes. In the case of contracting out, a contract is signed with the provider that submits the winning bid. In Östersund, the contract is awarded to the provider who can manage the nursing home in accordance with criteria specified in a tendering document at the lowest price. Sollentuna applies a different model, in which the sum received for operating the nursing home is fixed. The provider who can offer the best quality at the sum offered gets the contract.

The contract contains the criteria from the tendering documents as well as additional criteria, which makes it an important steering document for the municipality. For instance, it may include criteria about staff competence, safety, nutrition or influence for the elderly resident. If, during the tendering process, the providers promised to deliver other measures of quality—for example, staff with particular competences—then this is also included in the contract. Although public providers do not participate in the tendering process, their operations are also regulated in a contract of this type.

In Sollentuna, governing through contracts applies both to private and public nursing home providers. The public provider gets no special treatment. One head manager of the municipal administration said that every provider should be treated the same, regardless of whether they are private or public. This is motivated on the grounds that elderly care is offered in a competitive market. In reality, there are some differences due to the fact that contracts are written at different times. Nonetheless, the overall ambition of the municipal administration is to treat all providers the same (Interview, head manager, administration, 2013-12-13).

The head of elderly care administration in Sollentuna holds the view that the use of the contract implies rather hard steering of nursing homes. The municipality has many conditional requirements, which are included in all contracts, which suggests that services are largely the same, regardless of provider. In addition, this has implications for the possibility of choice for the elderly. Simply put, there is not much to choose from because there is little difference among nursing homes (Interview, head manager, administration, 2013-12-13). Politicians share this view. Therefore, one ambition for the future is that the conditional requirements focus more on what is to be done and less on how it should be done (Interview, conservative politician, 2013-12-11).

Managers of nursing homes in Sollentuna stress the importance of local guidelines, national guidelines and laws, and contracts with the municipality. The contract is seen as rather detailed, including, for example, guidelines for meals and the maintenance of the facilities. There are even instructions about financial responsibility if washing machines break down (Interview, site manager, public, 2014-02-14; site manager, private, 2014-04-14).

The situation is similar in Östersund. Every provider, regardless of whether they are private or public, must follow a number of quality criteria. These criteria are listed as conditional requirements in the contract with the nursing home provider. The implementation of the criteria ensures that the services provided at the nursing home are similar. Private nursing homes also have to follow an additional quality programme formulated by the company. Despite the fact that the operation of the private nursing home is governed from many different directions, the manager believes that there is some freedom to decide how to deliver the requested service (Interview, site manager, private 2014-04-14). At public nursing homes, the existence of quality criteria is mentioned alongside the budget provided for their operation (Interview, site manager, public, 2014-04-14).

In both municipalities, public administrators closely monitor nursing homes to ensure that they abide by their contracts. In Östersund, one of the politicians mentioned that the contracts and their criteria are not worth much if the homes are not monitored to ensure compliance (Interview, social democratic politician, 2014-04-07). Therefore, a special division within the administration conducts an annual follow-up of the nursing homes. It is conducted using a point system in which different scores require the home to undertake specific types of action. The procedure is carried out at both public and private nursing homes; everyone is treated the same (Interview, head manager, administration, 2014-04-07).

In Sollentuna, the monitoring of nursing homes takes place prior to the renewal of a contract. If the provider does not fulfil the criteria first agreed upon, then the contract may not be extended. This is not an empty threat because it has actually occurred. Instead of renewing a contract, a facility can be taken over by a municipal company (Interview, head manager, administration, 2013-12-13). A representative from the opposition party holds the view that this type of monitoring is insufficient, and that there is a need for more regular inspections both early on and in the middle of a contract period (Interview, social democratic politician, 2014-01-15).

In terms of future developments, the head manager of the elderly care administration in Östersund argues that one important task involves closely evaluating and scrutinising the criteria used. There might be some criteria that unnecessarily constrain operations (Interview, head manager, administration, 2014-04-07). Politicians have different views about the need to loosen up the governing of nursing homes in order to allow for greater variation in service supply. The politician representing the Centre Party wanted to see greater variation in the future, while the representative of the Social Democratic Party was more interested in a different goal. This representative argued that the purpose of having a mix of welfare providers is to be able to compare. How much does it cost to engage in an activity with a certain level of quality? What does a private operator cost in relation to a public operator? (Interview, social democratic politician, 2014-04-07).

The argument above illustrates the fact that politicians might support contracting out for different reasons. It is not necessarily about empowering the elderly and giving them a range of welfare providers with different profiles to choose from. Another motive might be formulated in terms of benchmarking, i.e. helping the municipality establish some point of reference about the cost of the elderly care provision.

In sum, evidence from the Swedish case suggests that there are no major differences between providers with regard to the services provided. This is explained by the fact that municipalities exercise hard rather than soft governing of nursing homes. Even though public providers do not participate in the tendering process, they are subject to the same steering as private providers. The rationale for this is that all providers should be treated the same by the municipal administration. In the next section, we use the same research questions to analyse the case of Norway.

Norway

Nursing Homes and Their Profiles

In the Norwegian case (the municipalities of Asker and Steinkjer), the welfare mix consists of public, for-profit and nonprofit nursing homes. Representatives from both for-profit and nonprofit nursing homes claim that they are distinct from their public counterparts. The for-profit nursing home refers to a particular 'service concept' that the company developed in its hotel management operations and subsequently introduced to nursing homes. The company has lauded its concept in its communication with both users and the municipality (Interview, site manager, for-profit, 2013-11-11).

Interestingly, neither users, staff or the municipality identified service as a special trait of this nursing home. Moreover, in the latest user survey, the for-profit nursing home had the lowest score on all service measures. When specifically asked what is uniquely special about the nursing home, the staff did not mention the service concept, which casts doubt on its importance. The elderly residents experience their nursing home through their interactions with care providers. If these providers are unaware of a concept, it cannot be seen as a defining trait of the home.

The nonprofit nursing home in this study has a diaconal approach to its operations; thus, according to the site manager, Christian values are a subject that is discussed when prospective staff are interviewed (Interview, site manager, nonprofit, 2014-01-27). Nevertheless, the municipality and elderly residents do not think that the diaconal approach influences care in important, substantive ways. As the administrative head at the municipality claimed, 'No, I don't think they have more visits from the priest and "stuff like that" than the other nursing homes' (Interview, head manager, administration, 2014-02-20).

In both municipalities, the interviewees from the municipal administration stressed that there are no differences between public and nonpublic nursing homes, and that no differences are indeed desired. All citizens have the same right to services, and the municipality allocates citizens to providers. Accordingly, from the point of view of the municipality, it is not possible to defend any difference in the content of the service provided. An elderly person can say that he or she prefers to live at a particular nursing home; but, in reality, capacity limitations will force him or her to take the first available slot. When an elderly person's health has deteriorated to the point of earning placement in a nursing home, then it is not usually possible to wait for a place in a preferred home to open up. Representatives of elderly residents of nursing homes stated that when someone prefers a particular home, the most important reasons for this preference are geography and proximity to a former home or where their relatives currently live. Some also mentioned general perceptions that a particular home has a reputation for offering high-quality service, but such perceptions are based on the anecdotal experiences of friends and families. Substantive differences among the nursing homes are not given as a prominent explanation.

In Asker, the municipality contracted the for-profit provider through a public tender in order to reap benefits from the tender itself. The tender provides a benchmark for how nursing homes should be run, something that the municipality can subsequently use in its steering of municipal nursing homes. The political and administrative leaders in the municipality as well as the head of the municipal nursing home alleges that the for-profit nursing home serves as a benchmark for public institutions. In addition, the municipality prefers to see some innovation in the form of differences in the administration and organisation of the private nursing home. However, elderly residents do not experience these differences as substantive differences in care.

In Steinkjer, the municipality does not want the nonprofit nursing home to be different from its public counterpart. On the contrary, the municipality wants it to operate largely the same as public nursing homes. In this sense, public nursing homes act as benchmarks for the nonprofit home. The municipality has a geographically dispersed population, and the geographic dimension trumps the issue of the type of welfare provider. At the same time, the interviewed actors were aware of the fact that the nonprofit nursing home is not part of the public hierarchy, and they were committed to ensuring that the municipality did not treat it as inferior.

The only tool for systematically comparing the nursing homes in the municipalities on objective quality indicators is the user survey carried out annually in Asker and twice a year in Steinkjer. Given the poor health of the residents, there were a number of methodological challenges involved in conducting the surveys. Nonetheless, the results consistently showed that there are no systematic differences between nonpublic and public nursing homes. The variation in results that did occur was not due to variation in the type of provider—i.e. public or private.

Governing of Nursing Homes

To understand the limited difference between public and nonpublic nursing homes, it is necessary to examine how the municipalities carry out local governance. National laws and regulations are the same for all providers, but differences across municipalities reveal the opportunities that municipalities have to influence the institutions for which they are responsible. Municipalities might exploit the opportunity available for local adaptation in order to allow for differences among various actors in the welfare mix. However, as discussed above, the interviews show that municipalities do not want differences.

The contracts that the municipalities have with private nursing homes govern their regulation. The nature of the contracts in Asker, which has a for-profit provider, and Steinkjer, which has a nonprofit, are different. Turning first to Asker, the contract is detailed with respect to a number of aspects of care to be provided. In the view of the head of the nursing home, 'I think that we are not completely private. The municipality sets the standard and is responsible for the care' (Interview, site manager, for-profit, 2013-11-13). This comment illustrates the fact that both parties find public control and intervention in the provision of services to be natural. However, the contractual relationship between the municipality and the for-profit home means that it is not natural for the municipality to intervene in the daily operations of the nursing home. With regard to the public nursing home, it has a frame budget and, in its experience, a certain amount of leeway for developing a particular profile. For example, one public nursing home has special expertise on severe dementia. The development of this profile was the result of an initiative at the nursing home itself. In this way, both public and for-profit nursing homes have some leeway to carve out profiles, but the resulting differences stem from factors other than the type of provider.

The contractual relationship between Steinkjer and its nonprofit home is different. The contract is less detailed in terms of content of care, but it does include a number of passages that force the provider to adapt to municipal standards and, crucially, entitles the municipality to intervene on a detailed level in the operation of the nursing home. The municipality could have opted for a hands-off approach; but in reality, the municipality is interested in detailed issues that go beyond care-related matters. For example, the municipality is involved in the number of people working in the administration of the nursing home as well as the wages of managers at the institution. The head manager of the municipal administration described a close relationship with a continuous discussion about detailed aspects of care. She concluded:

> The feedback [from the nonprofit nursing home] is that they think it is all right that we exercise oversight over the professional standards of care and that we are concerned that the product we pay for maintains a high standard, in the best interest of the citizens of Steinkjer. And they want to deliver a product that makes us willing to continue to use them. I have not experienced any conflict about this. (Interview, head manager, administration, 2014-02-20)

In spite of the fact that the for-profit nursing home has a more detailed contract, it seems as if it has more room to manoeuvre than its nonprofit counterpart. The contract of the for-profit facility shields it from certain forms of intervention by the municipality in matters that are not regulated in the contract. For example, while a cut in public spending on nursing homes would not affect the for-profit nursing home during the contract period, the nonprofit nursing home would be affected in the same way as the municipal ones. The larger the share of nursing home places located in for-profit nursing homes, the more severe the cuts on public institutions.

The municipal nursing homes in both municipalities are integrated into the municipal structure. This means that, formally, municipal politicians and administration can intervene in the institutions at any time. In reality, this occurs on issues such as the structure of care places. As the administrative head of Asker, which has the for-profit provider, explained:

> When I speak about dimensioning, it concerns the number of short-term and long-term places. It is important that this is dimensioned correctly [...] With municipal provision, I can make the change like this [snaps her fingers], immediately, but I cannot do that if it is on a contract. Then it is a longer process. (Interview, head manager, administration, 2013-11-19)

What this comment illustrates is that it is easier to force changes on municipal nursing homes than non-municipal ones. When it comes to issues relating to the content of care, however, things are different. Professionals at the nursing homes make decisions on these matters. For example, public homes for elderly care have tested alternative schedules for work shifts and the use of dogs to stimulate residents, all without consulting municipal authorities in advance. The central point is that the tools that municipalities use to govern nursing homes are different depending on whether the home is public or private, but the effect is more a matter of administrative differences than the content of care.

Within each municipality, each of the nursing homes reported the same indicators to municipal authorities in order to facilitate comparisons among them. Some of these indicators include staff sick leave, financial matters, changes in the educational composition of the staff, and other issues regulated in the contracts. The user surveys administered by the municipalities are the most important instrument for comparing the nursing homes. The surveys are the same for all homes, and they receive considerable attention from politicians and the municipal administration. Any nursing home, public or nonpublic, whose results are unsatisfactory is summoned to a meeting in order to explain the results and draw up plans for improving them. Since the survey is the same for all nursing homes, it provides an incentive for all of them to work on the areas raised in the surveys, because they know that these are the issues on which they will be measured and evaluated.

In Steinkjer, the governance model of elderly care is well established and no changes are imminent. This is a large, rural municipality, and ongoing debate about whether to centralise or maintain a broad range of services in all communities within the municipality has occurred as a result. Steinkjer's nonprofit nursing home is located on the outskirts of the municipality, and might therefore be vulnerable. Despite this, it has considerable political support, and both strategic plans and interviewees we spoke with agreed that major changes are unlikely.

In Asker, the municipality is currently preparing a new tender and its for-profit company must compete to retain its contract. According to both political and administrative leaders in the municipality, the price is not likely to be an evaluation criterion in the tender. According to the head of elderly care in the municipality:

> I do not think there is as much to gain from competition as there was earlier. The municipality has worked a lot on efficiency and closed the gap on average expenses compared to a few years ago. That is my experience, and that is why it is interesting to compete on quality, to see if the private sector can do it for the same price, but with better quality (Interview, head manager, administration, 2013-11-19).

Such a shift in strategy on the part of the municipality would invite private providers to offer additional areas that can be included in the contract. It also reveals an ambition on the part of the municipality to find private providers that deviate more from public nursing homes in their operations. However, the municipality has no plans to change the way it steers in order to obtain differentiation.

In conclusion, the evidence from Norway implies that there are no important differences in the content of care due to a nursing home being public or private. The explanation for this is partly that there is little room to deviate from the municipal standard within the municipal governance regime. A municipality can either use a detailed contract to impose its standard—as is the case for Asker's for-profit nursing home—or it can intervene more directly in the operation of a nursing home, as in the nonprofit case in Steinkjer. The greater the number of quality indicators, like user surveys, that the municipalities use, the stronger the convergence in how nursing homes operate.

Denmark

Nursing Homes and Their Profiles

Four nursing homes in two municipalities (Faaborg-Midtfyn and Herning) were examined—two public and two nonprofit. Both nonprofit nursing homes have a Christian profile and belong to the large nonprofit organisation, Danske Diakonhjem, which runs about 50 nursing homes in Denmark (www.danskediakonhjem.dk). Both of these homes have contracts with their local municipalities.

In the Faaborg-Midtfyn municipality, the municipal website makes no distinction between the nonprofit nursing home and the public nursing homes. This is in contrast to the situation in Herning, where a clear distinction is made between different types of nursing homes on the municipality's website. Moreover, the situation in Herning is different from the situation in Faaborg-Midtfyn, as the former includes two independent nursing homes. Both of these homes were established as a consequence of a municipal decision to cancel contracts with nonprofit nursing homes. The independent nursing homes were not closely examined in the empirical analysis presented here, but they played an important role in the interviews that were conducted with municipal actors. In addition, a single interview was conducted with the manager of one of the independent care homes in order to attain an overall understanding of their special status.

All four nursing homes have the same general principles for care, which focus on adapting care services as much as possible to accommodate personal needs and resources. The homes also strive to make the facilities homelike, and thus to involve the elderly in the daily life of the nursing home as much as possible. For instance, they have kitchens that allow elderly residents to participate in cooking activities. Not all nursing homes in the investigated municipalities have kitchens, but the ones selected for this study do in order to ensure that they all shared similar characteristics. The four homes are also of similar size. Three of the four are situated in small towns, and one is located in an urban area. In each of the nursing homes, interviews were conducted with managers, employees and representatives of user boards, primarily relatives of elderly persons living at the homes. None of the municipalities in the study administers user surveys on a regular basis, and no comparable surveys were available.

From the interviews, it is evident that there are no major differences between public and nonprofit providers with regard to the content of care. In all four nursing homes, great emphasis is placed on implementing homelike principles of care, as was mentioned above. However, the implementation of these principles is limited by the physical and mental condition of the elderly, as well as by the limited resources of the nursing homes (Interviews, employees, municipal nursing home, 2014-03-06). The weak condition of the elderly at the nursing homes is also important to keep in mind when considering the scope for freedom of choice. Although there is freedom of choice, it can in practice be limited by room availability combined with the urgency of care.

Some of the relatives in the interviews claimed that they were not able to wait for a vacant room at their first-choice home; therefore, they accepted the first available room. According to nursing home managers, while residents seldom move to a different facility, it does sometimes happen when an elderly person did not originally get their first-choice (Interview, manager, municipal nursing home, 2014-01-10). The interviews also reveal that the most important factor for choosing a nursing home is related more to geographical location and less to other characteristics of the homes:

> I think geography is the main reason. I wish I could say that it is because of us, but it is not. Of course people from the area want to stay here, because it is here that they have their social circles and their children. (Interview, manager, nonprofit nursing home, 2014-02-20)

Among the relatives we interviewed, it is also evident that the distinctive Christian profile is not the main reason why people choose nonprofit nursing homes. Again, geography and good reputation are mentioned as the main reasons (Interviews, user boards, nonprofit nursing home, 2014-03-12). However, according to some of the interviewees, kitchen facilities and a nursing home's principles for care also played a role in selection.

All nursing homes in the study hold an introductory meeting when a new resident arrives at the home. At this meeting, a care plan is drawn up, which includes information about personal needs and preferences. Another feature shared by all of the homes is that each elderly resident has a contact person who is responsible for maintaining contact between the resident, the staff and the relatives. These procedures do not vary across the different types of providers.

However, due to the Christian profile of the nonprofit nursing homes, there are some differences regarding specific activities for the elderly. This includes, for instance, services and other types of activities with religious elements (Interviews, employees, nonprofit nursing homes, 2014-03-01, 2014-03-12).

The managers of the nonprofit care homes also have other types of privileges by virtue of the fact that they run nonprofit facilities. These privileges are primarily related to the larger degree of freedom they experience as nonprofit actors. Although they must live up to municipal quality standards, they have more freedom in the overall running of the nursing home. A short journey from idea to implementation is one of the main strengths mentioned. In one of the nursing homes, the manager was considering buying some sheep for the green areas around the home, and he valued the possibility of being able to do so without having to ask anyone (Interview, manager, nonprofit nursing home, 2014-02-20). However, these kinds of differences are much more evident at the level of the manager than among employees and relatives, who do not experience any significant differences apart from Christian values.

Governing of Nursing Homes

From the interviews, it is evident that the municipal implementation of national framework legislation promotes similarities among different types of nursing homes with regard to the content of care. In addition to these quality standards, the interviews also revealed a strong norm for equality in services: All elderly residents should have the right to the same service standards (Interview, manager, nonprofit, 2014-02-12).

Since 1998, all municipalities have been legally required to formulate quality standards in the field of elderly care. These standards set the framework for the municipal governing of nursing homes. The standards cover both personal and practical care by, for instance, specifying the types of cleaning and other practical help included in and excluded from municipal service, as well as the types of personal care provided and exempted by the municipality (Faaborg-Midtfyn Municipality 2012; Herning Municipality 2008).

Monitoring of nursing homes takes place through regular inspections. For instance, the quality standards in Faaborg-Midtfyn state that unscheduled inspections are conducted once a year at all nursing homes in the municipality. These inspections include discussions with elderly residents, employees and managers regarding the quality of the care provided (Faaborg-Midtfyn Municipality 2012). Municipalities have contracts with nonprofit nursing homes, and these are used to apply the quality standards across different types of providers. The independent nursing homes are also obliged to provide services in accordance with municipal decisions in the field (LBK 897).

In the municipalities examined here, there is a high degree of satisfaction with collaboration with nonprofit nursing homes. In Faaborg-Midtfyn, the head of the nonprofit nursing home is invited to the same leadership seminars that heads of public care homes attend. In Herning, the municipality has more informal relations with the nonprofit nursing homes; but, according to the head of the elderly care administration, relations are very positive. For instance, they are offered the same courses as public nursing homes:

> If we have something special to offer – for instance, a seminar on dementia – the nonprofit nursing homes are also invited. They are not kept outside – not at all. (Interview, head manager, administration, 2013-12-18).

The manager of the nonprofit nursing home in this study reaffirmed the positive relationship with the municipality (Interview, site manager, nonprofit, 2014-02-12).

Although the independent nursing homes have not been investigated in detail in this study, they are mentioned repeatedly in interviews with the municipal actors. There are some differences between the independent nursing homes and other types. The independent homes are run on a freer basis, and the ability of local authorities to steer them is very limited (For a further discussion, see Chap. 3). This is evident in the case of Herning. The municipality decided to cancel its contract with two nonprofit nursing homes as part of a larger restructuring, which also included the establishment of new nursing homes in other parts of the municipality. Rather than close, the nonprofit nursing homes decided to continue delivering their services as independent nursing homes. As a result, the municipalities still shoulder the financial costs of these homes, but have no direct influence on them, apart from enforcing quality standards. This is also reflected in an interview with the manager of one of the nonprofit nursing homes, who has a high degree of freedom in the running of the facility (Interview, site manager, independent nursing home 2014-03-03).

While there is general support for the principle of freedom of choice, the establishment of independent nursing homes is considered problematic by municipal actors because of the financial pressures they create. Nonetheless, good relations are still maintained between the municipalities and the independent nursing homes, according to the head manager of the elderly care administration (Interview, head manager, administration, 2013-12-18; Interview, site manager, independent nursing home, 2014-03-03).

Thus, in Denmark, municipalities have the ability to directly steer nursing homes through contracts when they are traditional nonprofit nursing homes. Municipalities always have the right to cancel a contract if, for example, the service provision is not satisfactory or the municipality wants to restructure the field of providers. However, the ability of the municipality to steer nursing homes was significantly reduced with the introduction of the option to operate independent nursing homes in 2007. Today, nonprofit nursing homes can change their status to independent nursing homes if their municipal contract is cancelled. The municipal steering possibilities are very limited when it comes to independent nursing homes.

Evidence from the Danish case shows that there are no major differences between public and nonprofit nursing homes when it comes to the specific content of care.[6] This is due to statutory municipal quality standards, which are applied to both public and nonprofit providers. Municipalities can directly steer nursing homes through the use of contracts with traditional nonprofit facilities, which municipalities always have the right to cancel. However, their steering powers have been significantly limited as a result of the relatively new possibility of establishing independent nursing homes. On the whole, the differences between public and nonprofit providers are mainly value-based. However, nonprofit leaders also experience a larger degree of freedom to make local decisions at their nursing homes.

Welfare Providers from Different Sectors—A Comparison

Based on the results of the empirical investigation, it is evident that the welfare mix of different providers within the field of elderly care has not resulted in greater variety in the content of care. Whether nursing homes are run by public, nonprofit or for-profit organisations, the services they provide are generally the same. This conclusion can be drawn based on interviews with site managers about the content of care and the existence of distinct profiles for their operations. The empirical findings are also supported by the fact that surveys and interviews with relatives and nursing home residents do not point to any major differences among types of nursing homes. However, several minor differences can be noted; for example, a religious profile or the existence of specially trained staff to care for residents suffering from dementia. Nevertheless, differences like these do not seem to have any major impact on the types of services provided.

In all three countries, similarities cannot be explained in any significant way by regulation through national law. For instance, in Sweden, the national law creates a framework that gives the municipalities a great deal of power to make decisions on their own. Following a Scandinavian tradition of strong municipal self-rule, the situation is similar in Denmark and Norway. Rather, similarities can be explained by a high degree of local steering that takes several forms.

One of them, which can be regarded as an important underlying condition, is that there are only a limited number of rooms at each nursing home and a queuing system is thus administered by the municipality. This creates a problem for implementing a system of free choice in practice, as there might not be a room available at the chosen nursing home. One can, of course, wait for a room to become available, but considering the physical condition of the elderly, this is not as easy as it sounds.

Another form of steering is the use of quality indicators that are spelled out in contracts between the municipal administration and the nursing home. According to different categories of respondents who were interviewed, the contracts are very detailed, leaving site managers with limited room to manoeuvre regarding the content of the services provided. Quality indicators and contracts are used by municipal administrations regardless of whether nursing homes are run by public or private providers.

Another important tool for municipal steering is the evaluation of nursing homes. Such evaluations assess whether nursing homes are performing their work in accordance with quality indicators. If they are not, contracts can be terminated by the local administration. One part of municipal evaluations is the user survey. These surveys are sent to those receiving care as well as their relatives, and they ask questions about the overall performance of the nursing homes. The surveys can also influence the decision of the municipal administration to extend or terminate its contract with the provider. Another component of the evaluation process is inspection (i.e. site visits), which can be both announced and unannounced.

In sum, the level of administrative governance of nursing homes exercised by municipalities is 'high' regardless of the welfare provider. Denmark represents an exception to this overall pattern insofar as nonprofit providers can apply for status as 'independent nursing homes'. The broader implications of these research findings are considered below.

Conclusions

Scandinavian welfare states are currently being reorganised with the market as a model. The pace at which this development is occurring differs among the countries, with Sweden experiencing the most far-reaching changes. There are different rationales driving the development towards marketisation. One of the most common reasons is that the establishment of a market with different providers allows citizens to choose the 'best' alternative in terms of quality. By letting citizens choose, the government is steering the quality of welfare provision through the use of an 'invisible hand'. Simply put, only those welfare providers who can offer services with a sufficient level of quality to attract customers are able to survive in the long run. However, improving quality is not the only motive; another motive is the desire to strengthen user autonomy and enable citizens to choose among a variety of options depending on their own desires and needs.

If citizens are to have alternatives to choose from, then there obviously must be differences among service providers. Hence, it should matter whether the providers are public or private (nonprofit or for-profit). To make this possible, one might expect that there would be less local government steering of service providers. Whether this is actually the case is an empirical question, and little is known about the content and degree of local government steering. It is also possible that there are other reasons behind the development towards marketisation in the welfare field considered here, namely, nursing homes for the elderly.

Accordingly, the purpose of this chapter was to describe and analyse local government steering and how it affects the profile of nursing homes in six municipalities in Sweden, Norway and Denmark. The results of the empirical investigation show that the welfare mix within nursing homes for the elderly has not, to any great extent, resulted in distinct profiles of service provision. The explanation is found in the existence of a high degree of steering by municipalities at the local level, as has been discussed in the previous section.

These findings suggest that the discourse on 'active citizenship' and 'choice' discussed in the first chapter of this book is relevant to consider here only to a limited extent. Clearly, the rationale behind the development towards marketisation of nursing homes for the elderly is not foremost about creating a market in which citizens can choose among different alternatives.

Another interpretation of the underlying rationale is that it is about making it possible for the municipal administration to 'benchmark'. By contracting out, the municipality's administration gets a more comprehensive understanding of the costs of running a nursing home. This information can then be used to improve the efficiency of the services performed by the public provider. Following this alternative rationale, there is no need to allow for greater variation among service providers. It is foremost a question of facilities providing a particular service, one that is defined in advance by the municipal administration in the most efficient way.

Another interpretation of our findings is that the similarity in welfare provision across providers is an expression of a central principle of the Scandinavian welfare model—i.e. equality of welfare provision. According to this principle, every citizen is entitled to receive the same welfare content, regardless of place of residence or social stratum. Seen from this perspective, it comes as no surprise that quality indicators and contracts governing nursing homes for the elderly are the same with regard to content of care, regardless of whether the provider is public, for-profit or nonprofit. Simply put, they are important tools for ensuring the preservation of the principle of equality of welfare provision, even in the context of marketisation.

Although this study provides limited evidence of variation in the content of service provision, there is some evidence that things are about to change. In Denmark, nursing homes can apply for the status of 'independent nursing home'. In Sweden, the Freedom of Choice Act (LOV) has mainly been applied to home care services. However, the act can also be applied to nursing homes, and this has actually happened in some municipalities, which implies that a different routine of contracting out is being implemented. The consequences of these relatively new legislative acts must be investigated more closely. In the long run, in these two countries, we might see a development towards less local government steering and more distinct profiles among nursing homes.

Another topic for further research is the content of contracts and their development. A nursing home is often contracted out for a limited time period. At the end of that period, a new process is initiated in which municipal administrators reformulate old contracts and give them new content. In this process, one would expect that an element of policy learning would take place, i.e. participants would learn through past experiences of the implementation of policy. Whether this learning suggests that more or less detailed regulation is desirable remains to be seen. In several of the interviews, today's detailed regulations were openly questioned by both politicians and civil servants on the grounds that they are counterproductive because they fail to promote efficient solutions.

An additional question for further research concerns the role played by nonprofit organisations in a marketised welfare environment. There is a commonly held belief that nonprofit providers are better able to tailor their services to the particular needs of the elderly, i.e. they can offer a more distinct profile of services. However, the empirical investigation presented here provides little evidence that this is actually taking place. It would be interesting to determine how governance carried out by administrators in municipalities actually restricts how nonprofit providers conduct their operations. What is the potential for services provided by nonprofit providers and how is this potential restricted by local government steering?

As evident from this chapter, the Scandinavian model shows signs of divergence in light of the different speeds at which marketisation has taken place in the different countries. In addition, there are signs of divergence with respect to the role played by nonprofit providers, from their marginal role in Sweden to their more pronounced role in Denmark and Norway. However, this particular difference has been evident for a long time and has little to do with recent developments.

Although there are differences among Sweden, Norway and Denmark, it is still relevant to speak of a Scandinavian model within the field of care for the elderly. The main argument for this is that one of its chief characteristics, equality of welfare provision, is still very much alive at the local level. It is this particular value, expressed by some of the civil servants in the interviews, which constitutes one explanation as to why local governing of different welfare providers is very much the same, regardless of whether the provider is a municipal actor or a private one. There are also similar routines for elderly care; for example, implementation plans for each nursing home resident are developed in dialogue with the elderly person and his or her relatives. Besides this, the cornerstones of the Scandinavian model still exist—i.e. publicly financed care for the elderly, accessible to all citizens who need it.

Notes

1. In this chapter, the use of phrases such as 'content of service provision' refers to the content of care at nursing homes. In turn, content of care refers to various aspects of the activities taking place at the nursing homes; for example, medical care, cultural activities and physical activities such as walks.
2. In some countries, interviews have also been conducted with employees and elderly people living at the nursing homes or their relatives.
3. For a more elaborated definition of an 'independent nursing home', see Chap. 3 by Segaard and Saglie.
4. The figure for 2016 was calculated from statistics presented by the National Board of Health and Welfare (2017). In these statistics, there are municipalities with only a limited number of beds, one or two, which are run by a private operator. This may indicate that beds are purchased by another municipality, which, in turn, has decided to contract out their services. Hence, municipalities with less than five beds, run by a private operator, have not been included in the total number of 93 municipalities.
5. This is in accordance with a national regulation issued by the National Board of Health and Welfare (SOFS 2014:5). The regulation applies to all providers of elderly care regardless of being public or private.
6. For a similar conclusion regarding the Danish case, see Hjelmar et al. 2016.

References

Almqvist, Robert. 2001. 'Management by contract': A study of programmatic and technological aspects. *Public Administration* 79 (3): 689–706.
Anttonen, Anneli. 2002. Universalism and social policy: a Nordic-feminist revaluation. *NORA* 10 (2): 71–80.

Ascoli, Ugo, and Costanzo Ranci. 2002. *Dilemmas of the welfare mix: the new structure of welfare in an era of privatization*. New York: Kluwer Academic.

Béland, Daniel, Paula Blomqvist, Jørgen Goul Andersen, Joakim Palme, and Alex Waddan. 2014. The Universal Decline of Universality? Social Policy Change in Canada, Denmark, Sweden and the UK. *Social Policy & Administration* 48 (7): 739–756.

Bergman, Torbjörn, and Kaare Strøm. 2011. Nordic Europe in Comparative Perspective. In *The Madisonian turn: political parties and parliamentary democracy in Nordic Europe*, eds. Torbjörn Bergman, and Kaare Strøm. Ann Arbor: University of Michigan Press.

Bertelsen, Tilde Marie, and Tine Rostgaard. 2013. Marketisation in eldercare in Denmark: free choice and the quest for quality and efficiency. In *Marketisation in Nordic eldercare: a research report on legislation, oversight, extent and consequences*, eds. Gabrielle Meagher, and Marta Szebehely. Stockholm: Department of Social Work, Stockholm University.

Blomqvist, Paula. 2004. The choice revolution: Privatization of Swedish welfare services in the 1990s. *Social Policy & Administration* 38 (2): 139–155.

Blomqvist, Paula, and Bo Rothstein. 2000. *Välfärdsstatens nya ansikte: demokrati och marknadsreformer inom den offentliga sektorn*. Stockholm: Agora.

Boston, Jonathan. 2011. Basic NPM Ideas and their Development. In *The Ashgate Research Companion to New Public Management*, eds. Tom Christensen, and Per Laegreid. Farnham: Ashgate.

Burau, Viola, and Signy Irene Vabo. 2011. Shifts in Nordic welfare governance: introduction and outlook. *International Journal of Sociology and Social Policy* 31 (3/4): 140–147.

Dahl, Hanne Marlene. 2009. NPM, Disciplining Care and Struggles about Recognition. *Critical Social Policy* 29 (4): 634–654.

Dahl, Hanne Marlene, and Bente Rasmussen. 2012. Paradoxes in Elderly Care: The Nordic Model. In *Elderly Care in Transition: Management, Meaning and Identity at Work. A Scandinavian Perspective*, eds. Annette Kamp, and Helge Hvid. Copenhagen: Copenhagen Business School Press.

Dahler-Larsen, Elizabeth, et al. 2015. *Ældreomsorg i Norden*. Stockholm: Nordens Välfärdscenter.

Dølvik, Jon Erik, Tone Fløtten, Jon M. Hippe, and Bård Jordfald. 2015. *The Nordic model towards 2030: A new chapter? Fafo report 2015:07*. Oslo: Fafo.

Dunleavy, Patric, and Christopher Hood. 1994. From Public-administration to New Public Management. *Public Money & Management* 14 (3): 9–16.

Einhorn, Eric S., and John Logue. 2010. Can Welfare States Be Sustained in a Global Economy? Lessons from Scandinavia. *Political Science Quarterly* 125 (1): 1–29.

Elinder, Mikael, and Henrik Jordahl. 2013. Kontrakt, kostnader och kvalitet. In *Välfärdstjänster i privat regi: framväxt och drivkrafter*, ed. Henrik Jordahl. Stockholm: SNS Förlag.

Erlandsson, Sara, et al. 2013. Marketing trends in Swedish eldercare: competition, choice and calls for stricter regulation. In *Marketisation in Nordic eldercare: a research report on legislation, oversight, extent and consequences*, eds. Gabrielle Meagher, and Marta Szebehely. Stockholm: Department of Social Work, Stockholm University.

Esping-Andersen, Gøsta. 1990. *The three worlds of welfare capitalism*. Cambridge: Polity.

Faaborg-Midtfyn Kommune. 2012. Pleje og Omsorg, Kvalitetsstandarder 2012.

Feltenius, David, and Jessika Wide. 2015. Deltagardemokrati eller affärsangelägenhet? Om kollektivt deltagande i en marknadiserad äldreomsorg. *Statsvetenskaplig tidskrift* 117 (4): 587–615.

Ferlie, Ewan. 1996. *The new public management in action*. Oxford: Oxford University Press.

Gjevjon, Edith Roth, and Tor Inge Romøren. 2010. *Vedtak om sykehjemsplass– hvor høye er tersklene?*. Gjøvik: Senter for omsorgsforskning.

Gustafsson, Agne. 1999. *Kommunal självstyrelse: kommuner och landsting i det politiska systemet*. Stockholm: SNS Förlag.

Hartman, Laura. 2011. Inledning. In *Konkurrensens konsekvenser. Vad händer med svensk välfärd?*, ed. Laura Hartman. Stockholm: SNS Förlag.

Haugen, Per Kristian, and Knut Engedal. 2005. *Demens. Fakta og utfordringer, en lærebok*. Oslo: Aldring og helse.

Hermansen, Åsmund, and Heidi Gautun. 2011. *Eldreomsorg under press*. FAFO: Kommunenes helse- og omsorgstilbud til eldre. Oslo.

Herning kommune. 2008. Generelt tillæg til kvalitetsstandarder – praktisk hjælp. personlig pleje og træning.

Hirschman, Albert O. 1970. *Exit, voice, and loyalty: responses to decline in firms, organizations, and states*. Cambridge, MA.: Harvard University Press.

Hjemmehjælpskommisionen. 2013. *Fremtidens hjemmehjælp – ældres ressourcer i centrum for en sammenhængende indsats*. København: Social - og Integrationsministeriet.

Hjelmar, Ulf, et al. 2016. Kvalitet på offentlige og private plejecentre i Danmark. Forskningsprojektet "Dokumentation af effekter ved konkurrenceudsættelse af offentlige opgaver". Del-rapport 6. Roskilde: Roskilde Universitet.
Hood, Christopher. 1991. A public management for all seasons. *Public Administration* 69 (1): 3–19.
Jordahl, Henrik, and Richard Öhrvall. 2013. Nationella reformer och lokala initiativ. In *Välfärdstjänster i privat regi: framväxt och drivkrafter*, ed. Henrik Jordahl. SNS Förlag: Stockholm.
Kamp, Annette, and Helge Hvid. 2012. *Elderly care in transition: management, meaning and identity at work: A Scandinavian perspective*. Frederiksberg: Copenhagen Business School Press.
LBK 897, Law of independent nursing homes (LBK nr 897 af 17/08/2011).
Le Grand, Julian. 2007. *The other invisible hand: delivering public services through choice and competition*. Princeton: Princeton University Press.
Lindbom, Anders. 2001. Dismantling the social democratic welfare model? Has the Swedish welfare state lost its defining characteristics? *Scandinavian Political Studies* 24 (3): 171–193.
Loughlin, John, Frank Hendriks, and Anders Lidström. 2011. Introduction. In *The Oxford handbook of local and regional democracy in Europe*, eds. John Loughlin, Frank Hendriks, and Anders Lidström. Oxford: Oxford University Press.
Mariani, Laura, and Dario Cavenago. 2013. Redesigning welfare services for policies effectiveness: The non-profit organizations (NPOs) perspective. *Public Management Review* 15 (7): 1011–1039.
Osborne, Stephen P. 1998. *Voluntary organizations and innovation in public services*. London: Routledge.
Osborne, Stephen P. 2010. Delivering Public Services: Time for a new theory? *Public Management Review* 12 (1): 1–10.
Östersunds kommun. 2006. *Plan för vård och omsorg: Inriktningsmål och strategier*. Östersund: Östersunds kommun.
Östersunds kommun. 2013-06-13. Kommentarer – brukarenkät [A non-published report].
Östersunds kommun. 2013-09-16. Sammanställning av synpunkter från anhöriga. [A non-published report].
Östersunds kommun. 2014. *Din rätt till trygghet och ett värdigt liv*. Östersund: Vård- och omsorgsförvaltningen.

Petersen, Ole Helby, and Ulf Hjelmar. 2013. Marketization of welfare services in Scandinavia: A review of Swedish and Danish experiences. *Scandinavian Journal of Public Administrations* 17 (4): 3–20.

Pierre, Jon. 1995. The marketization of the state: Citizens, consumers and the emergence of the public market. In *Governance in a changing environment*, ed. Guy B. Peters, and Donald J. Savoie. Ottawa: Canadian Centre for Management Development.

Pierson, Paul. 1994. *Dismantling the welfare state? Reagan, Thatcher and the politics of retrenchment*. Cambridge: Cambridge University Press.

Pollitt, Christopher. 1995. Justification by work or faith? *Evaluation* 1 (2): 133–154.

Rambøll. 2012. *Evaluering af lov om friplejeboliger*. Rambøll Management (udarbejdet for Ministeriet for By, Bolig og Landdistrikter): København.

Salamon, Lester M., and A.J. Abramson. 1982. The Nonprofit Sector. In *The Reagan Experiment: An Examination of Economic and Social Policies Under the Reagan Administration*, eds. John L. Palmer, and Isabel V. Sawhill. Washington D.C.: The Urban Institute Press.

Salamon, Lester M. 1987. Of Market Failure, Voluntary Failure, and Third-Party Government: Toward a Theory of Government-Nonprofit Relations in the Modern Welfare State. *Nonprofit and Voluntary Sector Quarterly* 16 (1–2): 29–49.

Salamon, Lester M. 1993. The Marketization of Welfare: Changing Nonprofit and Forprofit Roles in the American Welfare-state. *Social Service Review* 67 (1): 16–39.

Sivesind, Karl Henrik. 2016. Endring av fordelningen mellom ideelle, kommersielle og offentlige velferdstjenster i Skandinavia. In *Mot en ny skandinavisk velferdsmodell? Konsekvenser av ideell, kommersiell og offentlig tjenesteyting for aktivt medborgerskap*, ed. Karl Henrik Sivesind. Oslo: Institutt for samfunnsforskning.

Socialstyrelsen. 2004. *Konkurrensutsättningen inom äldreomsorgen*. Stockholm: Socialstyrelsen.

Socialstyrelsen. 2017. *Statistik om äldre och personer med funktionsnedsättning efter regiform 2016*. Socialstyrelsen: Stencil med tillhörande datafil. Stockholm.

Sollentuna kommun., 2012. *Äldreomsorg: Kvalitetsbarometern*. Sollentuna: Sollentuna kommun.

SOSFS. (2014:5). Dokumentation i verksamhet som bedrivs med stöd av SoL, LVU, LVM & LS. Socialstyrelsens författningssamling. Socialstyrelsen: Stockholm.

Stolt, Ragnar, and Ulrika Winblad. 2009. Mechanisms behind privatization: A case study of private growth in Swedish elderly care. *Social Science & Medicine* 68 (5): 903–911.

Szebehely, Marta. 2011. *Insatser för äldre och funktionshindrade i privat regi*. Stockholm: SNS Förlag.

Traetteberg, Håkon Dalby, and Karl Henrik Sivesind. 2015. *Ideelle organisasjoners saertrekk og merverdi på helse- og omsorgsfeltet*. Oslo: Senter for forskning på sivilsamfunn & frivillig sektor.

Vabø, Mia. 2007. *Organisering for velferd*. Unipub: Hjemmetjensten i en styrningsideologisk brytningstid. Oslo.

Walsh, Kieron. 1995. *Public services and market mechanisms: competition, contracting and the new public management*. Basingstoke: Macmillan.

Weisbrod, Burton. 1977. *The voluntary nonprofit sector: an economic analysis*. Lexington, MA.: Heath.

Weisbrod, Burton Allen. 1988. *The nonprofit economy*. Cambridge, Mass.: Harvard University Press.

Vård- och omsorgsnämnden. 2013. *Äldreplan*. Sollentuna: Sollentuna kommun.

Author Biography

David Feltenius is Associate Professor at the Department of Political Science in Umeå, Sweden. In addition to studies on marketisation and the welfare state, his research focuses on central–local government relations and territorial politics. His recent publications include a chapter on subnational government in a multilevel perspective in the *Oxford Handbook of Swedish Politics*, as well as an article on parties and the politics of territorial reform published in *Scandinavian Political Studies*. Feltenius is currently working in a research project on inter-agency collaboration financed by the Swedish Research Council.

4 Towards a more diversified supply of welfare ... 157

Open Access This chapter is licensed under the terms of the Creative Commons Attribution 4.0 International License (http://creativecommons.org/licenses/by/4.0/), which permits use, sharing, adaptation, distribution and reproduction in any medium or format, as long as you give appropriate credit to the original author(s) and the source, provide a link to the Creative Commons license and indicate if changes were made.

The images or other third party material in this chapter are included in the chapter's Creative Commons license, unless indicated otherwise in a credit line to the material. If material is not included in the chapter's Creative Commons license and your intended use is not permitted by statutory regulation or exceeds the permitted use, you will need to obtain permission directly from the copyright holder.

5

Local Governing of Schools in Scandinavia—Between State, Market and Civil Society

Malene Thøgersen

Introduction

The education of future citizens is a fundamental welfare task, and therefore the school system plays a central role in relevant political debates (Arnesen and Lundahl 2006). In social democratic welfare states like the Scandinavian countries, the public sector is responsible for both financing and regulation in the field of education. The Scandinavian countries are also characterised by a high degree of decentralisation, with a large volume of welfare tasks carried out by the municipalities, including the responsibility for primary and lower secondary schools, which are the focus here (Kersting and Vetter 2003, 23; Baldersheim and Rose 2010; Nyhlén 2013, 158). However, municipalities are not the only providers of these schools. Nonprofit schools have a long history in the Scandinavian context. Moreover, increasing marketisation trends have affected the field. This trend has gone furthest in Sweden, where

---

M. Thøgersen (✉)
Danish Institute for Non-formal Education, Aarhus, Denmark
e-mail: malene.thogersen@vifo.dk

© The Author(s) 2017
K.H. Sivesind and J. Saglie (eds.), *Promoting Active Citizenship*,
DOI 10.1007/978-3-319-55381-8_5

159

for-profit providers today run schools side by side with public and nonprofit providers. Finally, across the Scandinavian countries, an increasing focus on freedom of choice has changed the conditions for local steering as well as citizens' opportunities to actively choose between different types of services, which can be seen as one important aspect of active citizenship (Chap. 1 in this book). Hence, the field of primary and lower secondary schools in Scandinavia is a complex mix of long historical traditions and recent trends from New Public Management (NPM) and market-based steering (Hood 1991; Donahue and Nye 2002). In other words, local governing in the field of schools takes place within a mix of tools and logics from both state, market and civil society.

This chapter will compare the field of primary and lower secondary schools in Sweden, Norway and Denmark and investigate the consequences of different national contexts for local governing in the field with a focus on different types of providers. The introductory chapters of this book leave no doubt that both the welfare mix and national legislation in the field of schools differ among the Scandinavian countries in spite of their belonging to the same welfare regime (Esping-Andersen 1990). The differences between the Scandinavian countries are evident in the various shares of welfare provided by private actors, as described by Sivesind in Chap. 2. In Chap. 3, Segaard and Saglie described the national legal framework for private providers, underlining important differences—and similarities—between the countries when it comes to the private provision of primary and lower secondary schools.

In this chapter, the focus shifts to the local level, where national policies are implemented. The overall aim is to investigate the consequences of different national contexts for the local governing of schools in Sweden, Norway and Denmark by comparing both countries and different institutional sectors.

The empirical focus will partly be on the municipal level, with a focus on how national legislation is interpreted and implemented, and partly on the school level in order to investigate how national and municipal governing and steering are experienced and dealt with in practice. The analysis will focus on the following research questions:

- How do municipalities implement national legislation, and which steering tools and types of regulation do they use?
- What are the consequences of national legislation and local steering and regulation for the schools?
- Do regulation and legislation promote or inhibit the development of a distinct profile of private schools compared with public schools? Are there any differences between the Scandinavian countries in this regard?

As is evident from these questions, the study is largely exploratory and has a strong empirical focus. All questions are addressed with a focus on comparisons across the Scandinavian countries and across different institutional sectors. The theoretical inspiration for the study is rooted in the literature on NPM, public steering and government–nonprofit relations. The empirical analysis will be based on data from case studies in two Swedish, two Danish and three Norwegian municipalities.

In the first part of this chapter, the theoretical background for the study will be presented. Afterwards, the characteristics of the welfare mix in the field of schools in the Scandinavian countries will be provided, including a view into the distinct development of alternatives to public schools. After a short presentation of data and methods, the empirical analysis will go deeper into the field of primary and lower secondary schools across the three countries, addressing the research questions above. This chapter concludes with a discussion of similarities and differences across countries and types of providers, including possible reasons for and consequences of these differences for future welfare provision in the field.

Public Steering and Relations between Government and Nonpublic Services

In the literature, much attention has been paid to various types of the welfare mix across countries (Gidron et al. 1992; Seeleib-Kaiser 2008; Alber 2010; Henriksen et al. 2012). However, relations between local governments and different types of local welfare providers in specific welfare fields are less well described empirically. In particular, there is a lack of attention on the role played by nonprofit organisations in local welfare provision (Pestoff 2009, 229). The concept of the welfare mix, which refers to new types of involvement by both for-profit and nonprofit actors in the welfare provision (Evers and Wintersberger 1990; Powell 2007; Anheier 2009; Dølvik et al. 2015) is therefore the underlying reason for investigating differences and similarities in the local governing of primary and lower secondary schools in Scandinavian countries. However, perspectives on public steering and government–nonprofit relations will provide the theoretical background for the empirical analysis.

During the 1990s and 2000s, ideas and tools inspired by New Public Management (NPM) influenced steering of the public sector across countries and welfare regimes. However, one of the challenges with NPM and its focus on the market, freedom of choice and competition, turned out in many cases to be increasing fragmentation of the organisation and the steering of the public sector. The subsequent need for coordination and collaboration led to an increased focus on 'collaborative governance' in the literature on public management. It has been argued that there has been a shift from NPM towards collaborative governance, characterised by less control and based on the assumption that less control will pay off in terms of better performance (Donahue and Zeckhauser 2011, 32).

However, others have argued that empirical evidence for this trend is lacking and that rule-based and regulatory systems, which are also a part of NPM, are still dominant (Phillips and Smith 2011, 28). According to Phillips and Smith, there is a cross-country tendency towards more accountability and transparency, which typically requires more regulation. Hence, the focus on regulation has persisted in spite of a similar trend towards more collaboration across sectors, resulting in a dual pressure on the relationship not only between government and service providers—e.g. third sector organisations (Phillips and Smith 2011, 23), but also between government and for-profit actors who are increasingly involved in the service provision. In relation to the involvement of for-profit actors, the consequence is the tendency that more market creates a need for more regulation and thereby more state involvement (Petersen and Hjelmar 2013, 6; Dølvik et al. 2015, 106).

The trends from NPM have been implemented in different ways across the three Scandinavian countries. A possible explanation for this can be found in the concept of *institutional layering*. The basic argument behind this concept is that although new tools and logics are incorporated into the agenda, they are often implemented on top of existing steering structures and historical traditions, resulting in large differences across countries and welfare fields (Thelen 2003). The impact of institutional legacies can, therefore, be seen as one possible explanation of the fact that the Scandinavian countries have implemented a more moderate version of NPM than countries with liberal welfare regimes (Politt and Bouckaert 2011, 64).

However, the impact of different institutional legacies can also be an important explanatory factor for the differing roles played by nonprofit providers across the Scandinavian countries. As it is argued in neo-institutional perspectives on nonprofit–government relationships, nonprofit organisations are largely a product of the institutional environment surrounding them (Smith and Grønbjerg 2006, 235).

In Scandinavian countries, there has been a long tradition of close collaboration between sectors, in spite of the government dominating welfare systems (Henriksen and Bundesen 2004). Traditional theories of nonprofit government relations—e.g. the literature on government, market and voluntary failures (the three-failures theory) which focus on how each sector compensates for each other's weaknesses—have not left much room for this kind of close collaborative relationship between the sectors (Steinberg 2006). However, increasing complexity in modern welfare states has prompted collaboration between sectors across countries and welfare regimes. Recent literature even suggests that government–nonprofit cooperation today is necessary to obtain effectiveness (Salamon and Toepler 2015).

The literature on public governance distinguishes between different ideas or ideal types of governance. A common distinction is between hierarchy, market and network (Jørgensen and Vrangbæk 2004; Meuleman 2008; Greve and Ejersbo 2013, 16). The three types of governance are not mutually exclusive. It is possible to find elements from all three types at the same time, although one of the types will often dominate (Jørgensen and Vrangbæk 2004, 83).

In hierarchical steering, rules and authority are the central elements. In market-based steering, order is to some extent left to market forces—for instance, through freedom of choice. Finally, in network-based steering, order is made through interaction and dialogue between interdependent actors in the system (Jørgensen and Vrangbæk 2004, 12).

The three ideal types can be reflected in municipal steering strategies. In a study of local governing of Swedish schools, Nyhlén (2013) identified three different types of local steering strategies in the relationship between municipalities and schools in a system with freedom of choice: control, competition and collaboration. *Control-based steering strategies* imply that the municipality takes initiatives to control the schools. *Competitive steering strategies* are at play when the municipality's awareness of competition is reflected in its steering. For instance, the municipality may seek to profile the public schools to prevent too big a flow of pupils to private schools—e.g. through marketing initiatives. Finally, *collaborative steering strategies* imply that the municipality actively seeks collaboration with the schools. According to Nyhlén, steering strategies vary across municipalities, and the different models affect the characteristics of the relationship between municipalities and schools (Nyhlén 2013, 157).

The three types of steering strategies identified by Nyhlén serve as a framework for the empirical analysis in this chapter (Table 5.1). However, it is important to note that control, collaboration and

Table 5.1 Analytical framework

Ideal types of governance	Hierarchy	Market	Network
Steering strategies	Control-based steering strategies	Competitive steering strategies	Collaborative steering strategies
Elements	Rules Inspections	Marketing initiatives Promotion of schools	Meetings and other formal relations Informal relations
Degree	Degree of control-based steering	Degree of competitive steering	Degree of collaborative steering

Inspired by Jørgensen and Vrangbæk (2004), Greve and Ejersbo (2013), and Nyhlén (2013)

competition are seen as analytical categories, not as an explicit choice of strategy made by the municipalities. The aim of using these categories is to structure the analysis and provide room for structured comparisons across countries and types of providers. Within each of the three analytical categories, the analysis will focus on concrete *elements* of steering but also the *degree* of steering: The extent to which elements of control, competition and collaboration are evident in the local governance of primary and lower secondary schools.

The Welfare Mix and Characteristics of the Field of Schools in Scandinavia

In Denmark, Norway and Sweden, the public sector accounts for the vast majority of primary and lower secondary schools, but private providers also play a role. However, there are interestingly different trajectories between the countries when it comes to the scope and type of private provision.

In Denmark, primary and lower secondary schools are either public or run by nonprofit providers, and there is a strong historical tradition of nonprofit schools. This tradition is rooted in the constitution, underlining compulsory education but not compulsory school attendance.

Regarding choice, all children belong to a public district school and have the right to attend this school, but it is possible to choose a nonprofit school or another public school within or outside the municipality, when available (Law on Public Schools, LBK 665). During recent years, there has been an increase in the number of nonprofit schools, from 460 in 2000 to 526 in 2011. Nonprofit schools also represent an increasing share of the total number of pupils; in 2011, their share was 15% (Thøgersen 2015).

Nonprofit schools in Denmark are subsidised by the state. The level of funding has been reduced during recent years, corresponding to 71% of the average expenses per pupil in public schools in 2015.[1] However, municipalities pay the state for each pupil in nonprofit schools,[2] and they therefore still constitute expenditures for the municipalities.

Nonprofit schools must charge the parents to receive public funding but are free to decide the level of parental payment.

Compared to many other types of nonprofit welfare providers in Denmark, nonprofit schools have some special privileges: Parents have the right to establish a new school and acquire public funding as long as the school fulfils national legal requirements. Moreover, nonprofit schools do not operate through a contract with the municipality, and they have a high degree of freedom when it comes to the content and structure of teaching and the running of the school in general. As an example, nonprofit schools have the right to decide which pupils they accept, and they are not obliged to do national tests or offer final exams. The school boards have the responsibility for both the finances and all other issues associated with the operation of the schools (Law of Independent and Private Schools, LBK 917).

In contrast, public schools are highly regulated at both the national and local level, and municipalities have full responsibility for public schools (Bogason 2001). The degree of national regulation has increased during recent years—for instance, through the implementation of national tests. However, municipalities still have many steering options (Law on Public Schools, LBK 665).

In Norway, there is also compulsory education and no compulsory school attendance. Like in Denmark, primary and lower secondary schools are run by municipalities or nonprofit providers. In the 2013–2014 school year, there were 195 nonprofit schools in Norway. This represents a doubling of the number since 2002–2003. However, most of the schools are quite small. In the same period, the share of pupils in nonprofit schools had only risen from slightly less than 2% to about 3% (Utdanningsdirektoratet 2014, 16). Consequently, nonprofit schools are still a marginal supplier compared to public schools.

To establish a nonprofit school, one must apply to a national directorate. For an application to be approved the school must fulfil certain criteria; among others, it must represent a 'recognised' alternative to public school—typically by being based on certain pedagogies, religious faiths or international dimensions. The municipality where the potential school is located is invited to give its opinion on its establishment, but the national directorate makes the final decision.

After their establishment, nonprofit schools are only regulated by national rules and regulations. Like in Denmark, the school boards have responsibility and authority over all major aspects of the operation of the schools, including budgets, hiring and other strategic decisions. However, Norwegian nonprofit schools are obliged to have objective criteria for selecting pupils and cannot reject certain pupils. By comparison, public schools are integrated into the municipality and are thus subject to municipal policies and regulations.

Nonprofit schools receive 85% of the funding level of municipal schools. The schools can thus charge the parents for the remaining 15%, but no more (Seegaard 2015, 40). The nonprofit schools get their funding directly from the state, and this money is deducted from the transfers that municipalities receive from the state. Thus, municipalities indirectly pay nonprofit schools for their pupils. Each municipality can decide if it wants to have user choice among the public schools. In all cases, the pupils are entitled to attend their local public school, but parents can choose a nonprofit alternative when available.

Sweden is similar to Denmark when it comes to the share of pupils attending private schools. Thirteen percent of the total number of pupils attended private (nonprofit or for-profit) schools in 2011. However, Sweden stands out from the two other countries because of a law that permits the transfer of profits to owners of primary school services with public funding. In 2013, the number of private schools was 792, which means that 16% of the schools were run by a private provider (nonprofit or for-profit). This number represents an increase compared to the situation in 2009 (Skolverket 2014). Across a longer time span, the increase has been even more considerable: At the end of the 1970s, less than 1% of the children of school age attended private schools (Lindström and Wijkström 1995, 20). Today, the majority of private authorities are joint stock companies, while nonprofit organisations play a limited role (Skolverket 2014).

Developments towards a 'welfare mix' in the Swedish primary and lower secondary school system began in the early 1990s. Before then, private actors mainly operated in a marginal part of the system— boarding schools. These schools were allowed by the government since they could provide an alternative, which the public schools could not.

In 1992, the non-socialist government had the opinion that parents should be able to choose between different types of providers. To make this possible, it was decided that municipalities had to pay private providers of schools at least 85% of the average cost per pupil attending a public school (Prop. 1991/92: 25). According to newer legislation, municipalities must treat public and private schools equally, i.e. private schools must obtain the same amount of money per pupil as public schools (Prop. 2008/09: 171).

A prerequisite for obtaining public funding for a private school is permission by the central state authority, the Swedish Schools Inspectorate. In the beginning, municipalities had little influence on this decision by central authorities. At present, municipalities have more influence but no formal veto on the final decision (Jarl and Rönnberg 2010, 81).

In spite of the differences between the three Scandinavian countries, a common feature is that approval for the establishment of private schools is a national task, but the standards and requirements that should be fulfilled to obtain this approval vary between the countries. Local governments do not have a formal say on the number of private schools in the municipalities, which highly affects steering possibilities in the field.

Freedom of choice is another common feature across the Scandinavian countries. In Denmark, parents have always had the right to choose private schools instead of public schools; and in 2002, freedom of choice among public schools was implemented. In Sweden, user choice was implemented through 'Friskolereformen' in 1992, which also made it possible to include for-profit actors in the provision of for-profit schools. In Norway, the possibility of choosing between different public schools varies between municipalities. However, if a nonprofit school is available, it is always possible to choose this school instead of a public school.

An important difference is that a common national law regulates all types of primary and lower secondary schools in Sweden, regardless of the type of provider. In contrast, nonprofit schools have their own law in both Denmark and Norway (Seegaard 2015, 94). This fact might be one of the reasons why conditions for different types of providers vary less in Sweden than in Denmark and Norway. For instance, private schools in Norway and Denmark are obliged to charge parental payment to get financial support from the state. In Sweden, all types of primary and lower secondary schools are provided free of charge for the users. However, there are also some differences between Denmark and Norway, as private schools have a higher degree of freedom regarding their curriculum and admissions in Denmark than in either Norway or Sweden (Segaard and Saglie, Chap. 3).

Altogether, in spite of their belonging to the same welfare regime, the three Scandinavian countries vary in a number of ways when it comes to the field of schools—regarding both the welfare mix and the national regulation the field. The following sections will take an empirical and analytical look into how these differences and similarities between countries and providers are reflected in the local governing of schools, with specific focus on elements of control, competition and collaboration.

The Case Study Design

The analysis will be based on case studies at the municipal level in Sweden, Norway and Denmark. Seven municipalities were selected for the case studies, and similar data gathering strategies and interview guides were used across countries and municipalities. The empirical data consist of qualitative interviews at both the municipal and school level, combined with written documents. A more detailed description of the selection of municipalities and schools is provided in the appendix to Chap. 1 in this book, including an overview of selected municipalities, schools and interviewees.

In each municipality, at least two schools were selected: One municipal and one private (nonprofit or for-profit). The case study design allowed for comparisons between different types of providers in the same local communities, thus controlling for many contextual factors. The analytical dimensions in this chapter will be structured, qualitative comparisons (Sivesind 2007) of data from interviews with actors in similar positions between countries and institutional sectors: public, nonprofit and for-profit schools.

Local Steering Trends in the Field of Schools

The following analysis will focus on local steering and types of regulations at play in the case municipalities in the field of primary and lower secondary schools. The analysis will be structured by the three analytical categories: control, competition and collaboration (Nyhlén 2013), corresponding to the three ideal types of governance: hierarchy, market and network (Jørgensen and Vrangbæk 2004; Meulenman 2008). The focus in the analysis will primarily be at the municipal level. However, experiences and practices at the school level will also be included.

Elements of Control

When it comes to elements of control in the local governing of schools, there are large differences across the different types of providers in the study. In all three countries, municipalities have very few steering possibilities when it comes to the number of private schools they contain. Private schools can be established as long as they live up to the national standards.

In the Danish case, some of the interviewees at the municipal level considered this lack of control problematic:

> They [the nonprofit schools] have become a natural part of the school system. However, they do give rise to challenges related to steering and planning. (Administrative leader, DK, 8.10.2013)

In contrast to many other welfare areas, there are no contracts between municipalities and nonprofit schools; which is, for instance, the case for nonprofit daycare. Moreover, there are very few restrictions in terms of inspections, which can either be conducted by the schools themselves or by an inspector chosen by the schools (LBK 917). The limited control is also evident in cases where a pupil is expelled from a nonprofit school and it is up to the municipality to find a suitable alternative. Finally, it can be a challenge in relation to efficient planning as, for example, when a nonprofit school is established as a consequence of the closing of a municipal school, and the municipality thereby does not achieve any cost reduction (Interview, administrative leader, DK, 18.12.2013).

In contrast to nonprofit schools, municipalities have a lot more control of public schools. Although national legislation sets the overall framework, there is still room for municipal steering and control. Responsibility for the inspection of public schools rests at the national level. However, municipalities typically make their own quality reports to document and follow the performance of the public schools (Interviews, administrative leaders, DK, 8.10.2013, 18.12.2013). Municipalities also have financial control of public schools and are free to decide both the number of schools and the limits of school districts. However, the freedom of choice also limits the degree of municipal control over public schools. Many parents use their freedom of choice, and there is a high degree of volatility between the schools. In one of the case municipalities, 56% of the pupils attend their district school, while the rest attend either a nonprofit school or another public school (Faaborg-Midtfyn kommune 2012). In some cases, this volatility can make it difficult to sustain schools in less populated areas:

> I find it problematic in relation to service in less populated areas, I really do. Both in the field of schools and in the field of daycare. If many pupils – or in some cases just a few – choose another school, they remove the basis for a school or a daycare institution. (Political chair of committee, DK, 4.10.2013)

At a more detailed level, municipalities have the option to promote and prioritise specific initiatives at the schools: An option that is used in both case municipalities. In Norway, the municipalities also experience that the possibility of establishing nonprofit schools can challenge efficient planning. For instance, it is difficult for the municipalities to save costs through the closing of small schools if parents choose to establish a nonprofit school instead:

> In the long run we have to look at the school structure in the municipality; it is a question of how small we can become [...] It is not like we necessarily have to close a school, but we can think differently about our

operation. But then the Montessori phenomenon is awaiting and can take over, and that becomes an expensive experience. Having two nonpublic schools in the municipality. (Administrative leader, N, 12.02.2014)

In this particular municipality, Løten in Norway, the nonprofit school has 45 pupils living within the municipality, while the rest come from neighbouring municipalities. According to the administrative leader, these 45 pupils could easily be integrated in the municipal school with few extra costs. In Steinkjer, one of the other Norwegian case municipalities, the municipal government decided to merge two public schools and has afterwards fought the establishment of a new Montessori school on the outskirts of the municipality. In this case, the Norwegian national directorate has so far accepted pleas from the municipality to prevent the school from being established. This will often be the case if the municipality can plausibly argue that a private school will weaken the basis for the public school. However, the municipality does not formally have a veto.

The public schools, by comparison, are entirely integrated within the municipality. Limited only by national regulations, the municipalities can run their schools as they wish. This includes decisions about school districts as well as the extent of user choice among public schools. Of the selected municipalities, Løten has no user choice, while parents in Steinkjer and Asker are able to choose between schools. In addition, the municipalities can decide the priorities of the schools. As an example, in Asker, the municipality has defined 15 detailed measures that the schools need to report on, in addition to both compulsory national tests and tests implemented by the municipality. Taken together, these targets and tests leave little room for local priorities at the schools.

Also in Sweden, municipalities have fewer steering possibilities and less control of private schools (nonprofit or for-profit) than public schools. However, the differences in the degree of control between different types of providers are less evident than in Denmark and Norway. One of the reasons for this is that all types of schools in Sweden are regulated by the same law. Highest in the regulation hierarchy is the Education Act, a law regulating the foundations for the Swedish education system. This act is followed by curricula adopted at the central level, which regulate the content of education in more detail. One of the requirements for obtaining permission for establishing a school is that it fulfil all the requirements of the law and curricula. In addition to central steering through national law and curricula, evaluations are performed by a central state authority, i.e. the Swedish Schools Inspectorate. This authority has the most far-reaching mandate since they can shut down a school because of an inspection. This goes for all schools regardless of provider.

Municipalities are heads of the primary and lower secondary schools, a task that implies a financial responsibility. The municipality calculates the price per pupil in a public school, and private schools then receive a corresponding compensation. In the municipalities investigated, meetings occur between the administration and private schools concerning the exact figure. However, these meetings do not concern the budget at each school nor how the money is used for different activities. This is an important difference compared to meetings held with the public schools, covering additional aspects. For instance, there is dialogue concerning areas for improvement at a particular school:

> What is good at the school, what is less well and which areas of development should be prioritised and how. (Administrative leader, S, 9.4.2015)

It could be asked whether the financial responsibility of the municipality for private schools actually constitutes a steering tool. According to one of the politicians interviewed, the national act is very clear on this issue—compensation should be the same for all types of schools, and therefore there is not really that much to discuss (Interview, social democratic politician, S, 9.4.2014).

Besides financial responsibility, municipalities have their own guidelines targeting schools. In Östersund, these guidelines include a mandate that all pupils leaving primary school should be qualified to apply to a secondary school, that the municipality should have a variety of programmes, and that staff should have a teaching licence and access to further education (Östersunds kommun 2013). Similar guidelines exist in Sollentuna, such as equal treatment of schools regardless of whether the provider is private or public, that no pupil should be a victim of bullying, and that a higher share of pupils should have their first choice of school approved (Sollentuna kommun 2008).

Formally, the guidelines only apply to public schools. However, in Sollentuna, private schools have voluntarily chosen to adopt them. In Östersund, the head administrator simply stated that there are no formal local guidelines from the municipality that apply to private providers (Interview, administrative leader, S, 9.4.2015).

In each of the municipalities, schools are also being governed through local evaluations. However, the target groups vary between municipalities. In Östersund, evaluations performed by the local administration only cover public schools and their fulfilment of learning requirements according to central regulation. Additionally, evaluations are made about what the schools are good at and how better activities can be developed. Part of this work is based on questionnaires sent out to both pupils and parents (Interview, administrative leader, S, 9.4.2014).

In Sollentuna, evaluations performed by the municipal administration targets all schools regardless of provider. One example of this is a questionnaire sent out to parents concerning the quality of the school. The result of the evaluation is displayed through the municipality's own website, making it possible for citizens to compare different schools (Interview, conservative politician, 13.12.2013; social democratic politician, S, 16.12.2013).

Summing up the Swedish case, private schools have the option to choose whether to follow municipal guidelines or not. Whether public evaluations only cover public schools or all schools also varies between the case municipalities. However, municipalities still have less control over private schools than public schools, specifically when it comes to financial control and local school priorities. Another important point from the Swedish case is that there are no differences in the degree of steering across different types of private providers. Hence, both for-profit and nonprofit providers are subject to the same regulations.

Experiences at the School Level—Elements of Control

The differences across providers in relation to elements and the degree of municipal control are also reflected in the schools' experiences and perceptions. The quote below from a nonprofit school leader in Denmark shows that this high level of self-determination and potential to create a school based on specific values, distinct from public schools, is valued. It is even underlined that it would be appropriate if nonprofit schools were obliged to develop a distinct profile:

> I find the freedom fantastic. I really do. And I do not understand that you do not want to make other types of demands. For instance, when we have the privilege of receiving financial support from the state, I think we ought to have a pedagogical profile where we do something different. (School leader, nonprofit school, DK, 5.2.2014)

In Norway, nonprofit schools are obliged to have a distinct profile, but the nonprofit schools still value the low level of control that sometimes frustrates the municipalities. As one school leader explained:

> My experience is that we have a lot of freedom, absolutely. Of course, we must follow the law, but besides that I think we pretty much have freedom when running the school [...] we are sort of our own little municipality, you know. Therefore, it is somewhat different; we do not have a school director to report to. (School leader, nonprofit school, N, 12.02.2014)

At the same time, this freedom exists within certain confines. According to national law, the schools must document how they are different from public schools. In the case above, the school has a Christian foundation. This framework narrows the amount of freedom in daily operations. As an example, the school only hires Christian, heterosexual employees. This demonstrates their level of freedom since a public school could never have such a policy.

Also in Sweden, private school leaders experience a high degree of freedom. The perception is that steering primarily comes from the national level and to a lesser extent from the municipality. One of the school leaders at a private school in Östersund concluded that there is no steering taking place, other than the money received from the municipality. Instead, the perception is that the school is almost entirely being governed from the central level through laws and regulations (Interview, school leader, for-profit school, S, 4.4.2014).

The perceptions above, across countries, stand in sharp contrast to the view held by school leaders at public schools. In Denmark, Norway and Sweden, the perception is that the level of steering and control from both the national and local level has increased over recent decades. A school leader of a public school in Norway described this development:

> This has changed a lot since I began. When I became school leader, there were two and a half people [in the municipal administration] who worked with school issues, and we had no school manager. Then, everything was left to us and at the same time, we received little support. Now, we are in a situation where I personally find that too many people work to support us, because how it works is that they make a list of how things should be, but then they do not have to do anything about it, if you see what I mean? (School leader, public school, N, 21.11.2013)

A school leader in one of the Danish case municipalities described how too much steering regarding local issues at the school can be problematic, because it leaves the school with less influence over daily life—for instance, regarding the completion of practical tasks at the schools. Earlier, such tasks had been completed by the school itself, but now it was a municipal task:

> Pedagogical leadership also includes the physical environment, and now we can see that they let the place be run down. We had a very nice new wooden terrace, but now it is full of water and leaves. Something that you would never accept at home without doing something about it, but all I can do is call and call [...] It is bad pedagogy towards the children. Why should they clean up then? (School leader, public school, DK, 9.1.2014).

Also in Sweden, a public school leader described how municipal steering implies detailed financial regulations on how to spend the budget for different parts of the operation of the school, leaving the schools with limited possibilities for local decisions (Interview, school leader, public school, S, 4.4.2014).

Summing up—Elements of Control

The results of the analysis of elements of control in the local governing of primary and lower secondary schools are summarised in Table 5.2.

It is evident in the table that municipalities across Scandinavian countries have few steering possibilities when it comes to private providers, regarding both financial and quality control. This is particularly evident in the Danish and Norwegian cases. The limited degree of control goes furthest in Denmark, where it is up to nonprofit schools to decide which pupils to accept. In Sweden, the degree of control is also relatively low, but the differences between providers are limited by common national regulation of all types of schools. This also implies that there are no differences in the municipal steering of nonprofit and for-profit schools. All schools have the same level of financial resources and have to live up to the same curriculum. Moreover, the municipal control of private schools in Sweden varies between the case municipalities because of different procedures regarding guidelines and evaluations.

Table 5.2 Elements of control in the local governing of schools

	Elements of control	Degree of control
Denmark		
Nonprofit schools	No municipal financial control No municipal quality control	Low
Public schools	Financial control through municipal budgets Quality control through quality reports and inspections	High
Norway		
Nonprofit schools	No municipal financial control No municipal quality control	Low
Public schools	Financial control through municipal budgets Quality control through tests, surveys, quality reports and inspections	High
Sweden		
Private schools	Limited financial control through municipal budgets, but no financial supervision Quality control through guidelines* and surveys*	Medium/Low*
Public schools	Financial control and quality control through guidelines and surveys.	High

* Some variation between the municipalities investigated

In contrast, municipalities exercise a rather high level of control when it comes to public schools, with respect to both financial control and quality control. Although national legislation sets the overall framework, there is still room for municipal steering and control, which takes place in all three Scandinavian countries. Moreover, the experience has been that the degree of regulation and control has increased during recent years, from both the national and local level.

Elements of Competition

Given the freedom of choice between different types of schools, elements of competition are an inevitable part of the municipal steering of primary and lower secondary schools in Denmark, Sweden and Norway.

In Denmark, local party programmes in both municipalities reveal relatively broad support for freedom of choice and various types of welfare providers. In spite of this and the general respect for the historical role of nonprofit schools, there has been a lot of focus on quality development in public schools to prevent parents from deselecting public schools and to make public schools as attractive as possible:

> There is no resistance towards nonprofit schools, but of course politicians wish to make public schools as attractive as possible to prevent a deselection of public schools. (Administrative leader, DK, 18.12.2014)

The focus on public schools is also evident in local party programmes; in most of them, nonprofit schools are hardly mentioned, even in Faaborg-Midtfyn where almost one-third of the pupils attend nonprofit schools. Both political and administrative leaders underline that nonprofit schools are seldom discussed politically. As an exception to this general picture, there was a proposal on one theme day on 'how to prevent people from choosing nonprofit schools'. The proposal was not accepted, and the day ended by focusing on how to profile public schools (Faaborg-Midtfyn Kommune 2012; Political chair of committee, DK, 4.10.2013). However, the example shows that some politicians find it problematic that so many parents choose nonprofit schools. The attitude towards nonprofit schools varies between political parties. According to an administrative leader, the classical political divide between left-wing and right-wing parties can also be identified in the field of schools. The Liberal and Conservative parties are generally more in favour of nonprofit schools and freedom of choice than left-wing parties (Interview, administrative leader, DK, 8.10.2013). However, across interviewees at the municipal level, there was some scepticism about the special privileges of nonprofit schools. Many interviewees had the opinion that when nonprofit schools opt for a free status, they cannot expect the same privileges as public schools. Moreover, some of the interviewees perceived unequal competition because nonprofit schools are allowed to refuse pupils, resulting in the risk of an unequal society with A- and B-schools (Interview, administrative leader, DK, 8.10.2013).

Also in Norway, nonprofit schools receive very limited attention in local party programmes. Primary and lower secondary schools are one of the core tasks of the municipalities, and therefore all programmes have policies for public schools. However, in all municipalities, only a minority of the parties mention the nonprofits. According to the interviewees at the municipal level, the only time the city councils debates about nonprofit schools is when the municipality is asked to voice its view on the establishment of a new school. One of the founders of the nonprofit school in Steinkjer experienced a negative attitude from the municipality when the school was in the process of being established 10 years ago:

> When we came up with the idea of establishing something in direct competition with the public providers, then the attitudes changed. That was a big surprise really [...] There was so much opposition to this. (Founder, nonprofit school, N, 13.02.2014)

It is evident from this statement that the founders experienced intense opposition to the establishment of their nonprofit school. Today, however, the school has been functioning for 10 years and, due to its limited size, its existence has not prompted the municipality or the public schools to change their behaviour. The following statement from an administrative leader in Steinkjer illustrates how the municipality sees nonprofit schools:

> We think they are a good supplement. I absolutely think there is nothing negative about it. It is most important that the children learn and do well at the Montessori school. That is the most important: the individual child. It is no point for me that all shall attend the public school. I just want it [the public school] to be good enough, so that no one wants to leave it. That is what I want. I think it is great that we have such a school, with regard to happy living. We might attract some [new residents] because we have an alternative to the public school. (Administrative leader, N, 20.02.2014)

This quote shows that municipalities want to offer high standards in order not to lose pupils. At the same time, the leader recognises that the nonprofit school offers something different, which can be attractive for some citizens.

As in Denmark, municipalities in Sweden cannot influence the degree of privatisation within education. If a private provider chooses to establish a school, they are free to do so, as long as the central authority grants their application. Nevertheless, the Swedish case municipalities cope with this new context of marketisation in different ways. These differences may reflect different degrees of political support for privatisation evident in the two municipalities.

In Östersund, the majority is foremost represented by the Social Democratic Party, and as such, the municipality has a negative attitude towards private providers within education. Every time the question of the establishment of a private school has been discussed in the committee of education, the Social Democratic Party has been against it. The chair of the committee declared in an interview that were his party to decide, only one alternative would be evident—the public one (Interview, social democratic politician, S, 9.4.2014). However, municipalities cannot stop the establishment of private schools, as long as they are approved by national authorities. The non-socialist parties in the committee hold the opposite view. According to a member of the committee representing the

Liberal Party, there should be more private providers and alternatives to choose from (Interview, liberal politician, S, 9.4.2014).

In Sollentuna, a municipality governed by non-socialist parties, the majority is clearly in favour of freedom of choice, while the opposition parties are more reluctant. The chair of the committee for education, representing the Moderates (Conservative Party), stated that the majority of members within the committee welcome new providers of schools to Sollentuna. The most important goal for them is that schools within the municipality have good quality regardless of provider (Interview, conservative politician, S, 13.12.2013).

The opposition parties are more hesitant about privatisation. A member of the committee, representing the Social Democratic Party, remarked that their position depends on the situation in each district of the municipality. If a new private school would pose a threat to an existing public one, then the party would vote 'no' (Interview, social democratic politician, S, 16.12.2013).

Different attitudes towards the welfare mix in Östersund and Sollentuna might have consequences for the practice of freedom of choice. In Sollentuna, the system of freedom of choice is promoted more clearly than in Östersund through a special website. During January and February each year, every parent makes a choice of school, regardless of the type of provider, on the municipality's website. Connected to this site are surveys which allow parents and pupils to compare different alternatives regardless of provider.

In Östersund, there are no similarities to the system practiced in Sollentuna. Instead, pupils automatically receive a place at the public school closest to their home (i.e. the proximity principle). If pupils and their parents prefer a private alternative, they must make a direct application to that particular school. In March each year, the private schools inform the municipality of how many and which pupils they have accepted. This makes it possible for the municipal administration to adjust their figures for the number of pupils in public schools.

In sum, Sollentuna actively promotes the system of freedom of choice, while Östersund practises a more traditional model in which pupils are placed at schools according to the principle of proximity. An interpretation of this difference is that Sollentuna acts as a facilitator of freedom of choice, making it easier for their citizens to compare, and then choose an appropriate school. The method practiced in Östersund, on the other hand, indicates that the municipality perceives itself as one type of provider on a competitive market, rather than as a facilitator of freedom of choice.

Experiences at the School Level—Elements of Competition

When it comes to experiences at the schools regarding elements of competition, the study shows some differences between the Scandinavian countries. In both Denmark and Sweden, the perception of the schools is that there is a competitive situation between them, particularly in areas with many schools within a limited geographical area.

In the Danish case, nonprofit schools see the primary focus of their municipalities to be on public schools, while very little attention is paid to them, even in Faaborg-Midtfyn, a municipality with a very high share of pupils in nonprofit schools:

> Politically, we do not have first priority here in the municipality. (Board member, nonprofit school, DK, 12.2.2014)

> No, we would be lying, if we said so. It is evident that public schools are given greater priority. (Board member, nonprofit school, DK, 12.2.2014)

> Yes, and especially here in the local community, we attract the same pupils as the public school. It is not very popular in the municipality that we attract so many pupils. (Board member, nonprofit school, DK, 12.2.2014)

The interviews clearly indicate that the nonprofit schools would like to be a more valued part of the school system in the municipality, and that the competitive situation is one of the reasons why municipalities pay very little attention to nonprofit schools. The interviews also show that nonprofit schools are very focused on being a high-quality alternative to the public schools.

Also in Sweden, all school leaders are well aware of the competition taking place between units. This is particularly evident at those schools that have or have had problems with attracting or keeping pupils. At one of the private schools in Sollentuna, the school leader believed that proximity was the most important factor when choosing a school. However, reputation was another important factor, with a negative or positive impact on the number of applicants (Interview, school leader, for-profit school, 3.4.2014). At one of the private schools in Östersund, pupils come from all parts of town. According to the school leader interviewed, this is due to the reputation of the school:

> People know the good environment, the good teachers, who work here and the results of it. (School leader, for-profit school, S, 4.4.2014)

Because of this reputation, there is no need to advertise for the school and its activities. At one of the public schools in the same town, there has been an outflow of pupils to private alternatives. To better understand this development, the school carried out a survey about the parents' motives for changing the school for their child. Many of the parents responded that they did not believe the public school was good enough for their child due to insufficient quality. The public school responded by not only improving quality, but also by improving communication about pedagogical activities taking place and the ideas behind them (Interview, school leader, public school, S, 4.4.2014). These examples show that the competitive situation can influence priorities locally at the schools.

The Norwegian case stands out from the other Scandinavian countries when it comes to the schools' perception of and experiences with competition. Neither the nonprofit nor the public schools perceived the other schools as competitors. For the public schools, the nonprofit schools are not big enough to pose a threat, as they cannot attract sufficient numbers of pupils to challenge the public schools. The nonprofit schools do not have the same natural pool of pupils who attend the school because they live close by, but they still do not experience competition—for instance as stated by this school leader of the Waldorf School:

I do not see our school as in a competition because we constitute a niche. We use an entirely different curriculum, we are an alternative, and for me that is motivation enough. Because I think we have a right to exist, since we are an alternative that I have experienced through many years has been important for many people. And I see no reason why we should not in the future continue to be important for many people. Not all, but for many, in sum over time, there are many people who have experienced crucial positive development by being able to choose something different from the public school. Not because the public school has been bad, but because this school has been suitable for them. (School leader, nonprofit school, N, 10.12.2013)

According to this claim, the degree of competition is perceived to be low because the nonprofit school represents a niche that attracts other types of pupils. This example shows that a high level of distinctiveness between providers might limit the level of competition.

Summing up—Elements of Competition

The results of the analysis of elements and degree of competition are summarised in Table 5.3.

Parents' option to choose between different types of schools will often lead to a certain level of competition. As the table shows, elements of competition in the field of schools are evident in both Denmark and Sweden. In Denmark, the municipalities actively seek to promote public schools to prevent deselection. The competitive situation is also experienced by the schools—in particular in one of the case municipalities,

Table 5.3 Elements of competition in the local governing of schools

	Elements of competition	Degree of competition
Denmark	Municipal strategy for promoting public schools	Medium
Norway	Nonprofit schools do not challenge public schools, but cater to different segments	Low
Sweden	Schools experience competition regardless of municipality and type of provider. The role of the municipal administration in this competition differs	Medium

where the geographical distance between the schools was limited. Also in Sweden, both municipalities and schools are aware of the competitive situation. However, the municipalities deal with the situation in different ways. While one of the municipalities actively promotes freedom of choice, the other municipality has a more passive approach. Interestingly, the degree of competition is far lower in Norway, where the perception at both levels is that nonprofit schools do not pose a threat to public schools, because of both their limited size and their distinctiveness.

Elements of Collaboration

Across the Scandinavian countries, the analysis shows that the degree of collaboration between municipalities and private schools is very limited, while there is more collaboration when it comes to public schools. However, there are some differences between the countries, regarding both the content and level of collaboration.

In the Danish case, elements of collaboration between municipalities and nonprofit schools are very limited in both municipalities, according to the administrative leaders. Due to state funding of the schools, there are no financial relations between nonprofit schools and the municipalities, and none of the municipalities have formal meetings with representatives from nonprofit schools (Interviews, administrative leaders, DK, 8.10.2013, 18.12.2013). The limited degree of collaboration is closely related to lack of steering possibilities and control in relation to nonprofit schools. Their possibilities for influencing the schools are very limited, which, from a municipal point of view, might minimise the motivation for collaboration. Specifically, at a time when limited financial resources are available:

> When a municipality has to plan efficient services in all fields – including schools – and we really need to do that in these years – it is a big challenge that one-third of the pupils are attending schools where we do not have any influence at all. (Administrative leader, DK, 8.10.2013)

In contrast, there is a much higher degree of collaboration between municipalities and public schools—for instance, through formal leader meetings. One of the municipalities even has a common school council, where school boards from all schools in the municipalities are represented. According to the administrative leaders, the municipalities strive to involve the schools in important decisions—for instance, in the restructuring of school districts, the closing of schools, etc. (Interviews, administrative leaders, DK, 8.10.2013, 18.12.2013).

In Norway, collaboration between municipalities and nonprofit schools is also limited, apart from practical issues associated with the transportation of pupils as well as on decisions regarding extra resources to pupils with special needs. These pupils are assessed by municipal professionals, who decide whether special attention or extra resources should be provided. When the professionals make such a decision, the pupils are entitled to these resources at their schools and the municipality must pay, regardless of whether it is a public or nonprofit school.

This latter point can make it difficult for municipalities to plan their costs. One administrative leader talked about this issue and concluded that nonpublic schools are 'a hassle and annoyance' (Interview, administrative leader, N, 12.02.2014). These steering challenges can be one explanation for the limited degree of collaboration.

However, some politicians actively embrace the nonprofit schools. The Conservative Party in Asker stated that it will 'develop cooperation with the nonprofits'. Challenged about how they would do this, their representative admitted that the tasks of the municipality are to 'make the operating conditions good enough so the schools want to continue. Yes, what we say is that we want to be positive towards the schools' (Interview, conservative politician, N, 22.10.2013). The inability of the politician to mention substantive steps the municipality could take to 'develop cooperation with nonprofits' illustrates the limited potential for collaboration between nonprofit schools and municipalities in Norway. The nonprofit schools provide schooling to a marginal fraction of citizens, and most interaction between the schools and the municipality is demanded and regulated by law.

However, one formal bond is that all nonprofit schools—according to the law—must have a school board responsible for their operation; and a representative from the municipality must be on the school board. This representative does not hold a vote but is entitled to meet and speak at all meetings. This representative is normally a politician involved in the school sector. This policy functions differently between the schools depending on the interest and efforts of individual politicians. The schools, therefore, report that some representatives are hardly ever seen at board meetings, while others make constructive contributions to the discussions.

Overall, there is little voluntary cooperation between nonprofit schools and the municipality. According to the analysis, this limited degree of collaboration can be explained by the lack of obvious areas for collaboration as well as the steering challenges experienced by the municipal actors. In contrast, collaboration between municipalities and public schools is more developed and includes both formal networks and meetings between school leaders and municipal administrators.

In Sweden, collaboration between municipalities and private schools is more common than in Denmark and Norway, although its level and content vary between the two case municipalities. In one of the municipalities, Sollentuna, private schools are included in several aspects. Three of the most striking examples of this have already been mentioned: First, the inclusion of private schools on a special website where citizens can make their own choice of school. Second, private schools have chosen to adopt local guidelines, which is a sort of collaboration with the municipality. Third, all schools in Sollentuna participate in a quality survey—targeting both parents and pupils—carried out by the municipality.

An additional element is the quality project *Våga visa!* (Dare to show!), which covers all schools. The project consists of school visits performed by teachers or other pedagogical leaders from neighbouring municipalities. Through these visits, attention is paid to how schools are working with different parts of national regulation such as learning, grading, norms and values, and pupils' influence. The information obtained from these visits is documented in a report summarising the strengths and weaknesses of the school (Interview, conservative politician, S, 13.12.2013).

Collaborations such as these do not exist in Östersund, but cooperation between public and private schools is not entirely absent.

According to the Education Act, all pupils should be ensured access to school nurses and counsellors. In Östersund, private schools do not provide for this on their own, since they have been granted access to the public system. This is an important form of collaboration between private and public schools which does not exist in Sollentuna (Interview, school leader, nonprofit school, S, 8.4.2014).

In both municipalities, there is dialogue between the administration and the schools; for instance, on budget issues. This dialogue takes place in regard to all types of schools, but seems to be more comprehensive between the municipal administration and public schools. For example, in Sollentuna, all school leaders from public schools meet within a working group referred to as *Rektorsgruppen* to discuss joint efforts (Interview, school leader, S, 16.1.2014). A similar dialogue takes place between the administration and the public schools in Östersund. This indicates that the collaborative ties—also in the Swedish case—are stronger when it comes to public schools.

Experiences at the School Level—Elements of Collaboration

Also at the school level, the picture from the analysis above is clear. In all three countries, public school leaders perceive a higher degree of collaboration than private school leaders.

In the Danish case, nonprofit schools feel that a collaborative attitude on the part of the municipalities is limited. For instance, nonprofit schools do not have equal opportunities for attending municipal seminars, and relevant information, such as information about changes in bus timetables, does not always reach them (Interview, school leader, nonprofit school, DK, 9.1.2014). On the other hand, one of the public schools has the opinion that nonprofit schools receive too many of the same opportunities as public schools, since they do not have the same obligations (Interview, school leader, public school, DK, 9.1.2014).

A similar picture can be seen in Norway, where nonprofit schools feel ignored by the municipalities. They are in many instances not cooperatively included. Sometimes this is natural, since they operate on different terms, but all of the nonprofit schools would have preferred closer ties to the municipality (Interview, school leader, nonprofit school, N, 24.4.2014).

In Sweden, there are different views on the extent to which collaboration takes place with the municipal administration. In Östersund, a meeting with the administration is held twice a year. During these meetings, a discussion takes place on issues such as financial compensation and collaboration on health care for pupils (Interviews, school leaders, for-profit, S, 4.4.2014; nonprofit, S, 4.8.2014). In Sollentuna, similar meetings take place between the private school and the administration. Additionally, collaboration includes other types of activities, such as surveys and quality projects like *Våga visa!* (Interview, school leader, for-profit, S, 3.4.2014). Private schools in Sweden experience a more collaborative attitude from the municipalities than nonprofit schools in Denmark and Norway.

In all three countries, municipalities appear to have a more collaborative attitude when it comes to public schools. School leaders of public schools believe that they are a more integrated part of the municipality than leaders of private schools. However, in the Danish case, the extent to which public schools actually feel involved and heard in decisions made by the municipalities, varies. In one of the municipalities, the public school perceives a limited degree of responsiveness, while there is a higher degree of satisfaction in the other municipality (Interviews, school leaders, DK, 9.1.2014, 14.3.2014; board members, DK, 26.2.2014, 30.4.2014).

Summing up—Elements of Collaboration

The results of the analysis of elements and degree of collaboration in the local governing of primary and lower secondary schools are summarised in Table 5.4.

As the table shows, the overall result of the analysis is that collaboration between municipalities and private schools is limited in all three countries. In Denmark, there are no formal meetings and limited contact, while in Norway there are few meeting points. Sweden stands out from the other countries by having some degree of collaboration between

Table 5.4 Elements of collaboration in local governing of schools

	Elements of collaboration	Degree of collaboration
Denmark		
Nonprofit schools	No formal meetings and limited contact	Low
Public schools	Formal meetings and networks	Medium*
Norway		
Nonprofit schools	Few meeting points	Low
Public schools	Formal meetings and networks	Medium
Sweden		
Nonprofit schools	Formal meetings, common guidelines*, common surveys*, common projects* and joint health care*	Medium/Low*
Public schools	Formal meetings and networks	Medium

* Some variation between municipalities investigated

municipalities and private schools. However, the content and degree of collaboration vary between the case municipalities. A number of factors can explain the limited degree of collaboration: For instance, the limited formal bonds and limited municipal opportunities for controlling and influencing the field of private schools. The competitive situation in some of the countries as well as financial pressures are also possible explanations. On the other hand, municipalities have more formal bonds to public schools. They are an integrated part of the municipal administration and therefore naturally collaborate more with the municipalities through formal meetings and networks.

The Field of Schools—Between Control, Choice and Room for Distinctiveness

What are the similarities and differences across countries and types of providers when it comes to municipal steering and regulation in the field of schools? What are the consequences for the schools? And finally, does the legislation and regulations promote or inhibit distinctive profiles at the schools?

The answer to these questions will provide the basis for a discussion of possible implications for future welfare provision in the field of schools in Scandinavia. Although the results of the case studies not necessarily can be generalised to all municipalities and schools in the three countries, the strength of the analysis is the in-depth character of the data, making it possible to identify mechanisms between the regulatory frameworks and the actions and experiences at the local level.

The overall picture from the analysis is that there are profound differences in the local governing of primary and lower secondary schools across private and public providers in the case municipalities. Moreover, national legislation is to a large extent reflected in the local governing of and attitudes towards different types of schools.

When it comes to elements related to *control*, there are similar trends across the Scandinavian countries. In general, administrative supervision in private schools is limited compared to public schools. Because of the national approval of private schools, municipalities have less direct control over them and limited steering possibilities, across all three countries. This goes furthest in Denmark and Norway, where municipalities have neither financial control nor quality control when it comes to nonprofit schools. It is up to national authorities to make sure that public support is used for educational purposes. In Sweden, municipalities have limited control through municipal budgets, but no control over the economy of private schools. They do have some potential control through different types of guidelines. However, it is voluntary for schools to join the common guidelines. Therefore, the extent of quality control varies between the Swedish municipalities.

These differences leave varying room for distinctiveness between the countries. The room for distinctiveness is particularly large in Denmark and Norway but less so in Sweden, where the same law regulates all schools. The municipal role in the national approval process also varies. In both Norway and Sweden, municipalities are heard when a private actor wishes to establish a school in the municipality, yet they have no veto power. In Denmark, it is an entirely national process.

The limited degree of control is to some extent reflected in sceptical attitudes towards nonprofit schools from the municipal point of view. Again, this holds particularly true for Denmark and Norway. In spite of overall support for nonprofit schools, there is frustration regarding the steering challenges experienced. This is less evident in the Swedish case, where attitudes towards private schools are more a result of ideological positions than practical steering challenges. These ideological positions are also evident in Denmark, but to a lower extent than in Sweden, probably because of the opportunities for for-profit providers in Sweden and the long historical tradition of nonprofit providers in Denmark.

When it comes to elements of *competition*, there are some overall differences between the three countries. First, freedom of choice between all schools is defended by national legislation in both Denmark and Sweden. In Norway, opportunities for choice between public schools are largely a municipal decision, while it has always been possible to choose between public schools and nonprofit schools. Therefore, it is also possible to have competition in municipalities that—as in one of the case municipalities—have not implemented freedom of choice.

However, in the Norwegian case, the argument is that public and nonprofit schools attract different segments of the population and that there is, therefore, a low degree of competition and no municipal attempts to attract more pupils to public schools in the case municipalities. In contrast, there are clear signs of political interest in promoting public schools in both case municipalities in Denmark. In spite of general support for nonprofit schools, preventing the deselection of public schools is a primary ambition. In Sweden, municipalities are also aware of the competitive situation. However, the two case municipalities reacted in very different ways: One of the municipalities reacted by promoting transparency for parents in their choice of schools, while the other promoted public schools, similar to the Danish case municipalities.

Across the three Scandinavian countries, elements of *collaboration* are much more widespread in the relationship between municipalities and public schools than nonprofit schools. This is not surprising as public schools are a part of the municipal structure. There are, however, some differences across countries. The tendency is that collaboration between private schools and municipalities is closer in Sweden than in Norway and Denmark, where collaboration is very limited in the cases studied. However, also in Sweden, there is large variation across the case municipalities. In one of the municipalities, collaboration is limited to formal meetings, while there is more collaboration in the other municipality—for instance, through common guidelines and common surveys.

The case studies also show that the trends identified at the municipal level are to a large extent reflected at the school level. In all three countries, private providers perceive a large degree of freedom regarding the running of the schools, and this freedom is highly valued. In contrast, public schools experience a high and increasing degree of control, especially from the national level, but—particularly in Denmark—at the local level as well, although this varies between the case municipalities.

Regarding elements of *competition*, this is clearly experienced at the school level in both Denmark and Sweden. Whether the schools just accept the situation as it is or take specific actions to attract new pupils varies. In the Norwegian case municipalities, neither the schools nor the municipalities perceive nonprofit schools as competitors. However, this might be different in other local communities where private schools make particular public schools redundant.

Finally, regarding *collaboration*, perceptions are very similar to perceptions at the municipal level: Collaborative relations are more widespread when it comes to public schools than private schools. Nonprofit schools in both Denmark and Norway would like to have closer relations with their municipalities than is currently the case. In contrast, private schools in Sweden do have formal meetings with the municipality; and in one of the municipalities, private schools have voluntarily chosen to participate in more collaborative activities.

Altogether, the analysis shows important similarities between the three countries: Among the most important of these is the fact that the degree of municipal control is much lower when it comes to private schools than public schools. Another common trend is that there is a higher degree of collaboration between municipalities and public schools than nonprofit schools. However, there are also important differences, indicating that variation in national legislation, as described in detail in Chap. 3, is to a large extent reflected in actions and attitudes at the local level, in terms of both the municipal level and school level.

First, sector distinctiveness varies between the countries. Sweden is the most marketised of the three Scandinavian countries given its opportunities for for-profit providers to establish schools. At the same time, Sweden has the largest degree of control and regulation over private schools, supporting the theoretical assumption that more market creates more regulation (Dølvik et al. 2015, 106). Second, the analysis shows a larger focus on equal services in Sweden than in Denmark and Norway, where nonprofit schools are often based on specific principles or values. In Norway, distinctiveness is even a criterion for establishing a nonprofit school. This leaves private schools in Sweden with less room for distinctiveness than in Norway and Denmark, which makes it more difficult for citizens to make an active choice between services with distinctive profiles. In relation to this, it is interesting that there are no significant differences between for-profit and nonprofit providers in Sweden when it comes to the local governing of schools.

Possible reasons for the identified differences across the Scandinavian countries can be found in different historical legacies. Both in Norway and Denmark, there has been a long historical tradition of nonprofit schools (Ibsen and Habermann 2006; Thuen and Tveit 2013). This historical tendency towards autonomy has remained very strong in spite of overall trends towards more regulation. In Sweden, the vast majority of primary and lower secondary schools has been under government control for many decades (Lundström and Wijkström 1995, 20); and until the 1990s, private schools only played a minimal role. The historical weight of equality in the Swedish welfare state (Bunar 2010, 56), together with newer trends of market principles, have been dominating the field of schools in Sweden, leaving less room for distinctiveness.

Altogether, the local governing of schools in Scandinavia does not show any clear signs of collaborative steering relations—at least not in the sense of dialogue and learning relations, which are some of the central characteristics of collaborative governance (Donahue and Zeckhauser 2011). Although the national steering of private providers can be characterised as indirect steering, where both the state and private providers influence the service provision (Segaard and Saglie, Chap. 3), collaborative steering relations at the local level are very limited. In relation to private schools, there is very limited collaboration, especially in Denmark and Norway, but also less control, leaving room for distinctiveness. When it comes to public schools, the control-based regime seems to be dominating, but there are elements of involvement and dialogue between municipalities and public schools.

The results of the analysis show a number of trade-offs worth discussing in relation to the implications of different types of welfare mix and local governing of different types of providers. These issues clearly show that the local governing of schools takes place in a complex mix of logics and tools from state, market and civil society.

First, there is a trade-off between the autonomy of schools and collaboration between schools and municipalities, particularly evident in Denmark and Norway. On the one hand, private schools value their independence and potential for developing a distinct profile. On the other hand, they would like to have more collaboration with the municipalities and be more accepted as alternative providers. In Sweden, private schools are to a larger extent integrated into the school system, but they also have less autonomy. However, there are local variations in the extent to which private schools are integrated.

Second, there is a related trade-off between equivalent quality and distinctiveness. Part of the reason why nonprofit schools are not fully accepted as an integrated part of the school system in Danish and Norwegian municipalities seems to be the clash between strong norms for equivalent quality and strong norms for autonomy and distinctiveness. In Sweden, another path has been chosen: A heavy focus on equivalent quality and services, resulting in less room for distinctiveness.

Third, there is a trade-off between autonomy and accountability. When schools have a high degree of autonomy, tools for accountability are limited, which is the case in Norway and Denmark. Again, the situation in Sweden is different, because all schools are subject to the same law and have to follow the same national curriculum. This creates better possibilities for accountability, but less room for autonomy (Gustafsson et al. 2016, 56).

These points are interesting to discuss in relation to the role played by nonprofit actors in welfare services. The nonprofit sector is often—and has historically been—seen as a 'field of experimentation' and as providers of distinct, innovative and specialised services (Weisbrod 1977;

Anheier 2009, 1092; Mariani and Cavanego 2013). However, possibilities for experimentation vary due to the level of control, and control is often implemented to ensure a legitimate accountability structure (Smith and Grønbjerg 2006).

The issues above are also relevant for the arguments surrounding the implementation of freedom of choice. One of the arguments is that citizens should be able to choose between different types of services (Petersen and Hjelmar 2013, 6). However, if the level of control is too high, it is clearly more difficult to have providers with a high degree of distinctiveness (Gustafsson et al. 2016, 48, 56). This paradox is particularly evident in the Swedish case: Although Sweden is the most marketised of the three countries, it is also the country with the least room for distinctiveness. With such a limited potential for distinctiveness, it can be debated whether citizens actually have real opportunities for choice which is a relevant point in the discussion of possibilities for active citizenship.

The country-specific differences above can be related to the fact that some of the Swedish private schools are run by for-profit actors, while all alternatives in Denmark and Norway are nonprofit schools. According to the classic literature, the non-distributional constraint is likely to create trust in nonprofit organisations (Hanssmann 1987), which might lead to lower demands for accountability. However, the high level of autonomy for nonprofit schools in Denmark and Norway also has to be seen in light of the long historical tradition of nonprofit organisations in these countries (Henriksen and Bundesen 2004; Ibsen and Habermann 2006; Thuen and Tveit 2013).

Altogether, the results of the case studies show that local governing in the field of primary schools largely reflects national legislation in the field. Moreover, local governing has clear implications for the local perceptions and actions of the schools. Finally, it is evident that there are large differences in the local governing of schools across public and private providers; to some extent, there are also variations between the three Scandinavian countries in spite of their other similarities, especially when it comes to the type of welfare regime. However, the results also suggest the institutional sector does not alone create the differences between the different types of providers. The complex interplay between regulation, funding and norms in the field are also of crucial importance. Together with local governing, national legislation has a large impact on the potential for distinctive services, accountability, equal quality and equal competition in the field of schools in Scandinavia. The balance between these elements is central to discuss in the future development of the welfare state in the three countries. In the concluding chapter, the importance of institutional legacies and political strategies for regulating the welfare mix and the distinctiveness of for-profit and nonprofit services will be further discussed.

Notes

1. www.friskoler.dk
2. In practice, this payment refers to a repayment of the block grant municipalities receive for each school-seeking child in the municipality (www.friskoler.dk).

References

Alber, Jens. 2010. What the European and American Welfare States have in common and where they differ: facts and fiction in comparisons of the European Social Model and the United States. *Journal of European Social Policy* 20 (2): 102–125.
Anheier, Helmut K. 2009. What Kind of Non-profit Sector? What Kind of Society? *American Behavioral Scientist* 52 (7): 1082–1094.
Arnesen, Anne-Lise, and Lisbeth Lundahl. 2006. Still Social and Democratic? Inclusive Education Policies in the Nordic Welfare States. *Scandinavian Journal of Educational Research* 50 (3): 285–300.
Baldersheim, Harald, and Lawrence E. Rose. (eds.). 2010. *Territorial choice: The politics of boundaries and borders.* Basingstoke: Palgrave Macmillan.
Bogason, Peter. 2001. *Forvaltning og stat.* Aarhus: Systime.
Bunar, Nihad. 2010. The controlled school market and urban schools in Sweden. *Journal of School Choice* 4 (1): 47–73.
Donahue, John, and Joseph Nye. 2002. *Market-based governance.* Brookings: Washington D.C.

Donahue, Johna, and Richard Zeckhauser. 2011. *Collaborative Governance.* Princeton: Princeton University Press.
Dølvik, Jon Erik, T. Fløtten, J.M. Hippe, and B. Jordfald. 2015. *The Nordic model towards 2030. A new chapter?* Fafo report 2015:07. Oslo: Fafo.
Esping-Andersen, Gösta. 1990. *The three worlds of welfare capitalism.* Cambridge: Polity.
Evers, Adalbert and Helmut Wintersberger. 1990. *Shifts in the welfare mix. Their impact on work, social services, and welfare policies.* Frankfurt am Main: Campus Verlag.
Faaborg-Midtfyn Kommune. 2012. Børne-og Undervisningsudvalgets Årsplan 2012 [Annual calendar of the committee on children and education]. Denmark.
Gidron, Benjamin, Ralph M. Kramer, and Lester M. Salamon. 1992. *Government and the third sector.* San Francisco: Jossey-Bass Publishers.
Greve, Carsten and Niels Ejersbo. 2013. Udviklingen i styringen af den offentlige sektor. Baggrundspapir til Produktivitetskommissionen. Copenhagen Business School & Syddansk Universitet.
Gustafsson, Jan-Eric, Sverker Sörlin, and Jonas Vlacos. 2016. *Policyidéer för svensk skola.* Stockholm: SNS Förlag.
Hansmann, H. 1987. Economic theories of non-profit organizations. In *The Nonprofit Sector: A Research Handbook*, ed. W.W. Powell, 27–42. New Haven: Yale University Press.
Henriksen, Lars Skov, and Peter Bundesen. 2004. The Moving Frontier in Denmark: Voluntary-State Relationships since 1850. *Journal of Social Policy* 33 (4): 605–625.
Henriksen, Lars Skov, Steven R. Smith, and Annette Zimmer. 2012. At the eve of convergence? Transformations of Social Service Provision in Denmark, Germany, and the United States. *Voluntas* 23 (2): 458–501.
Hood, Christopher 1991. A Public Management for All Seasons? *Public Administration* 69 (1): 3–19.
Homepage for Danish association for nonprofit schools. www.friskoler.dk.
Ibsen, Bjarne, and Ulla Habermann. 2006. De selvejende institutioner. In *Frivillighed og nonprofit i Danmark - Omfang, organisation, økonomi og beskæftigelse*, eds. Thomas Boje, and Bjarne Ibsen, 97–136. København: Socialforskningsinstituttet.
Jarl, Maria, and Linda Rönnberg. 2010. *Skolpolitik: från riksdagshus till klassrum.* Stockholm: Liber.
Jørgensen, Torben Beck, and Karsten Vrangbæk. 2004. *Det offentlige styringsunivers. Fra government til governance?* Aarhus: Magtudredningen.

Kersting, Norbert, and Angelika Vetter. 2003. *Reforming Local Governments in Europe*. Opladen: Leske + Budrik.
Law on independent and private schools (LBK 917 13/08/2014). Denmark.
Law on public schools (LBK 665 20/06/2014). Denmark.
Lundström, Tommy, and Filip Wijkström. 1995. Defining the non-profit sector: Sweden. Working Papers of the Johns Hopkins Comparative Non-profit Sector Project, no. 16. Baltimore: The Johns Hopkins Institute for Policy Studies.
Mariani, Laura, and Dario Cavenago. 2013. Redesigning welfare services for policies effectiveness: The nonprofit organizations' (NPOs) perspective. *Public Management Review* 15 (7): 1011–1039.
Meuleman, Louis. 2008. *Public management and the metagovernance of hierarchies, networks and markets. The feasibility of designing and managing governance style combinations*. Heidelberg: Physica-Verlag.
Nyhlén, Jon. 2013. Kommunen och skolmarknaden—Strategier och förhållningssätt. In *När förvaltning blir business: - Marknadiseringens utmaningar för demokratin och välfärdsstaten*, eds. L. Rönnberg, U. Strandberg, E. Wihlborg and U. Winblad, 153–168. Linköping: Linköping University Electronic Press.
Östersunds kommun (2013-11-28). Plan för kunskap och lärande. Östersund: Östersunds Kommun.
Pestoff, Victor A. 2009. *A democratic architecture for the welfare state*. Routledge, London & New York.
Petersen, Ole Helby, and Ulf Hjelmar. 2013. Marketization of welfare services in Scandinavia: A review of Swedish and Danish experiences. *Scandinavian Journal of Public Administration* 26 (5): 3–20.
Phillips, Susan. D., and Steven R. Smith. 2011. Between governance and regulation. Evolving government-third sector relationships. In *Governance and Regulation in the Third Sector. International Perspectives*, eds. Susan D. Phillips and Steven R. Smith, 1–36. New York: Routledge.
Pollitt, Christopher, and Geert Bouckaert. 2011. *Public management reform: A comparative analysis—new public management, governance, and the Neo-Weberian State*. Oxford: Oxford University Press.
Powell, Martin A. 2007. *Understanding the mixed economy of welfare*. Policy Press.
Prop. 1991/92:25. Om valfrihet och fristående skolor [Government bill]. Sweden.
Prop. 2008/09:171. Offentliga bidrag på lika villkor [Government bill]. Sweden.

Salamon, Lester M., and Stephan Toepler 2015. Government-non-profit cooperation: anomaly or necessity? *Voluntas* 26 (6): 2155–2177.
Seeleib-Kaiser, Martin, ed., 2008. *Welfare state transformations: Comparative perspectives*. Palgrave Macmillan.
Segaard, Signe Bock. 2015. *Skole og eldreomsorg i Skandinavia. Nasjonale føringer for ikke-offentlige aktører*. Rapport 2015:07. Oslo: Institutt for Samfunnsforskning.
Sivesind, Karl Henrik. 2007. Structured, qualitative comparison: Between singularity and single-dimensionality. In *Data analysis*, vol. 1, ed. Sotirios Sarantakos, 113–134. Los Angeles: Sage Publications.
Skolverket. 2014. Privata aktörer inom förskola och skola: En nationell kartläggning av enskilda huvudmän och ägare. Stockholm: Skolverket.
Smith, Steven. R., and Kirsten Grønbjerg. 2006. Scope and theory of government-non-profit relations. In *The non-profit sector. A research handbook*, eds. Walter W. Powell and Richard Steinberg, 221–242. London: Yale University Press.
Sollentuna kommun. 2008. Skolplan/utbildningsstrategi för Sollentuna kommun. Sollentuna: Sollentuna kommun. Adopted by the municipal council 2008-05-21.
Steinberg, Richard. 2006. Economic theories on nonprofit organizations. In *The non-profit sector. A research handbook*, eds. Walter W. Powell and Richard Steinberg, 117–139. London: Yale University Press.
Thelen, Kathleen. 2003. How institutions evolve. Insights from comparative historical analysis. In *Comparative historical analysis in the social sciences*, eds. James Mahoney and Dietrich Rueschemeyer, 208–240. Cambridge: Cambridge University Press.
Thuen, Harald, and Knut Tveit. 2013. Privatskolane: vere eller ikkje vere? Fire hundre år i motgang og medgang. *Tidsskrift for samfunnsforskning* 54 (4): 493–508.
Thøgersen, Malene. 2015. Explaining collaboration and commitment in Danish non-profit organizations: Linking institutional environments to outcomes. *Voluntas* 26 (5): 1639–1665.
Weisbrod, B.A. 1977. *The voluntary non-profit sector, an economic analysis*. Lexington, Mass: D.C. Heath.
Utdanningsdirektoratet. 2014. Utdanningsspeilet. Oslo. Utdanningsdirektoratet.

Author Biography

Malene Thøgersen has a Ph.D. in Political Science from University of Southern Denmark. Today, she is a researcher at the Danish Institute for Non-formal Education, Aarhus. Her main research interests are the nonprofit sector and relations between the voluntary and the public sector, primarily at the local level. Her publications include articles in *Scandinavian Political Studies* and *Voluntas*, as well as contributions to a number of anthologies within the fields of local government reforms, voluntary associations, and sports policy.

Open Access This chapter is licensed under the terms of the Creative Commons Attribution 4.0 International License (http://creativecommons.org/licenses/by/4.0/), which permits use, sharing, adaptation, distribution and reproduction in any medium or format, as long as you give appropriate credit to the original author(s) and the source, provide a link to the Creative Commons license and indicate if changes were made.

The images or other third party material in this chapter are included in the chapter's Creative Commons license, unless indicated otherwise in a credit line to the material. If material is not included in the chapter's Creative Commons license and your intended use is not permitted by statutory regulation or exceeds the permitted use, you will need to obtain permission directly from the copyright holder.

6

Active Citizenship in Scandinavian Schools and Nursing Homes

Håkon Solbu Trætteberg

Introduction

The preceding chapters in this volume have documented how welfare services in Scandinavia are changing. An insight gleaned from the chapters by Sivesind and Segaard and Saglie is how marketisation, national legislation and regulation are important drivers behind changes in the welfare mix—the composition of public, for-profit and nonprofit providers. In this chapter, I am concerned with how the users of services funded by the public sector are affected by the different providers in the welfare mix. By taking the perspective of the citizen, I document through a comparative case study analysis how the institutional sector of the provider and the use of policy instruments have relevance at the ground level of services.

A fundamental principle in western understandings of democracy is that citizens are different in all sorts of ways, and that these differences are

H.S. Trætteberg (✉)
Institute for Social Research, Oslo, Norway
e-mail: h.s.tratteberg@socialresearch.no

© The Author(s) 2017
K.H. Sivesind and J. Saglie (eds.), *Promoting Active Citizenship*,
DOI 10.1007/978-3-319-55381-8_6

important for the organisation of society but have no relevance when it comes to the right of all citizens to have autonomy and control over their own lives (Olsen 1990, 24). This is a fundamental feature of the Scandinavian citizenship model, where moving power as close as possible to the citizen is considered ideal (Hernes 1988; Andersen and Hoff 2001). Expectations of citizens, however, have been continuously growing over recent decades (Rothstein 1994, 232; Hvinden and Johansson 2007b).

In the face of the documented changes in governance tools and the welfare mix, it is vital to identify how Scandinavian users of public, for-profit and nonprofit providers differentially control their lives when they use public services. In developed welfare states, citizens have extensive interactions with welfare providers. Their ability to control their own lives in these meetings is, therefore, an important part of their citizenship (Andersen and Rossteutscher 2007). This aspect of service quality is a high priority in political documents on welfare policy in all Scandinavian countries (Rostgaard 2015, 4).

The concept of *active citizenship* can be used to analyse the consequences of welfare policy for individuals or groups in society (Hoskins 2014; Jensen and Pfau-Effinger 2005). The concept goes beyond a traditional understanding of citizenship that primarily emphasised social rights and entitlements (Marshall 1950). It emphasises possibilities for active participation through representative democracy, civil society and freedom of choice (Hvinden and Johansson 2007a). Analytically, I use the concept of active citizenship as a way of looking at the opportunities citizens have to use *choice* before they become users, *empowerment* as users at institutions and *participation* as users in local policy processes that frame operations at the institutions. Based on this analytic approach, the central questions of this chapter are: Do citizens exercise active citizenship differently in public, for-profit and nonprofit service providers? if so, what can explain it?

In this chapter, active citizenship is examined at institutions at the local level. Municipalities are instrumental in providing welfare services to citizens in Scandinavia to the extent that the welfare model has been said to be based on 'welfare municipalities' (Kröger 1997; Kjølsrød 2005). I compare the experiences of users of municipal primary and lower secondary school and nursing homes in Norway, Denmark and Sweden. Through these comparative case studies, I examine the differences between the three institutional sectors: public, for-profit and nonprofit. I also compare the consequences of different conditions regarding the governing structures that were analysed in the preceding chapters focusing on schools and nursing homes. Therefore, in addition to the institutional sectors, the cases were selected to make it possible to compare across countries and service areas. For further information about the selection of cases, see Chap. 1.

Studies of increased marketisation and changes in the welfare mix have often focused on efficient provision and economic savings for the public purse (Domberger and Jensen 1997; Hood and Dixon 2015), or on different forms of quality such as the number of staff and use of physical restraints in elderly care (Comondore et al. 2009), and test scores in schools (Hanushek et al. 2013). Relevant to this study is research that shows how marketisation and changes in the welfare mix have impacted the relationship between citizens and the state (Clarke 2006; Clarke et al. 2007), as well as how Scandinavian countries are particularly exposed to such changes due to their tradition of universal public services (Anttonen and Meagher 2013; Kröger 1997). Judgments about the consequences of marketisation vary. Some studies have warned of deteriorating solidarity between and powerlessness of users when faced with market entrepreneurs (Christensen 2012; Eriksen and Weigård 1993). Others have pointed that the potential users have to achieve more control when they obtain consumer or customer rights (Rothstein 1998; Kumlin 2004).

The relevance of using an active citizenship approach to study this issue is accentuated by a report from the Norwegian Centre for Human Rights, which documents breaches of human rights in Norwegian nursing homes. The report identified users' inability to make their voices heard as one explanation for unsatisfactory action to improve the citizen-rights situation (Norsk senter for menneskerettigheter 2014). Given that user power and opportunities for active citizenship are important for the quality of services, I examine these aspects in light of the local governance of services and the use of providers from different institutional sectors. To set the stage for this discussion, the following section presents and subsequently operationalises the analytic concept of active citizenship. The empirical approach used in this chapter overlaps with that used in the preceding two chapters, but a short reminder is also included before the analysis is presented.

Active Citizenship

Active citizenship is a contested concept that scholars and policymakers have used in a number of different ways (Hoskins 2014). Before using active citizenship as an analytic tool, it is necessary to first establish the concept in relation to the existing uses of the term, and to show how it is useful for the analytic purposes of this chapter.

Within the context of local service delivery, the content of publicly financed services is decided by actors in three different roles: the user and their next of kin, the staff and leaders at the institutions and the policymakers and administrators at the municipal level (Daly and Lewis 2000, 287). Users and their next of kin can influence the content of services in meetings with both staff and managers, as well as with policymakers and administrators at the municipal level. An analytic approach based on the capacity users have to exercise an active citizenship role can deepen understanding of these relations.

I use the concept of active citizenship to analyse services from the perspective of users (i.e. citizens) and to map how users can control and influence their lives when using public services. The extent to which users can influence their own lives is directly related to their potential to influence services at three different levels. First, if and how they can choose a provider before they become users. This choice also includes the option to change providers. Second, if and how they can influence the institution's services while they are users. Third, if and how they can influence the municipality that sets the frames for the service provider. Based on this tripartite understanding of users' capacity to control their lives in relation to service providers, I develop three dimensions of active citizenship in order to analyse differences in the capacity for active citizenship for users (and their next of kin) of public, for-profit and non-profit welfare services: *choice, empowerment* and *participation*.

Investigating the experiences users have when interacting with welfare providers can provide insight into the functioning of the welfare model in terms of the autonomy of citizens, the division of labour, responsibility and influence. The concept of active citizenship allows us to evaluate these features or functions from the users' point of view (Jensen and Pfau-Effinger 2005; Boje and Potucek 2011b). Although hailed as a universal and solidary welfare regime, the Nordic welfare states are also remarkably individualistic in the sense that different welfare instruments are consistently based on individual autonomy (Trägårdh 1997, 253). The welfare programmes are tied to individuals, and through them the state seeks to give individuals autonomy from alternative structures such as charities, families and employers (Trägårdh 2008). This perspective on the state's role in the welfare society reveals a longstanding tradition of striving to expand the individuals' control of their everyday lives, also when dependent on public transfers or services. When new instruments are used in the welfare state, individual rights can be expanded with correspondingly new duties, which is a natural process in societies with a more skilled and individualistic population both able and willing to enjoy a growing level of individual autonomy (Andersen 2005, 87).

If growing individual rights and room for influence in the implementation stage of the political process are observed, this may enhance the individualistic features of the social democratic model. At the earlier stages of social democracy, the strategy of granting cash assistance and not only benefits in kind to single mothers was an example of the belief that individuals have the right to make decisions concerning their own lives (Rothstein 1998); thus, the expansion of active citizenship can be viewed as a continuation and further development of this feature of the social democratic model. At the same time, equality in service quality is also an important value in the social democratic model. Whether these mechanisms are compatible, or whether they pull in opposing directions, is an empirical question.

The capacity for active citizenship can have wider implications. When the power of users influences the implementation of policies, the experience of the citizenry as a whole can change; small, incremental steps can, over time, change the welfare arrangement, almost as if by stealth (Hinrichs and Kangas 2003). A growth in the importance of policy implementation at the expense of electoral politics is a common finding in Scandinavian power studies (Andersen 2006, 580). Strong electoral legitimacy is a cornerstone of Scandinavian democracy, but much of this legitimacy is determined on the output side where the citizens experience the results of decisions made by policymakers, and one such important result is the public welfare services (Rothstein 2009; Gustavsen et al. 2014). What happens on this side of the democratic process is thus also important to consider.

Currently, citizen involvement in forming welfare services is becoming a critical issue in international scholarly debates (Boje and Potucek 2011b; Evers and Guillemard 2013a, 24). Evers and Guillemard (2013a) emphasised how using active citizenship as an analytic tool gives insight into the 'responsibility mix': the division of rights and obligations between the state, civil society and individual citizens. This division involves deciding which tasks should be assigned to different actors, and also provides a basis for normative perceptions about the suitable size of each institutional sector. In Western Europe, the governments' redistributive role is increasingly being supplemented by attempts to motivate citizens, as the states assume the role as orchestrators of last resort. In this capacity, the states must balance their interest in the individual autonomy of citizens, commercial enterprises and other special interests in the welfare fields, with their economic goals, including social investment agendas (Evers and Guillemard 2013b). At the same time, variations in user preferences are arguably also growing as societies become more diverse (Boje and Potucek 2011a, 13; Phillips and Smith 2011). This calls for the active involvement of users and citizens in forming the content of services.

The concept of active citizenship can elucidate these developments and show how welfare states are dynamic entities in spite of their stability on many variables (Palier 2007). In using the concept, I recognise that users can seek to influence both staff at the level of local institutions and local policymakers. Active citizenship thus maps the landscape of user control and, in our case, this landscape is limited by borders established by national and EU laws, regulations and policies. Therefore, analyses focusing on active citizenship connect the individual experiences of users with overarching changes in the welfare model.

Operationalisation of Active Citizenship

Hirschman (1970) identified two main strategies for users to obtain changes from an organisation: exit and voice. The first strategy involves either exiting or threatening to exit an organisation. This will give the organisation an incentive to accommodate the wishes of users and is thus an empowering instrument for users. This strategy is related to the use of *choice* in my framework. The second strategy involves the use of voice by users who stay in an organisation, and who advocate changes within them. Here, users do not leave the organisation but try to produce changes by identifying aspects they believe to be unacceptable. This relates to my notions of user *empowerment* and *participation*, whereby users voice their interests at the institutional or municipal level, respectively.

In terms of choice, the central features are whether the option to choose can enhance the power of citizens as customers, and whether the available alternatives are distinctive enough to increase variation in the services offered to citizens. For choice to be an important aspect of power relations, alternatives must exist that are real options and not just formal possibilities. The most powerful action taken by a user who is dissatisfied with a service is to exit an institution altogether (Hirschman 1970). This is the solution Blomqvist and Rothstein (2008, 18) recommended for amending the asymmetrical power relationship between users and staff at the institution and the policymakers' ultimate lack of control over policy output. In addition, letting users choose institutions can also increase the capacity for active citizenship by expanding the scope of public services. When users can choose between different institutions with their own distinctive content, the chances of getting services in line with the users' interests and needs also increases (Smith and Grønbjerg 2006, 224). Distinctive alternatives are therefore an essential component of choice. For the citizen, a central prerequisite for exploiting a broader range of services is knowing what is available. Information is therefore also an important aspect of choice (Le Grand and Bartlett 1993). From a citizen's perspective, the capacity for active citizenship expands when public services are more diverse and cater to minorities and other groups whose preferences and interests deviate from the majority.

Empowerment is a matter of how users and their next of kin voice their concerns about what happens at an institution and what changes they can obtain. This can take place formally or informally (Andersen 2004, 25). Arenas set up by institutions or users (e.g. user boards) comprise formal mechanisms for voice. Central to these are how they are included in the overall steering of an institution (Rose 2007). Circumstances or settings in which users can affect their situations through day-to-day interactions with staff or other official members of institutions constitute informal mechanisms for voice. Interaction between users and providers is a fundamental aspect of services, and in this sense co-production is a feature of all services (Osborne et al. 2013, 139). Since the study by Parks et al. (1981), the focus on co-production has dealt with costs for the government and the improvement of service quality (OECD 2011; Alford 2014, 300). In this study, I am more concerned with how co-production affects power relations between users and providers, as well as how users can influence services. When citizens involve themselves in institutions that are part of their everyday lives, they become 'everyday makers'. They may have no ambition to influence what happens in the large-scale democracy, but when various individuals take steps to make changes in their close surroundings, it becomes something 'democracy cannot afford to dismiss, neither in theory nor in practice' (Bang and Sørensen 1999, 336).

Choice and empowerment pertain to active citizenship in the implementation of public policies. The third dimension, participation, involves participation in the development of public policies at the local level. This dimension concerns user involvement in relevant political settings and how users perceive their level of influence or their political efficacy (Andersen 2004, 25). When users influence the interpretation of public policies, they operate within politically defined frames. When they are able to influence local policymaking, they influence the frames themselves: The resources held by users when approaching the municipal level, the arenas set up to facilitate such approaches, and the responsiveness of the municipality decides the scope of this influence. The fundamental issue regarding active citizenship is that the experiences made at the institutions have real influence on policymaking. In practical terms, this is an issue of the advocacy role of institutions and individual users vis-à-vis the municipal political and administrative level. User surveys are not part of the advocacy efforts of users, but represent the only tool for the municipalities to directly collect the views of many users at the same time and are thus a relevant aspect to consider.

The definition of active citizenship covers what we may refer to as the basic level or background concept (Goertz 2006; Adcock and Collier 2001). The second level consists of the three dimensions. These dimensions are ontological in the sense that they constitute the background concept. Based on these dimensions, I developed indicators than can be evaluated. These indicators are not necessarily internally correlated, but can be functionally equivalent, which means that the strong occurrence of one indicator can substitute for the lack of occurrence of another indicator of the same dimension (Goertz 2006, 15). The qualitative data gathering process was designed to capture variations in the dimensions of active citizenship and to be able to conduct qualitative comparisons between institutions. The scores on the indicators are therefore qualitative. What is interesting is the value on one provider's indicator as compared to the other providers. Table 6.1 illustrates the relationship between different levels of the concept.

Table 6.1 Active citizenship, dimensions, and empirical indicators

Background concept	Dimensions	Empirical indicators
Active citizenship	Choice	Promoting a broader range of services where more users obtain services that cater to their interests
		Formal and real exit opportunities give power to users
	Empowerment	Influence through collective representation in user boards
		Influence through individuals' day-to-day contacts with staff
	Participation	Interactions between user representatives and municipal decision-makers, either directly or mediated by civil society organisations

For each dimension, I developed indicators that allow for the observation of variations as well as comparisons. For the dimension of *choice*, I looked at the capacity users have to choose a provider when they initially become users of a service and to what degree they may exit an institution. I developed two indicators for this dimension. First, I assessed if the opportunity to choose and exit providers is important for power relations. Choice gives power to users if municipal or institutional representatives report changing the content of a service in order to avoid user exits or attract more users. Likewise, users' perception of exit as a tool for obtaining changes indicates that they have power as opposed to situations where there is no exit opportunity. There is a continuum between no exit opportunity and full exit opportunity. Second, I evaluated whether the opportunity for choice leads to a wider range of services for citizens. If users are able to choose alternatives that constitute distinct services from those offered by public providers, the entire scope of public service becomes broader. When public services can cover a broader range of citizen preferences, the capacity for active citizenship is expanded.

Indicators of empowerment focus on two forms of user influence. First, I mapped how user boards take part in steering and influencing the activities of institutions. The accessibility of user boards and their level of influence are central components of this measure. Second, I examined how users experience the opportunities they have to obtain changes through day-to-day interactions with other users.

I evaluated participation by looking at arenas where users have access to decision makers at the municipal level, and I examined how representatives and decision makers perceived user influence in these arenas. I also looked at municipal interest organisations, like councils for the elderly, which channel the interests of users toward the municipal level. In some cases, these channels were missing altogether.

The Importance of Individual Characteristics of Staff and Users

Even if the institutional sector of a provider matters for active citizenship, it is not the only factor explaining variations in active citizenship. The actions of individuals who operate within the frames of institutions make up the capacity for active citizenship. The capacity for active citizenship is affected by which sector an institution belongs to because it frames the decision making of its leaders, staff and users (Thornton et al. 2012). How individuals choose to use the flexibility that exists within the frames influences much of the variation between institutions. If nonprofit institutions generally have more space than public institutions to promote empowerment, institutional leaders at public institutions can still, due to their individual abilities, empower users more than leaders of nonprofit institutions. Accordingly, what this study sets out to reveal are differences in the potential for active citizenship that exist between the different types of providers. This potential is sometimes exploited fully, while at other times we can only speak of latent control of everyday life.

In addition to variations in how leaders and staff at providers exploit the capacity for active citizenship within their institutional frames, user characteristics are another factor to consider when evaluating active citizenship (Bang et al. 2000). When it comes to welfare services, one central characteristic is the health of users. Users of nursing homes have health problems that make it difficult for many of them to exploit the capacity for active citizenship. This renders users unable to seek more active citizenship and makes facilitating more active citizenship less relevant for providers. In the school sector, the parents of students are primarily the ones who enjoy active citizenship. They are often able and willing to pursue as much influence as they can obtain.

The latent or potential capacity for active citizenship says something about how users can influence services. Some users do not wish to be active citizens, but their interest in good services is nevertheless just as acute as any other citizen. If the capacity for active citizenship leads to some citizens being able to obtain better services than others, then this constitutes a relevant aspect of the analysis. At the same time, opportunities for user influence can also be important for those who do not actively use it at any given time. The existence of such channels for influence is like 'security valves' in the system. They may not be in use at all times, and they may seem insignificant on a day-to-day basis, but they can make a huge difference once users feel that things need to change.

Data and Methodology

The empirical analysis in this chapter is based on the same material as in the preceding chapters. I will therefore not repeat all of the details of the design, which are presented in the appendix to Chap. 1. In each country, we selected two municipalities (plus a third municipality in Norway where only schools were studied). In each municipality, one public institution and one nonpublic institution were compared in both the school and the nursing home sectors. National experts in each country carried out the qualitative investigation with a shared field guide as the basis for data gathering. The primary sources of data were semi-structured interviews and focus groups. In total, we conducted 35 interviews in Denmark, 21 in Sweden, and 57 in Norway. These data were triangulated with studies of central documents in the investigated municipalities and institutions, in addition to local user surveys where relevant. There is no room for statistical generalisations from these case studies, but they do highlight some mechanisms that help us understand conditions that expand the capacity for active citizenship.

Analysis and Findings

For each service area, I analysed the different dimensions of active citizenship—choice, empowerment and participation—across the analytic dimensions by country and institutional sector. I start by presenting an analysis of the nursing home sector in the three countries before turning to an analysis of the school sector in the same three countries.

Nursing Homes

Choice—Diversity in Services and Exit Opportunities for Users?

In the Norwegian and Swedish municipalities, the users of nursing homes do not have user choice because the municipalities allocate citizens to the nursing homes. Users can request certain homes, but due to excess demand, they must normally take the first slot that opens. The consequence of this system can be frustrating for users. The daughter of a user in Norway explains:

> I was at the counter at the grocery store when my phone rang. The person tells me: your mother can have a place [in the nursing home] now, but you must decide within an hour. You know what I felt, I was so angry. Am I supposed to turn everything upside down? We had applied many months before and then we get one hour to change your life, take it, or leave it. [...] Am I supposed to take this decision without talking to her? (Interview, user representative, municipal nursing home, Norway)

Since 2005, Danes have had user choice between nursing homes in the same municipality. The poor health of users means that the choice is mainly exercised by their next of kin. The effectiveness of this right is limited by the lack of a sufficient number of nursing home places. When a slot in a nursing home opens up, a user will typically take that slot. Thus, in spite of the formal user choice opportunity in Denmark, actual differences between the Scandinavian countries in terms of user choice in nursing homes are negligible.

Even if users are not free to choose nursing homes, they can make requests. As much as possible, all municipalities claim to try to accommodate user requests. Interviewees from different positions stress geography as the most important factor for users. The leader at one of the Danish diaconal nursing homes sums up the importance of geography:

> I believe geography is most important. I wish I could say that it is because of us, but it is not. People live in this area, and of course, they want to stay

because here is where they have their social environment and their children. When they first are here, they are happy to be here, and their children are happy. Yet it is mostly geography, no doubt. We can see the same with ourselves. No matter where we live, we do not want to move to the other side of the country if we were to move to a nursing home. We want to be in a well-known, safe environment where we belong. (Interview, site manager, nonprofit nursing home, Denmark)

Even though some of the studied municipalities have introduced open tenders, there are no differences between municipalities in terms of how nursing homes compete to attract users. There is thus no sense of competition between the different options and no exit opportunity that could affect power relations. The staff and leaders at the different nursing homes did not perceive of themselves as providers who attract users in a market.

The lack of user choice also complicates the opportunities nonpublic providers have for providing services distinct from those of the public sector. With the high demand for nursing home slots, municipalities want all available nursing homes to provide a uniform service so that deciding which homes to allocate users to is a non-issue. Since the interviewees specified geographic proximity to their home or their relatives' homes as the primary factor in requesting a particular nursing home, it is in their interest that the nursing homes do not represent different concepts, as they do not want to risk that the closest nursing home does not provide a service that suits them.

Therefore, when municipalities present information about their nursing homes, they do not point to substantive differences, since effectively there are none. In some cases, municipalities do not even differentiate between public and nonpublic options on their websites. The administrative leader of one of the municipalities suggested that citizens do not know which nursing homes are public and which are nonpublic, a claim which underscores how difficult it is for users to choose providers based on institutional sectors.

Still, leaders at all the nonprofit nursing homes stressed that they found *their* nursing home to be distinct from the public option. All nonprofit nursing homes in our study were faith-based. Their Christian values are demonstrated in how they operate, albeit with respect for non-Christian residents. Since their users have not specifically chosen Christian nursing homes, administrators cannot impose their faith on them. As the leader of one of the Danish nursing homes put it:

> It is the diaconal, the spiritual care, that is in focus. A good thing about spiritual care is that it is not measurable. It is lovely that we have one field where one cannot measure everything. Because how do you measure that we have read the Lord's Prayer today? [...] for me the importance of this has increased over the years as I have experienced that the elderly want this. They need the space for reflection that spiritual care provides. In reality, this is mostly about reflection. (Interview, site manager, nonprofit nursing home, Denmark)

The user representatives at this nursing home share this view, but point out the conditions for the employees, and not the users, when referring to the particular diaconal institution. They found that the diaconal respect for individuals makes the nursing home a good employer, but they do not find that the diaconal basis of the nursing home affects the content of the care.

The staff members also recognised the particular aspects of spiritual care, but qualified them by claiming that represented minor differences:

> Well, I do not know what to say, but I do not notice the big difference. I simply do not. Of course, there is worship in the afternoon. Moreover, we have the services. I do not know if this is more than in other nursing homes, but in my daily life, I do not notice any difference. (Interview, staff member, nonprofit nursing home, Denmark)

The for-profit nursing homes do not have the same inherent alternative values as the public option. The Norwegian for-profit nursing home still claims to be distinctive by employing a 'service concept' imported from the hotel business branch of the firm. Interestingly, none of the users, staff or municipal representatives found that the for-profit nursing home demonstrated any distinctiveness from public institutions.

Yet, the importance of institutional sectors for local policymakers is evident. One of the Swedish municipalities has gone the furthest by introducing market mechanisms. It uses tenders to allocate contracts, and within the public structure, it has an autonomous unit that operates like a provider entity. The Conservative leadership in the municipality allocates contracts to it because they regard having a public option as 'important for the user choice'. It is difficult to understand this reasoning as the users cannot themselves choose institutions, and the municipalities themselves claim there are no substantive differences. At the same time, it recognises the potential differences between different institutional sectors. In addition, by having providers from different institutional sectors, this municipality has benchmarks that can be useful for assessing the different providers.

In conclusion, the regulatory regime of nonpublic nursing homes gives some freedom to operate according to local institutional initiatives. It is, however, unclear if this room for local initiatives is bigger for nonpublic than for public institutions. The lack of user choice means that there is no power based on opportunities users might have to exit a provider.

Empowerment—How Users Can Influence at an Institution

All nursing homes in this study have tried, with or without success, to establish user boards. In all cases, the formal arenas for user involvement in nursing homes are based on the participation of relatives. Eighty percent of nursing home users in Norway suffer from dementia (Haugen and Engedal 2005), and reports from staff and municipalities suggest the situation is similar in Denmark and Sweden.

When it comes to the functioning of user boards, there is no systematic difference between homes belonging to different sectors. The functioning of user boards is in all cases somewhat up to the users themselves. As one Norwegian municipal manager puts it:

> User board, it is almost dangerous to say, because we had a project, you may have heard about it, at the municipal nursing home. It was very

dependent on some vital persons to run it on such an advanced scale as they expected. When these persons no longer had their loved ones at the nursing home, the user board, I will not put it explicitly, was transformed into a friend's organisation [that encourages volunteer efforts]. (Interview, administrative leader, municipality, Norway)

The situation today is that the user board mostly coordinates volunteer activities and does not play an important role in the steering of institutions, even though they are sometimes consulted.

In Denmark, both nonprofit nursing homes have closed their user boards due to lack of interest from relatives; the same thing has happened to both nursing homes in one municipality in Sweden. The lack of user boards in the municipality does not concern any of the leaders of the institutions, but they find it somewhat frustrating that there are no relatives willing to contribute: 'I understand completely [that people have busy lives], but we have 52 residents, it should be possible to find 3–4 persons' (Interview, site manager, municipal nursing home, Sweden).

At the same time, there have been successful attempts to establish user boards. In the for-profit nursing home in Norway, the leader of the user board believed that the leader of the institution felt threatened by how the user board interfered in how the institution was run, implying that the user board's influence was real. In this municipality, municipal guidelines instruct the head of the nursing home to discuss important plans and changes with the user board before making final decisions. When initiatives come from user representatives, they normally concern detailed aspects of care, not the long-term development of the institutions themselves. Likewise, in Denmark, a municipal leader describes the importance of their user board:

> It is a demand that we involve the next of kin and the residents in what happens, and why should we change something that works? Therefore, we will keep our user board and we will keep elections for who can be in it. We have elections almost every time because there are more people running than we need in the board. We do not have any problems getting people to participate in the board, and as the representatives from the staff say: 'everyone should experience a user-next of kin board.' Imagine all our

old users who are immobile and can almost do nothing, and then they appear [in the board meetings] with pen and pencil. (Interview, site manager, municipal nursing home, Denmark)

Generally, the interviewees agreed that there were variations over time in the nursing homes, but the willingness and ability of the user board members to take an active role explains these variations. Accordingly, it is difficult to conclude that variations in the functioning of user boards can be attributed to the institutional sector.

The interviewees cited day-to-day contacts as the most important route for obtaining changes on behalf of users. Most users in all institutions were content with the possibility of exerting influence via this channel. The exception were those who would have liked more services, such as follow-ups from physiotherapists, which are limited due to cost issues. This exemplifies how changes with budgetary consequences are difficult to obtain, while other changes are easier to achieve. Changes in budgetary frames are decided at the municipal level. To obtain these sorts of changes, users need to try to participate in arenas which channel their interests to this level.

Some interviewees among the staff and leadership at nonprofit nursing homes pointed to increased flexibility outside of the public hierarchy, which allows more adaptation to user needs. It seems difficult, however, to infer if this is an effect of ownership or of variation in how nursing homes exploit their ability to manoeuvre. Users at public institutions were also happy with the possibilities they had to influence services, as illustrated by a user at a municipal institution:

> I find that both leaders we have here are very open to us in the user-next of kin board. In addition, I have the impression that they are very open to all the users and want to do a lot to make sure this is a good place to live.
> (Interview, user representative, municipal nursing home, Denmark)

There is no contradiction between collective and individual empowerment, but there is the perception that individual empowerment can compensate for a lack of collective empowerment. One leader of a nursing home found that the lack of a user board was no problem because of individual empowerment:

> This is why one does not miss the user board. One has good contact with them [the relatives] and they come here to visit. The nurse and the designated contact staff talk to the relatives and ask if they have any questions. (Interview, site manager, municipal nursing home, Sweden)

On the other hand, we were unable to collect data from users with the most fragile health. There is, therefore, a risk that their interests are not as well represented as the interests of those who can articulate themselves better. It is not possible to affirmatively conclude that providers belonging to a specific institutional sector have better levels of individual empowerment.

Participation—How User Experiences are Translated to the Municipal Level

The dimension of participation is where the biggest differences between the three countries were observed. In all three countries, local politicians stressed that they wanted input from users, and they all gave users and other citizens access to their meetings. The differences observed included how local policymakers actively invited users to provide their input and how users sought to directly influence the municipal level.

One thing the Scandinavian countries have in common is municipal elderly councils or associations that speak on their behalf. One example from Norway shows how interactions between this type of council and nonpublic providers can be mutually reinforcing, as the council uses the professional expertise of the nonprofit nursing home to strengthen their arguments with the municipality. The leader of the nonprofit nursing home explains:

> They are quite good at approaching us, perhaps because they see that we think somewhat differently in certain areas, and then they ask. I let them know if I want to try out something […] and when big issues for the

council for the elderly arise, it is obvious that we discuss them. What are the needs? They have many opinions themselves, but sometimes I think they need some help with some additional arguments. (Interview, site manager, for-profit nursing home, Norway)

The presence of a nonprofit nursing home thereby empowers the elderly in the municipality by giving them access to professional opinions that may challenge the municipal structure.

In Norway, both nonpublic nursing homes are integrated with the public system when it comes to this issue. The public and nonpublic nursing homes administer the same user surveys, which thus have the same potential for leading to changes in all institutional sectors. One of the municipalities holds annual meetings between user boards and the relevant committee in the municipal council. Opinions differ between municipal representatives and users in regards to how constructive these meetings are. Both the administrative and political leadership were very clear, as in this statement from the administrative leader:

> The dialogue meetings are the basis for the budget process. The CEO of the municipality has the results as the fundament of the priorities in the strategic plans. He often uses the input from these dialogue processes when he suggests future focuses and priorities. That is what can happen, and it does not happen seldom. (Interview, administrative leader, municipality, Norway)

Users, on the other hand, were more sceptical:

> Afterward, we concluded that [the meeting] had little commitment. The politicians said something, we said something, but there were no minutes of the meeting. Moreover, many issues were raised that had no place in the municipal budget. (Interview, user representatives, municipal nursing home, Norway)

It seems like users had no information about the consequences of the meeting and had no way of knowing how their input could make an impact. In this sense, they might have more influence than they make use of or realise.

In Denmark, at both the nonprofit and municipal nursing homes, the user boards have had an active role in defending the interests of the nursing homes in relation to the municipality. There are examples from both forms of nursing homes of incidents where active lobbying from the user boards has prevented municipal budget cuts. The leader of a municipal nursing home gives a telling example of the role the user board can play:

> At one point, in 2010, it was suggested by politicians that our kitchen should close, and that we should get food from Aulum [a central kitchen] like the other nursing homes. I must say, at that time we had some fine next of kins. They are the ones we can thank for having our kitchen today. That is for sure. They were present at the town hall, sent letters to the editors of newspapers, and called politicians. They were the ones who did the job. (Interview, site manager, municipal nursing home, Denmark)

This clearly shows how the user board takes responsibility for the nursing home in its relations with the municipality. Interestingly, the nonprofit nursing home chose to stand outside of the public structure, but users still found it natural to lobby the municipal level when they wanted changes. The leader of the user board gives one example:

> I told the leadership at one point: we have to write a letter and send it to all the members of the city council because I do not think they know what is going on here [...] and that is what we did, and then – I promise – things started to happen. I spoke on the phone with some of the members of the council and they did not know what they had said yes to. (Interview, user representative, nonprofit nursing home, Denmark)

As we can see from these examples, the fight for resources is what interviewees at the nursing homes pointed to when describing their external role, and this role is the same for both public and nonprofit nursing homes. It is up to the nursing homes themselves to be active in approaching the municipal level, since there are no formal arenas where

Table 6.2 Active citizenship in the nursing home sector

	Norway	Denmark	Sweden	Shared findings
Choice				
Creation of diverse service options	Little diversity in content across institutional sectors	Little diversity in content across institutional sectors	Little diversity in content across institutional sectors	Little diversity in content across institutional sectors
Exit opportunities give power to users.	No user choice and thus no power from exit opportunities	Formally user choice, but limited by lack of capacity. No power from exit opportunities	No user choice and thus no power from exit opportunities	Little to no power to users stemming from exit opportunities
Empowerment				
Collective	Limited by user health, but little difference due to institutional sectors	Limited by user health, but little difference due to institutional sectors	Limited by user health, but little difference due to institutional sectors	Limited by user health, but little difference due to institutional sectors
Individual	Small differences between institutions	Small differences between institutions	Small differences between institutions	Small differences between institutions
Participation	Small differences due to institutional sectors. Possible to obtain changes	Small difference due to institutional sectors. User boards can engage actively with the municipality, mainly to obtain resources	Open door policy for all citizens, but little direct interaction between the municipality and users at institutions	Differences between countries, but not institutional sectors

representatives from the user boards can interact directly with municipal leaders.

In Sweden, politicians practice an 'open door' policy where committee meetings are open to the public, and citizens are welcome to make statements to politicians. Politicians report that few citizens use this opportunity, but they still believe it is a good way of promoting transparency in the municipality. In addition, both municipalities have politicians dedicated to following up with the different nursing homes and keeping in touch with the user boards, where these exist.

The more prominent form of citizen involvement in Sweden is through councils for the elderly that influence local policymaking. They have no formal ties to users of the nursing homes and do not work differently with institutions based on their institutional sector. In sum, Sweden has fewer formal routes for user participation in municipal policy formulation.

Table 6.2 summarises the findings for active citizenship in the nursing home sector. The table shows that there are small differences between the different institutional sectors as well as between countries. For citizens, their ability to control services did not vary that much across different institutions in Scandinavia.

Schools

Choice—Diversity in Services and Exit Opportunities for Users?

All countries have user choice where families are free to select nonpublic schools. In Sweden, these schools can come from all three institutional sectors. In Denmark, nonpublic schools that receive public funding must be self-owned and thus nonprofit. In Norway, nonpublic schools that receive public funding may not distribute profits or channel funds out of the schools in any way. All income from the state and user fees must benefit the students. These regulations entail that practically all nonpublic schools in Norway are nonprofit. In all municipalities, families have a local school where they belong to and have the right to attend.

To choose to attend a nonpublic school thus represents an active choice to exit this local alternative. How much the families use this opportunity varies. In one Danish municipality, only 56% of students attended their local schools; while in Norwegian municipalities, more than 90% of students attended their local schools.

In Norway, the main motivation for selecting a nonprofit school are the special services they offer. For the religion-based nonprofit schools, the view of this parent is typical: 'The Christian influence and the values we have, they get them both at school and at home; the values we have, they get them at school also' (Interview, parent, nonprofit school, Norway). The other schools, which have alternative approaches to teaching as their basis, point to their holistic approach to each student and relaxed approach to testing and competition as examples of their special qualities.

At the same time, there was a large minority of families whose choices were not determined by the schools' conceptual framework. Rather, they actively make a choice away from the public schools. These families shared a negative experience with the public schools, and approached nonprofit schools as a last resort. One mother gives a telling example about her daughter:

> She has had some difficulty concentrating throughout her schooling. As parents, we have seen it, but the school has not taken it seriously and handled it as we wanted. In the end, the girl practically perished. It was a matter of surviving. (Interview, parent, nonprofit school, Norway)

In Denmark, which has a bigger share of students in nonprofit schools, there are many reasons for choosing a specific school. The distinctiveness of a school is one reason among several, and the importance of this factor varies substantially. One parent who found the distinctiveness of a school to be of great importance states:

> No, it is not my experience that to go to a nonprofit school is a conscious decision. Unfortunately, seen from my perspective, I experience that at least in the grade of my youngest child, that in selecting the school many think it is a for-profit school [something that does not exist in Denmark].

At least it is a negative choice, away from the public school. (Interview, parent, nonprofit school, Denmark)

Disappointment about the lack of conviction on the part of some parents was shared by teachers who found that there were two kinds of families: the classical 'nonprofit family' that treasures the distinctiveness of nonprofit schools, and the kind of family that seeks an alternative to public school with little concern for the actual content of the alternative. In order for this latter group to be pleased with a nonprofit school, deviation from public schools cannot be too pronounced. The share of students attending nonprofit schools seems to reflect how much these schools deviate from the public option.

Nonprofit schools take active measures to defend their distinctiveness. They vary in terms of their particular type of distinctiveness, but share an emphasis on the collective, which is an important finding in our case study schools. In these schools, parents are expected to be involved in different aspects related to their operation. One headmaster made it a point to be explicit about this expectation in his first conversation with potential parents in order to maintain loyalty to the principles of the school:

> I know that I have scared away parents and they have simply said: it is so much collectivity and participation; it is simply not us. (Interview, site manager, nonprofit school, Denmark)

In the same way that nonprofit values are important for some of the families who choose this kind of school, values also underpin the decision to select municipal schools. Denmark has traditionally had many non-public schools, which has caused some parents to rally around the public option. One parent at a municipal school explained: 'When we moved here we were aware that there was a nonprofit school here, but in our family we are by principle against opting against the public school' (Interview, parent, public school, Denmark). This parent went on to describe the effect on social integration when students from different families in the same neighbourhood attend the same local school; something he contrasted with nonprofit schools, where he found that the group of parents were more homogeneous. In sum, the motivation for choosing a specific school can be based on values in both public and nonprofit schools.

Interestingly, for-profit schools in Sweden are not perceived as offering something substantively different when it comes to teaching methodology, religion or ideology. Here, when families make their initial decision, geography is the most important factor. In addition, the administrative leader in one municipality mentioned other factors that were revealed in an internal investigation in the municipality. What was surprising was that the profiles of the nonpublic schools, like a special orientation toward sports, were hardly mentioned by the parents. Instead, they mentioned quality, group pressure and opting out of the public option.

Moreover, the lack of distinctiveness between Swedish schools makes changing between them an available option for families that do not want something substantively different from their local schools, and this creates a competitive dynamic. In all Swedish schools, staff members report that parents use the threat of changing schools when arguing their case. According to the schools themselves, changing schools is more of a problem for students than it is for schools, as it does not occur often enough to affect the schools but can be disruptive for students. Still, the schools reported that their operation was dependent on attracting students, and headmasters in different schools reported that they believed that competition inspired them to remain competitive: 'We feel the competition and that has made us clearer and better' (Interview, site manager, public school, Sweden).

A similar effect was seen in Denmark, where competitive pressure is growing. The number of students in Denmark is set to decrease in coming years since the total number of children in each generation is getting smaller. In combination with substantial reforms to public schools that have increased the number of lessons given per week, a competitive environment has been created where leaders of both types of schools must make active choices in order to stay competitive. A statement by a teacher at a nonprofit school exemplifies this trend:

> We tell ourselves that we are a collective and such things, and that is obviously true, but it is also a business. We need some customers in the

shop; if not, there is no money to run the collective. So yes, we are in competition with local municipal schools to attract students. I do not find that there is any bad blood between the two institutions, but it is something we have to deal with – e.g., with the new reforms and the new number of lessons a week, we need to be on par with local public schools. I strongly doubt that this is needed for nonprofit schools in more densely populated areas. (Interview, staff member, nonprofit school, Denmark)

In spite of the blunt admission that competition is altering how schools are run, this teacher concluded that the distinctiveness of the school can be preserved: 'That is exactly what we fear, but I doubt it. The big challenge is to follow the development while at the same time not becoming too similar. I do not really think so because there are certain things that make us unique' (Interview, staff member, nonprofit school, Denmark).

In Norway, competition between public and nonprofit schools is an unfamiliar concept. Families choose nonprofit schools primarily because they give them services better suited to their preferences. Interestingly, although some parents expressed discontent with public schools, none used the exit option as a tool for obtaining change at their former public schools. Moreover, headmasters at the schools did not regard the threat of exit as a potential instrument for students to obtain changes. One headmaster at a public school pointed out that they tried to keep their students and would accommodate them to avoid changes, but that it was to a certain degree unavoidable. At the same time, more students enter the school than leave it, as the headmaster observes: 'It is not always we get star students, to speak plainly. Often there is 'something' when you change school' (Interview, site manager, public school, Norway). This suggests that often it is the weaker, more demanding students who change schools, especially when the change is between public schools, since these families do not seek distinctiveness or wish to opt out of public school. Since these students demand many resources, it might not be beneficial for schools to attract them in the first place.

Information is pivotal for parents to make an active choice when choosing schools and making use of the alternatives they have. Differences in this sense reflect the tradition of school types in the different countries. In Denmark, the law requires all nonprofit schools to publish their values on their websites, but as the preceding quote demonstrates, parents are sometimes still uninformed about the schools before they approach them directly. In Norway, there are no such rules, but nonprofit schools belong to three categories: Christian, Montessori and Waldorf (Steiner), and most families that consider opting out of public school have an idea about what they consist of. There is no information readily available about them though, so one can speculate that more families would be interested in the nonprofit option if they knew what they had to offer. In Sweden, schools from different institutional sectors have less distinctive profiles, so such information is deemed irrelevant. However, parents actively searching for information can find quality indicators, such as results from user surveys and test results from the schools.

A different aspect of choice seems to involve a contradiction between giving users power through exit opportunities and broadening services. If there is to be a level of competition that moves power from the institution to the user, services cannot be too distinctive. If different actors cater to different students, many families will only find one suitable institution for themselves. This empowers them as they do find good options, but it does not give them improved opportunities for asking for changes from the institutions.

Generally, the opportunity for choice is associated with somewhat different effects in the three countries. In Norway and Denmark, which only allow nonprofit schools, choice spurs the development of schools that are distinct from the public option. In Sweden, there is less variation between schools across institutional sectors; one can, however, observe competition between schools, which is also increasingly seen in Denmark but is absent from Norway.

Empowerment—How Users Can Influence at an Institution

Parents have more influence in schools than users and their relatives have in nursing homes. This is partly because students and parents are more willing to use their latent influence, and partly because of laws giving parents more influence in schools. All three Scandinavian countries have laws that govern the composition of user boards in public schools and the issues about which they must be consulted.

In the selected municipal schools, user boards function as arenas where representatives for the parents obtain relevant information and provide input on general issues. Parents typically describe them as places 'where we can give input'. The headmasters who also attend these meetings share this description. When asked to give an example of a case where a user board has had influence, the headmaster mentioned work done on IT solutions, but then qualified the statement by adding, 'It is not completely true because I had already decided to make these changes. But it is good to use the parents as support when I argue with the teachers, even if it is not always a good argument' (Interview, site manager, public school, Norway). This latter example illustrates how collective empowerment can have real, albeit limited, effects. The Swedish for-profit schools function practically the same way as public schools in this regard.

Formal arrangements give parents more influence over nonprofit schools. The law guarantees their representation in the school board, and in reality, they dominate user boards as the primary stakeholders in the institutions. In municipal schools, the municipal administration makes important decisions, such as hiring headmasters, adopting budgets and planning long-term strategies for the schools. In nonprofit schools, the board makes these decisions.

Indeed, one parent member of the school board questioned if he had too much power: 'That was probably what surprised me the most: that as a board member you are so much involved. In many ways, it is a great responsibility. One does not have any other qualifications to be in the board other than the fact that you are a parent' (Interview, user representative, nonprofit school, Denmark). This overwhelming feeling can come from overall administrative and economic responsibility, not all of which impacts teaching directly. At the same time, overarching decisions regarding values, teaching philosophies and school–parent cooperation are decided at this level. One example of how administrative decisions play an important role is the nonprofit school that experienced a cutback in public transfers and then decided to increase the number of students in each class and not raise the fees. The parents themselves took this decision through to the school board.

A parent who was one of the founders of a nonprofit school illustrates the importance of parental influence in nonprofit schools. She explains that parental influence was an important reason why she helped established the school:

> It is the real opportunity the parents have to have influence on the content in the school [...] We saw that this teaching methodology, and that one could do this under the auspices of the parents, gives opportunities that you want as an active parent. To participate in creating something that in many ways is better then what you had to begin with. (Interview, user representative, nonprofit school, Norway)

There seems to be universal agreement that the room for influence is greater in nonprofit schools, both in principle and in reality. One Swedish public school demonstrates, however, that there is no determinism in this relationship. Here the school board makes the major decisions. The board consists of staff and parents, but the parents have the majority of the votes and the chairman. The parents show real interest in the board, and the headmaster states that the present board was elected with about 100 votes, a figure that makes up the lion's share of parents at the school.

Yet, informal contact between teachers and parents is the more important form of influence. A reason for this is that in spite of its strong legal backing, there is still some doubt about how the user board should function, as one board member explains:

> It happens in cases with complaints about teachers, grades or something else; I am very unsure about what the user board can say about professional matters. We have no role. We have no competence to speak about the teaching methodology. However, as a parent, you have the right and the duty to follow up on the teaching of your child ... and the teacher and all that, but as a user board, I do not know. (Interview, user representative, public school, Norway)

Regarding informal contact, there are smaller differences between public and nonpublic schools. Both have structures in place to allow students' and parents' voices to be heard, and there is a shared understanding among interviewees from different groups that these structures are useful and available. In the public schools, users and staff do not experience any lack of user involvement. They stress that personal contact between teachers and parents is fluid, and that the school is receptive to input from parents. The relationship between teachers and parents is important, and personal chemistry is not dependent on one type of institutional sector.

Yet, the flexibility of the structures can be different. Nonprofit schools are based on an ideology that entails more user input and different teaching methods than in for-profit and public schools. A teacher at a nonprofit school explains the difference:

> That is the major, decisive difference from the public school. The children are involved in what goals we have for them and what ambitions we have for their development. We continuously set goals on three levels: the professional, the personal, and the social. They are themselves involved, so the old concept of self-management exudes from our school. (Interview, staff member, nonprofit school, Denmark)

One part of the explanation for more room for user empowerment, both individual and collective, at nonprofit schools stems from how these schools use test scores and measurable indicators in their governance. These schools generally have a relaxed approach to tests, unlike for-profit and public schools. A headmaster at a public school explains:

> Then comes the PISA-test that tells people: 'You do not perform well enough. This is simply too bad'. Then there is even more focus on us not having enough projects, themes and 1000 other things. We must stick to the book. Oh, now I am harsh, but sometimes it annoys me that one governs [the school] this way and thus kills some of the creativity. (Interview, site manager, public school, Denmark)

With more emphasis on PISA scores and quantifiable goals, there is less room for influence from parents. From all municipalities, increased emphasis on these measures was reported, and the same can be said of for-profit schools. In this regard, nonprofit schools are in a freer position. These schools are not part of a bigger structure and thus have fewer limits to making changes based on user input. On the other hand, one of the for-profit firms has an ombudsman at the level of the firm. Students and teachers can report incidents and situations to the ombudsman, who is tasked with making sure the school follows up appropriately on reports that the school is not performing according to standards. This gives users an extra outlet to reach out to if they are unhappy with the school's services.

Participation—How User Experiences are Translated to the Municipal Level

Just as the participatory role of relatives varies between countries in the nursing home sector, parental participation in the school sector is the dimension which exhibits the greatest differences between Scandinavian countries.

In Norway, all municipalities have mechanisms in place for conveying the opinions of students and their parents to the municipal level. Chief among them is that in all municipalities a municipal-level body exists which consists of selected parents from different schools. In one municipality, the leader of this body is paid by the municipality to enable her to spend sufficient time to efficiently promote the voice of the parents. Asked whether such leaders are able to influence school policy, one leader remarks: 'Yes. That is my experience. I find that they are very interested in our opinions'. The same message comes from other municipalities. Debates about issues that are not strictly related to school policy but concern wider elements of municipal policies for the young also find a place in this body. In one municipality, an advisory committee exists for 'family and child protection' where representatives of school parents meet. The parents therefore have the opportunity to influence a range of municipal policies. Even though no formal power is allocated to these bodies, politicians, administrative leaders and parents agree that they exert real influence.

In addition, a municipal politician is also present at meetings at each school. This is meant to inform local policymakers about the operations of different schools, and the law requires it. How this provision functions varies substantially, as some politicians eagerly participate in school meetings while others are seldom present. Variations seem to be solely based on the level of personal enthusiasm of individual politicians.

In Norwegian nonprofit schools, state law requires a local politician to participate as an observer in their user boards. The interest levels of these politicians also vary, but in all cases they have less room for formal influence. Nonprofit schools are controversial in some parts of the municipalities, among some administrative leaders who find interaction and competition with nonprofits to be 'a hassle and an annoyance' and among some politicians who hold a more ideological approach. This partly explains why nonprofit schools are excluded from municipal arenas with policymaking influence, even when these include wider perspectives than just school policies. Nonprofit schools see this as a negative since they feel unrecognised and unheard. As one mother says: 'It is an underlying factor that we are an outsider in the municipality. I think that feels very negative for the teachers. It takes so long to get accepted' (Interview, user representative, public school, Norway).

Like in Norway, the external role of collective user bodies in Danish public and nonprofit schools is the opposite of its internal role. Municipal schools are more active in their relationship with municipalities. They provide input at local hearings, write open letters to editors of local newspapers and work directly with local politicians. Most of the time their goal is to make visible the need for funding at the schools. Indeed, one parent pointed to this form of lobbying effort vis-à-vis the municipality as the most important task of the school board:

> Formally, we do not have much influence. Some of the things we have done the last few years are related to traffic and other things where we try to influence the municipality through different channels than the ones available to the leaders in the school. We can approach the politicians directly, that is something the leaders cannot do. They must go through their superiors. In situations where we want to put pressure on their superiors, we approach the politicians [...] I see it as one of our most

important roles, that we can speak the case of the school. The leadership of the school is part of the municipality and must fall in line. If the municipality makes a decision, they must loyally carry it out. We are not bound by this. We can speak the case of the school. (Interview, representative, public school, Denmark)

In nonprofit schools, user boards play a lesser external role. This is partly because headmasters have more freedom to occupy this role since they are not part of the municipal hierarchy. The loyalty of headmasters is, therefore, more clearly defined as belonging to the schools. Another reason for the limited external role of nonprofits schools is that they receive very little attention from municipalities. However, this is a natural consequence of nonprofit students opting out of the municipal option, and municipalities have limited opportunities for steering. On the other hand, about 30% of students in Faaborg Midtfyn, less in Herning, attend nonprofit schools, which consequently means that local politicians are only informed about a limited portion of the educational system in the municipality. This is something that users of nonprofit schools find frustrating: 'No, there is no attention from the politicians. That is my impression. Neither when I am here at the school nor when I am at work [in the local newspaper] do I get the impression that the politicians are concerned about the nonprofit schools' (Interview, user representative, nonprofit school, Denmark). This stands in stark contrast to the experiences expressed by public school users.

In Sweden, contact between users and local policymakers is less organised. User influence on the municipal level is not all that different from influential channels available to other citizens, such as elections, local political parties and direct approaches to politicians.

Information about schools typically flows through the headmaster in the municipal hierarchy, and direct contact is not formally organised, except from user surveys which are subject to scrutiny at the municipal level. Parents have every opportunity to make further contact with politicians. In municipalities, meetings of the political committee responsible for schools are open events where all citizens can attend. In reality, few citizens use this opportunity. To make politicians better informed about situations at the schools, a politician from the municipality is present at user board meetings of all municipal schools. This makes local politicians more informed about public schools than nonpublic schools, an imbalance which reflects where politicians have room for influence.

There are few initiatives from parents that seek changes at the municipal level. In one municipality, some parents expressed discontent with the lack of opportunities to express their voices in relation to a large overhaul of the school structure. According to politicians, the opportunity to 'vote with the feet' and change schools, should amend this problem.

Table 6.3 summarises the findings from the school sector. As is evident from the table, this service area displays more differentiation between different institutional sectors. Nonprofit institutions, in particular, tend to be associated with more potential for user control through choice and empowerment, while users of public institutions tend to participate more in policy influencing.

How Can We Explain Different Potentials for Active Citizenship?

To make the comparison between service areas easier to grasp, Table 6.4 compares the shared findings from schools and nursing homes.

This table illustrates some patterns of similarities and differences across the analytic dimensions. In the following sections, I will identify the most important aspects of these patterns for the different dimensions of active citizenship. By analysing variations and consistencies across countries, institutional sectors and service areas, I am also able to suggest some mechanisms that could expand or limit the capacity for active citizenship.

Choice—The Importance of Capacity in Supply

Two mechanisms that contribute to explaining differences between service areas are the functioning of user choice and the importance of passing a threshold in capacity. In Danish municipalities, the nursing home sector formally has user choice, whereas their counterparts in

Table 6.3 Active citizenship in the school sector

	Norway	Denmark	Sweden	Shared findings
Choice				
Creates diverse service options	Yes, nonprofit schools provide distinctive services and expand the available options	Yes, nonprofit schools provide distinctive services and expand the available options	Not much diversity between public and for-profit schools	More diversity in Denmark and Norway than in Sweden
Exit opportunities give power	No	Schools adapt to competition	Yes. Schools adapt to competition and users use exit opportunities as leverage	Not in Norway, more in Denmark, most in Sweden
Empowerment				
Collective	More room for influence and control for parents in nonprofit schools than public schools	More room for influence and control for parents in nonprofit schools than public schools	A municipal school which is parent-run stands out as collectively empowered. Also, nonprofit schools are more empowered than municipal and for-profit schools	More in nonprofit schools than in public schools. Special 'parent-run' schools in Sweden show municipal potential

(continued)

Table 6.3 (continued)

	Norway	Denmark	Sweden	Shared findings
Individual	Smaller differences between schools from different institutional sectors. More local room for adaptation in nonprofit schools	Smaller differences between schools from different institutional sectors. More local room for adaptation in nonprofit schools	Small differences between schools from different institutional sectors. For-profit firms have ombudsman	Smaller difference between the institutional sectors. More local room for adaptation in nonprofit schools
Participation	More arenas for advocacy for users of public schools. Users of public schools are more content with their participation than users of nonprofit schools	Public schools have an active external role in trying to influence the municipality. Nonprofit schools have little involvement with the municipality	Only passive participation, filtered through hierarchical channels in the municipality or via user surveys	More arenas for advocacy for users of public schools in Denmark and Norway. Less so in Sweden and in nonpublic schools

Table 6.4 Key variations in nursing homes and schools

	Shared findings	
	Nursing home	School
Choice		
Diverse service options	Not much diversity in content	More diversity in Denmark and Norway than in Sweden. In all cases, more so than in nursing homes
Change in power balance	Little to no effect	More so than in nursing homes. More in Sweden, less in Norway, with Denmark in between
Empowerment		
Collective	Limited by user health. Small differences between the institutional sectors	More in schools than nursing homes and more in nonprofits than in public schools. Special 'parent-run' schools in Sweden show possibilities for collective empowerment in municipal schools
Individual	Small differences between the institutional sectors	Small differences between institutions from different institutional sectors. Somewhat more local room for adaptation in nonprofit institutions
Participation	Differences between countries, but not institutional sectors	More arenas for advocacy for users of public schools in Denmark and Norway. Less difference between institutional sectors in Sweden

Norway and Sweden do not. Potential nursing home users in Norway and Sweden can ask for a specific nursing home, but public bureaucrats make the final decision. In reality, the lack of available nursing home slots restrains Danish user choice, so user experience in the nursing home sector is very much the same across all three countries. Nursing homes are an area for cost reduction, something that together with the recalibration of the elderly care structure results in insufficient capacity (Hermansen and Gautun 2011). The consequence is that every new available space in nursing homes—public, for-profit or nonprofit—is immediately filled. Variations between nursing homes cannot be too large since one cannot know the preferences, interests and needs of users. In addition, users mentioned geography and proximity to home and family as the most important considerations when reporting preferences for nursing homes. Thus, it becomes problematic if the local nursing home has a profile that does not match a potential user. Moreover, users can be temporarily admitted to a nursing home before getting a permanent place elsewhere. This means that differences between institutions cannot be too large. From the users' perspective, the lack of capacity makes any talk of choice irrelevant, as this user representative from Norway explains:

> My mother in law was diagnosed with dementia in 2001, it almost killed me, and she lived next door. He [my husband] worked in Sweden and I had to take care of her in all ways. Then we were so 'lucky' to be rude, that she fell and broke her upper femur. She had surgery and was granted a short time stay [in a nursing home] and after much begging, she got a place at [name of nursing home]. [...] It is not like you will get a place when you need it. (Interview, user representative, for-profit nursing home, Norway)

When users experience a shortage of available places at nursing homes, it is impossible for them to make demands regarding a single nursing home in particular. In the above example, the user was first temporarily admitted to one institution before being moved to a permanent one; this underlines the need for different institutions to have limited variation in terms of content. We found similar examples in different institutions and municipalities in all three countries. Given this situation, there are no credible nursing home alternatives for users and their next of kin, and thus exit opportunities are not available to them either.

The contrast with the school sector is striking. Municipalities in all three countries are responsible for providing enough school places for all children. Students automatically belong to their local school unless they actively seek out a different school. Nonpublic schools represent an addition to this system, as their establishment is not dependent on approval from municipalities, but is decided instead at a national level by meeting certain criteria. Unlike nursing homes, all children are entitled to a place in school. Inability to meet the necessary capacity is therefore not an option. In reality, nonpublic schools secure a certain level of overcapacity of school places since the public schools must accept students that want to return from a nonpublic school. This makes the choice option real and gives families the opportunity to choose which schools they like best and to change schools when appropriate. Thus, nonprofit schools develop distinctiveness without these characteristics being forced upon anyone.

Empowerment—Nonprofit Schools Use Administrative Freedom to Empower Users

In this investigation, the main finding regarding empowerment is that users of nonprofit schools enjoy more empowerment than users of other types of schools and nursing homes. This can be explained by the administrative freedom afforded to nonprofit schools. Legal instruments and formal arrangements at the national and municipal level also contribute to explaining levels of empowerment. Individual forms of empowerment are perceived as more important for users than collective forms of empowerment.

It is a reasonable assumption that limited access to user choice would inspire nursing homes to develop their own instruments for empowerment. This is not the case, and generally speaking, schools have more empowered users. In schools, there is no shortage of volunteers to participate in user boards. Their role also has stronger legal backing, and on certain issues, school leaders must consult user boards before making final decisions. The role of user boards is in most cases well established, and users do not reflect much on their power. They generally share the feeling that they have influence and that this makes it worth their time. The collective influence of the user board varies, but it is a shared feature that users exploit this arena when they have strongly held opinions on issues.

In nursing homes, there are small differences in terms of empowerment between institutions belonging to different institutional sectors. For schools, on the other hand, there are important differences. Nonprofit schools seem to consistently offer more room for empowerment and a broader range of services for users. One central explanation for this is the administrative freedom these schools enjoy. Nonprofit schools are located outside of larger structures of hierarchical governance, such as municipalities and for-profit firms. This gives nonprofit schools fewer sources for steering, and thus more decision-making power rests locally at these schools. Fewer stakeholders mean a greater share of power for existing stakeholders, and parents are the principal stakeholders. Ben-Ner (1986) has shown how nonprofits are often founded by entrepreneurs who have strong convictions in terms of their missions and methods. They, therefore, construct mechanisms that protect what is distinctive about their services, their steering capacity, and the room they allocate for user empowerment. As we have seen in this study, parental influence is also part of the reason why nonprofit schools have been established. There may also be an aspect of self-selection involved, since families who seek nonprofit schools often wish to actively influence how the schools are run. However, for the potential agency of these families to blossom, it is necessary to allow it to develop, which nonprofit schools do.

Two further arguments underline the importance of administrative freedom. First, the Swedish example of a public school governed by parents displays as much empowerment as nonprofit schools. Accordingly, when public schools have the same administrative room for manoeuvring, they can empower their users in the same fashion as nonprofits. However, this potential is seldom used as this school model is uncommon. A likely interpretation of this is that granting public schools a significant degree of freedom from public hierarchy undermines the input channel of the local democracy—the votes cast in elections. Local politicians are evaluated by how they run schools; thus, appearing to lean back and leave school operations to parents may be seen as a failure to assume a central part of their responsibility. This represents a dilemma between different forms of democratic legitimacy. The dilemma is, however, not present when nonprofits run schools, since in these cases local politicians are not held responsible. It is also an indication that even though earlier reported studies suggested that a growing number of decisions are being made at the output side of the democratic process

(Andersen 2006), there is a limit to this development when politicians seek to remain in charge of services. Aside from the issue of democratic legitimacy, politicians also seek to safeguard the model of a unitary school system that all children attend. The idea is that this model promotes social integration across economic, cultural and religious cleavages in society. The willingness to give freedom to nonpublic schools may depend on the willingness to give up or downsize ambitions for a unitary school system as an arena for social integration.

Second, nonprofit nursing homes do not offer the same level of diversity and empowerment as schools. This demonstrates how nonprofit institutions are dependent on the public sector's approach to service areas when they are part of the public service system. In all municipalities, nonprofit and for-profit nursing homes have about the same room for collective user empowerment as their public counterparts, while variation does exist between municipalities. This implies that municipal-level regulations are important for influencing levels of empowerment, which suppresses any potential nonprofit or for-profit providers may have to deviate from the public approach to empowerment. Illustrative of this is a statement from an administrative leader in a Swedish municipality who pointed out that the number of compulsory demands made of nursing homes tends to lead them to become 'all the same' (Interview, administrative leader, municipality, Sweden).

What is shared between service areas is the agreement that individual empowerment is experienced by users as being more important than collective forms of empowerment. Most users are satisfied with their level of individual empowerment, both in nursing homes and schools. There is somewhat more discontent among users at nursing homes, but such users tend to add that it is not based on lack of will from the staff, but instead on the shortage of staff and resources. There are few important differences in this respect across institutional sectors, municipalities and countries. These differences seem more dependent on the individual attributes of staff members. In addition, municipal-level regulations and institutional arrangements in companies or institutions influence individual empowerment. A telling example is the for-profit school in Sweden that has its own ombudsman. Students at this school have additional opportunities to voice complaints. The commercial interests of for-profit schools may also compel them to be more diligent in following-up on complaints. Whether these incentives work in this way is an empirical question we do not have the data to answer at this time. Either way, they demonstrate the potential for increased individual empowerment in different steering structures.

Participation—Administrative Integration Gives Arenas for Participation

The main findings regarding participation mirror the findings about empowerment. When institutions become detached from the public hierarchy, their users participate less in local policy processes. This means that, unlike for empowerment, the lowest levels of participation in local policy processes are found among users of nonprofit schools. Formal arrangements for user involvement are important as they can explain variations in user participation between service areas and municipalities.

The countries were uniform in their stated aims regarding user participation in policymaking. Open meetings among policymakers, and regular meeting points between users and policymakers, occur in many places. The users most capable of taking advantage of these spaces are at institutions integrated with the public administration. These include nursing homes, public schools and, interestingly, for-profit schools. When municipalities outsource services, they do so without reducing their perceived responsibility for the services. Nursing home users have no option to opt out of services from for-profit providers, and local policymakers, therefore, retain their ability to involve themselves in them. Users of nonprofit schools have consciously opted out of the realm of local policymakers, and are thus less of a concern for the municipality. Since decisions regarding opportunities to open up these schools rest at the national level, there is no process whereby the electorate can hold local policymakers responsible for the service content of these schools. Swedish for-profit schools are approved nationally, but are somewhat more attached to the municipal structure and are thus in a middle position.

This dimension exhibits fewer differences between service areas. All municipalities conduct user surveys, and these are administered in all institutions except nonprofit schools. User surveys are the only opportunity for direct communication between users and local policymakers. In addition, municipalities have arenas for representatives of institutions to participate. For nursing homes, there is no difference between public, for-profit and nonprofit institutions when it comes to their participation in these arenas. For schools, the more detached nonprofit schools are more isolated when it comes to participation. This is partly because local policymakers have less influence over what happens at nonprofit schools. It is a curious situation, since issues discussed in these arenas often include more than municipal school policies and are thus of interest also to the parents of children in nonprofit schools.

The implication here is that a trade-off exists between empowerment at institutions and participation and influence in local policy process. The institutions where users have more local influence get less attention and less room for influence from the municipal level. This gives them more room to manoeuvre locally but also gives them less administrative support. Albeit to varying degrees, municipalities are important for all these institutions, and so to be excluded from the municipal decision-making structure undermines the opportunities citizens have to influence decision making in their communities. For policymakers, the exclusion of citizens from platforms for communication with them can present a skewed view of the opinions of citizens, especially those who by definition have taken an active stance on particular welfare issues.

There is some variance between countries. In Denmark, user boards at nursing homes can report about successes in changing municipal policy, and interactions with local policymakers are a natural part of their tasks. This also happens in Norway, but to a lesser extent, while in Sweden it is all but absent. For schools, divisions between the strong influence of public schools and the lack of influence of nonpublic schools are evident across countries. The greater presence of participation in Denmark can be seen in the light of Scandinavian countries' respective 'power studies', where the Danish research team drew more optimistic conclusions about the state of democracy on the basis of investigations into the implementation of policies (Andersen 2006).

Conclusions

Effect of Institutional Sector Depends on User Choice and Administrative Freedom

This chapter used experiences from 27 institutions in seven municipalities in three Scandinavian countries to explore whether it matters who provides publicly funded and regulated services. There is accordingly a wealth of data underlying the inferences made in this study, but they are not representative in any statistical meaning of the word. The results in this chapter must, therefore, be regarded as *exploratory*. There are many potential approaches to a comparison of service providers from different institutional sectors. Here I have chosen *active citizenship*: the ability for users to take control over their own lives when they are dependent on services.

There are differences between public, for-profit and nonprofit providers when it comes to active citizenship. However, these differences vary between the dimensions of active citizenship and service areas. Generally, nonprofits deviate more than for-profits in terms of public options. These deviations include providing more room for active citizenship along the dimensions of choice and empowerment, and less so for participation. What is needed is an understanding of these variations.

The first step is to look at the interaction of administrative freedom and user choice. Illustrative in this respect are the differences between Norwegian and Danish nonprofit schools and the elderly care sector in all three countries. In all three countries, this study shows nursing homes are closely integrated with the municipal hierarchy. Municipalities have ample room to intervene in nonprofit nursing homes, a power that undermines their autonomy and ability to be different from municipal nursing homes. For for-profit nursing homes, tender documents are very detailed and thus leave little room to develop distinctive characters. Furthermore, they are measured by the same parameters as municipal nursing homes and provide incentives to strive for the same goals. Overall, this means that nonpublic nursing homes have little administrative freedom and limited opportunity to develop distinctiveness.

This is in contrast with what we find for nonprofit schools in Norway and Denmark. These schools are outside municipal control since they are approved at the state level. The directorate for education collects the opinions of a municipality about establishing a nonprofit school, but the municipality will not be able to prevent its establishment. Moreover, municipalities do not supervise or inspect nonprofit schools. In addition, nonprofit schools are governed by different laws than public schools and thus have different legal elbow rooms than nonpublic nursing homes. In comparison, Swedish nonprofit schools can be established without municipal approval, but municipalities monitor them more extensively than they do in Norway and Denmark. For example, nonprofit schools are included in some municipal quality surveys. Moreover, nonpublic schools in Sweden are governed by the same laws as public schools, which provide less space and incentives to develop distinctive characteristics. The result is that there is less variation between schools in Sweden than in either Denmark or Norway. The other side of this point is that we find competition between schools to be stronger in Sweden than it is in Norway, with Denmark occupying an intermediate position. When distinctive characteristics of a school are not used as selection criteria, general perceptions of school quality determine which school families ultimately choose. The struggle to create quality perceptions invites competition and pits schools against each other. Therefore, Swedish interviewees reported that unhappy families often used competition between schools as a means of changing schools.

This study suggests that user choice is decisive for establishing distinctiveness in public, for-profit and nonprofit institutions. User choice is what enables the state and municipalities to let providers develop distinctive profiles from public options, since this implies that distinctiveness is not forced upon any user. This distinctiveness is an important factor in its own right, but allowing for institutional distinctiveness has two further implications for empowerment and participation. First, institutional arrangements that allow for diversity are also more flexible in how they are run. Institutions can use this flexibility to make changes based on input from users. The potential for obtaining real changes through arenas for empowerment at institutions is, therefore, greater since the room for change is larger. We see this effect in nonprofit schools, where their detachment from public hierarchy creates possibilities for the democratic involvement of parents to a larger degree than in the other institutions.

Second, users involved in nonpublic, and especially nonprofit, institutions have often obtained the service they preferred by selecting a provider that was distinct from the public provider. If they had been forced to remain with a provider within the public hierarchy, they would be more likely to use voice to seek changes from policymakers. The existence of a broad range of service providers therefore weakens the motive for using political channels to influence the content of services. Moreover, many of the arenas currently in place to inform local policymakers about the views and opinions of users exclude users of nonprofit schools. Local politicians are more concerned with nonpublic nursing homes, since the lack of user choice there makes it a political–administrative decision which citizens use against them.

Emphasis on governance tools must be balanced with an examination of the characteristics of the users. Of the three analytic dimensions, I found the greatest variation in active citizenship between the different service areas. Users of schools have more capacity for active citizenship than users of nursing home services. They are also more willing and able to exploit the existing capacity. Part of the explanation for this can be found in the nature of services and users. Parents are more inclined to involve themselves in school services than elderly users at nursing homes who typically are in poor health and do not always have relatives available to speak on their behalf.

Implications for the Scandinavian Model

A part of the Scandinavian welfare model is that municipalities have broad and comprehensive responsibilities for providing services to citizens. A reason for this is that assigning decision-making power to the municipal level is expected to yield services better tailored to the needs of citizens. When decisions are made at the local level, they are more compatible with the local context and local priorities (Kjølsrød 2005). Moreover, Norwegians find local democracy to be an important part of the democratic system, but they mainly regard municipalities as service providers, a belief that underscores the importance of this aspect of their functioning (Rose 2011). However, this study shows that nonpublic schools which are removed from the municipal decision-making sphere can better tailor their services to the interests of users. This demonstrates how detaching service providers from the municipal level gives them more room to manoeuvre and enables them to develop distinctive services and increased flexibility in order to heed signals from users. The challenge for the Scandinavian welfare model is whether this development challenges the demand for equality in services.

The term 'welfare municipalities' describes the trade-off between universalism and local decision-making capacities (Kröger 1997; Burau and Kröger 2004; Grønlie 2004). State oversight is normally seen as a limiting room for both local policymakers and street-level bureaucrats and thus creates uniform services across municipalities (Henriksen et al. 2012, 471, Tranvik and Selle 2005). Strong, autonomous municipalities supposedly undermine the universality of services as they create variations between municipalities. This study gives nuance to this finding since it demonstrates how the state can also obtain service differentiation by *weakening* municipal control—when nonpublic school approval takes place at the national level. When the state grants freedom to a nonpublic provider to develop the content of their services, it diminishes municipal power and increases diversity. In turn, universalism in the context of the content of services is also reduced.

At the same time, the nursing home case studies also show that there are no necessary advantages for active citizenship that automatically come from provider plurality. Rather, the potential for active citizenship is demonstrated under certain conditions. In the school sector, nonprofit providers stand out by giving increased autonomy to users both in the form of catering to niche preferences and enabling user influence in the operation of schools. In this way, nonprofit providers can be understood as the prime exponents of a core feature of what has been labelled the Scandinavian form of citizenship, which democratize[s] all aspects of society (Hernes 1988; Janoski 1998, 20). It might be a paradox that in a welfare model dominated by public providers, nonprofit providers arguably represent the most advanced example of one of its most successful tenets. This implies that a natural next step in developing Scandinavian welfare societies based on core citizenship values is to actively use the welfare mix to give influence to citizens and curb the power of public bureaucrats.

On the other hand, the democratising effect of nonprofit providers is dependent on the state yielding its responsibility and influence to smaller groups of citizens. It is an individual choice to opt for a nonpublic school, but collective efforts are necessary in order to obtain such alternatives. Fundamental to Scandinavian state individualism is that the state guarantees services to citizens and thus liberates them from smaller collectives in society (Trägårdh 1997). A future welfare society where providers are granted more liberty in the welfare mix may make services more dependent on initiatives of smaller collectives, and the individual's integration into alternative structures such as families and religious groups may become more important, a possibility which could weaken a central and distinctive value of the Scandinavian welfare model.

Diversity in terms of providers and service content is beneficial for active citizenship, but it is important not to lose sight of those citizens who do not want or are unable to exercise active citizenship. Their interests are as important as the interests of the ones who continuously and actively seek to influence services for their own benefit. Some studies from Sweden have shown that user choice schemes in schools have led to increased differences between schools (Böhlmark and Holmlund 2012; Lindbom 2010). The goal of for-profits and their incentives—to prioritise profit over quality—has been identified as a threat to the equal and high quality of the welfare provision (Steinberg 2006). In earlier studies, Meagher and Szebehely (2013) found that due to tight regulation of services, Scandinavian elderly care has avoided many of the negative effects of marketisation that have occurred in the US. Tuning down the level of public regulation in order to enhance diversity between providers may accordingly have unwanted consequences for service quality involving aspects not included in this study.

In a study of Danish home care, Rostgaard (2006) found that the new 'consumer citizens' can have more influence over services, but that there are differences in the ability of users to exploit this opportunity. This is an issue we are not able to answer satisfactorilyin this study, and further research on this issue in Scandinavia is needed. Likewise, it is an independent value in the school system that children from different backgrounds with different values and interests meet in a public arena, which increases integration between different groups in society. This type of value must always be assessed against different dimensions of active citizenship.

One can envisage that the more individual constituents of active citizenship, such as user choice and individual empowerment, may sometimes conflict with equality values in Scandinavian welfare. The collective aspects of active citizenship, such as a user council and close contact between users and decision makers, are more easily compatible with an equity ideal. Moreover, the mentioned violations of human rights in Norwegian nursing homes affect some of the weakest users. This underlines that it is not sufficient with mechanisms for the individual advancement of one's own interests. Collective arrangements are necessary for the whole range of users' interests to receive attention. The private resources of individuals cannot decide the level of service for citizens.

In the nursing home sector, differences between public, for-profit and nonprofit providers are not large in terms of active citizenship. Here the differences are rather between municipalities and countries. This shows how important legislations, regulations and choices made by local policymakers can affect the capacity for active citizenship. The legal position of user boards at public schools gives influence to the users. Similarly, municipal guidelines concerning the role of user boards can secure user influence in relevant nursing homes. Active citizenship can be promoted by providing nonpublic, particularly nonprofit, providers a framework that will promote their user influence models; it can also be extended through government legislation and directives for the advancement of user influence at all institutions.

Finally, does it actually matter who performs services? Yes, but not if there are capacity problems, little real user choice and tight municipal governance. The state and municipalities decide who will perform public welfare tasks. If the public sector chooses, it can use nonpublic actors strategically to promote more and different values than what public institutions deliver. To get maximum benefit from the diversity that nonpublic institutions offer, one must ensure adequate capacity and it is thus beneficial to have a user choice system. Further, it is necessary to be conscious of the autonomy institutions should have. They should be given the opportunity to develop distinctiveness, but at the same time they should be required to establish venues for user influence. By using these tools, the public sector can use the welfare mix to promote active citizenship. However, it is necessary to balance measures to promote active citizenship against the effects they have for equality values in Scandinavian welfare. What this study demonstrates is the broad range of options that exist when designing welfare services and some of the mechanisms involved in determining the outcome of active citizenship. Governments can regulate shares of providers in the welfare mix and the activities of the providers in the welfare mix. The division of strictness and lenience on those two dimensions is decisive for active citizenship.

References

Adcock, Robert, and David Collier. 2001. Measurement validity: A shared standard for qualitative and quantitative research. *American Political Science Review* 95 (3): 529–546.

Alford, John. 2014. The multiple facets of co-production: Building on the work of Elinor Ostrom. *Public Management Review* 16 (3): 299–316.

Andersen, Jørgen Goul. 2004. *Et ganske levende demokrati*. Århus: Aarhus universitetsforlag.

Andersen, Jørgen Goul. 2005. Citizenship, unemployment and welfare policy. In *The changing face of welfare*, eds. J. Goul Andersen, J.-G. Guillemard, Per H Jensen, and Birgit Pfau-Effinger. Bristol: Policy Press.

Andersen, Jørgen Goul. 2006. Political power and democracy in Denmark: Decline of democracy or change in democracy? *Journal of European Public Policy* 13 (4): 569–586.

Andersen, Jørgen Goul, and Jens Villiam Hoff. 2001. *Democracy and citizenship in Scandinavia*. New York: Palgrave Macmillan.

Andersen, Jørgen Goul, and Sigrid Rossteutscher. 2007. Small-scale democracy: Citizen power in the domains of everyday life. In *Citizenship and involvement in European democracies: A comparative analysis*, eds. Jan W Van Deth, José Ramón Montero, and Anders Westholm. Oxon: Routledge.

Anders, Lindbom. 2010. School choice in Sweden: Effects on student performance, school costs, and segregation. *Scandinavian Journal of Educational Research* 54 (6):615–630.

Anttonen, Anneli, and Gabrielle Meagher. 2013. Mapping marketisation: Concepts and goals. In *Marketisation in Nordic eldercare: A research report on legislation, oversight, extent and consequences*, eds. Gabrielle Meagher, and Marta Szebehely, 13–22. Stockholm: Department of Social Work, Stockholm University.

Bang, Henrik P., Allan Dreyer Hansen, and Jens Hoff. 2000. Demokrati fra neden: problematikker og teorertiske overvejelser. In *Demokrati fra neden. Casestudier fra en dansk kommune*, eds. Henrik P Bang, Allan Dreyer Hansen, and Jens Hoff, 9–36. København: Jurist- og Økonomiforbundets Forlag.

Bang, Henrik P., and Eva Sørensen. 1999. The everyday maker: A new challenge to democratic governance. *Administrative Theory & Praxis* 21 (3): 325–341.

Ben-Ner, Avner. 1986. Nonprofit organizations: Why do they exist in market economies. In *The economics of nonprofit institutions: Studies in structure and policy*, ed. Susan Rose-Ackerman, 94–113. New York: Oxford University Press.

Blomqvist, Paula, and Bo Rothstein. 2008. *Välfärdsstatens nya ansikte: demokrati och marknadsreformer inom den offentliga sektorn*. Stockholm: Agora.

Böhlmark, A., and Holmlund, H. 2012. *Lika möjligheter. Familjebakgrund och skolprestationer 1988–2010*. Uppsala: Institutet för arbetsmarknads- och utbildningspolitisk utvärdering.

Boje, Thomas P., and Martin Potucek. 2011a. Introduction. In *Social rights, active citizenship and governance in the European Union*, eds. Thomas P Boje and Martin Potucek. Baden-Baden: Nomos Verlagsgesellschaft mbH & Co. KG.

Boje, Thomas P., and Martin Potucek (eds.). 2011b. *Social rights, active citizenship and governance in the European Union*. Baden-Baden: Nomos Verlagsgesellschaft mbH & Co. KG.

Burau, Viola, and Teppo Kröger. 2004. Towards local comparisons of community care governance: Exploring the relationship between policy and politics. *Social Policy & Administration* 38 (7): 793–810.

Christensen, Karen. 2012. Towards a mixed economy of long-term care in Norway? *Critical Social Policy* 32 (4): 577–596.

Clarke, John. 2006. Consumers, clients or citizens? Politics, policy and practice in the reform of social care. *European Societies* 8 (3): 423–442.

Clarke, John, Janet Newman, Elizabeth Vidler, Louise Westmarland, Nick Smith, and Janet E Newman. 2007. *Creating citizen-consumers: Changing publics and changing public services.* Pine Forge Press.

Comondore, Vikram R., P.J. Devereaux, Qi Zhou, Samuel B. Stone, Jason W. Busse, Nikila C. Ravindran, Karen E. Burns, Ted Haines, Bernadette Stringer, and Deborah J. Cook. 2009. Quality of care in for-profit and not-for-profit nursing homes: Systematic review and meta-analysis. *BMJ* 339: b2732.

Daly, Mary, and Jane Lewis. 2000. The concept of social care and the analysis of contemporary welfare states. *The British Journal of Sociology* 51 (2): 281–298. doi:10.1111/j.1468-4446.2000.00281.x.

Domberger, Simon, and Paul Jensen. 1997. Contracting out by the public sector: Theory, evidence, prospects. *Oxford review of economic policy* 13 (4): 67–78.

Eriksen, Erik Oddvar, and Jarle Weigård. 1993. Fra statsborger til kunde. *Statsvetenskaplig tidskrift* 9: 111–131.

Evers, Adalbert, and Anne-Marie Guillemard. 2013a. Introduction: Marshall's concept of citizenship and contemporary welfare reconfiguration. In *Social policy and citizenship: The changing landscape*, eds. Adalbert Evers, and Anne-Marie Guillemard. New York: Oxford University Press.

Evers, Adalbert, and Anne-Marie Guillemard (eds.). 2013b. *Social policy and citizenship: The changing landscape.* New York: Oxford University Press.

Goertz, Gary. 2006. *Social science concepts: A user's guide.* Princeton, NJ: Princeton University Press.

Grønlie, Tore. 2004. Fra velferdskommune til velferdsstat–hundre års velferdsvekst fra lokalisme til statsdominans. *Historisk tidsskrift* 83 (4): 633–649.

Gustavsen, Annelin, Asbjørn Røiseland, and Jon Pierre. 2014. Procedure or performance? Assessing citizen's attitudes toward legitimacy in Swedish and Norwegian local government. *Urban Research & Practice* 7 (2): 200–212.

Hanushek, Eric A., Susanne Link, and Ludger Woessmann. 2013. Does school autonomy make sense everywhere? Panel estimates from PISA. *Journal of Development Economics* 104: 212–232. doi:10.1016/j.jdeveco.2012.08.002.

Haugen, Perk Kristian, and Knut Engedal. 2005. *Demens. fakta og utfordringer, en lærebok*, vol. 4. utgave. Oslo: Aldring og helse.

Henriksen, Lars Skov, Steven Rathgeb Smith, and Annette Zimmer. 2012. At the eve of convergence? Transformations of social service provision in Denmark, Germany, and the United States. *VOLUNTAS: International Journal of Voluntary and Nonprofit Organizations* 23 (2): 458–501.

Hermansen, Åsmund, and Heidi Gautun. 2011. *Eldreomsorg under press*. FAFO: Kommunenes helse- og omsorgstilbud til eldre. Oslo.
Hernes, Helga M. 1988. Scandinavian citizenship. *Acta Sociologica* 31 (3): 199–215.
Hinrichs, Karl, and Olli Kangas. 2003. When is a change big enough to be a system shift? Small system-shifting changes in German and finnish pension policies. *Social Policy & Administration* 37 (6): 573–591. doi:10.1111/1467-9515.00359.
Hirschman, Albert O. 1970. *Exit, voice, and loyalty: Responses to decline in firms, organizations, and states*, vol. 25. Cambridge, MA: Harvard University Press.
Hood, Christopher, and Ruth Dixon. 2015. *A government that worked better and cost less? Evaluating three decades of reform and change in UK Central Government*. Oxford: Oxford University Press.
Hoskins, Bryony L. 2014. Active citizenship. In *Encyclopedia of quality of life and well-being research*, ed. Alex C. Michalos, 14–16. Springer Netherlands.
Hvinden, Bjørn, and Håkan Johansson (eds.). 2007a. *Citizenship in Nordic welfare states: Dynamics of choice, duties and participation in a changing Europe*. London: Routledge.
Hvinden, Bjørn, and Håkan Johansson. 2007b. Opening citizenship. Why do we need a new understanding of social citizenship? In *Citizenship in Nordic welfare states: Dynamics of choice, duties and participation in a changing Europe*, eds. Bjørn Hvinden and Håkan Johansson. London: Routledge.
Janoski, Thomas. 1998. *Citizenship and civil society: a framework of rights and obligations in liberal, traditional, and social democratic regimes*. Cambridge: Cambridge University Press.
Jensen, Per H., and Birgit Pfau-Effinger. 2005. Active citizenship: The new face of welfare. In *The changing face of welfare*, eds. J. Gould Andersen, J.-G. Guillemard, Per H. Jensen, and Birgit Pfau-Effinger. Bristol: Policy Press.
Kjølsrød, Lise. 2005. En tjenesteintens velferdsstat. In *Det norske samfunn*, eds. Ivar Frønes, and Lise Kjølsrød, 184–209. Oslo: Gyldendal akademisk.
Kröger, Teppo. 1997. Local government in Scandinavia: Autonomous or integrated into the welfare state? In *Social Care Services: The Key to the Scandinavian Welfare Model*, ed. Jorma Sipilä, 95–108. Avebury: Aldershot.
Kumlin, 2004. *The personal and the political: How personal welfare state experiences affect political trust and ideology*. New York: Palgrave Macmillan.
Le Grand, Julian, and Will Bartlett. 1993. The theory of Quasi-markets. In *Quasi-markets and social policy*, eds. Julian Le Grand, and Will Bartlett, 13–34. London: Macmillan Press.

Marshall, T.H. 1950. *Class, citizenship and social development: Essays*. New York: Doubleday.
Meagher, Gabrielle, and Marta Szebehely. 2013. Four Nordic countries—Four responses to the international trend of marketisation. In *Marketisation in Nordic eldercare*, eds. Gabrielle Meagher and Marta Szebehely. Stockholm: Department of Social Work, Stockholm University.
Norsk senter for menneskerettigheter. 2014. *Menneskerettigheter i norske sykehjem*. Oslo: Juridisk fakultet, Universitetet i Oslo.
OECD. 2011. *Together for better public services: Partnering with citizens and civil society*. Paris: OECD.
Olsen, Johan P. 1990. *Demokrati på Svenska*. Stockholm: Carlson Bokförlag.
Osborne, Stephen P., Zoe Radnor, and Greta Nasi. 2013. A new theory for public service management? Toward a (public) service-dominant approach. *The American Review of Public Administration* 43 (2): 135–158.
Palier, Bruno. 2007. Beyond retrenchment: Four problems in current welfare state research and one suggestion on how to overcome. In *Welfare state reader*, 2nd ed, eds. Christopher Pierson, and Fracis G. Casltles, 358–374. Cambridge: Polity Press.
Parks, Roger B., Paula C. Baker, Larry Kiser, Ronald Oakerson, Elinor Ostrom, Vincent Ostrom, Stephen L. Percy, Martha B. Vandivort, Gordon P. Whitaker, and Rick Wilson. 1981. Consumers as coproducers of public services: Some economic and institutional considerations. *Policy Studies Journal* 9 (7): 1001–1011.
Phillips, Susan D., and Steven Rathgeb Smith. 2011. Between governance and regulation. Evolving government—Third sector relationships. In *Governance and regulation in the third sector: International perspectives*, eds. Susan D. Phillips and Steven Rathgeb Smith. New York: Routledge.
Rose, Lawrence E. 2007. User boards and user control: Increment or detriment to local democracy? In *Towards DIY-politics: Participatory and direct democracy at the local level in Europe*, eds. Herwig Reynaert, Kristof Steyvers, Pascal Delwit, and Jean-Benoit Pilet, 127–164. Brugge: Vanden Broele.
Rose, Lawrence E. 2011. Den krevende borger: Kveles lokaldemokratiet? In *Lokalt demokrati uten kommunalt selvstyre?*, eds. Harald Baldersheim, and Eivind Smith. Oslo: Abstrakt forlag.
Rostgaard, Tine. 2006. Constructing the care consumer: Free choice of home care for the elderly in Denmark. *European Societies* 8 (3): 443–463.

Rostgaard, Tine. 2015. *Når fortiden er længere end fremtiden*. Stockholm: Nordens Välfärdscenter.
Rothstein, Bo. 1994. *Vad bör staten göra*. Stockholm: SNS Förlag.
Rothstein, Bo. 1998. *Just institutions matter: The moral and political logic of the universal welfare state*. Cambridge: Cambridge University Press.
Rothstein, Bo. 2009. Creating political legitimacy: Electoral democracy versus quality of government. *American Behavioral Scientist* 53 (3): 311–330. doi:10.1177/0002764209338795.
Smith, Steven Rathgeb, and Kristen A. Grønbjerg. 2006. Scope and theory of government-nonprofit relations. In *The nonprofit sector: A research handbook*, eds. Walter W. Powell and Richard Steinberg, 221–242. New Haven, CT: Yale University Press.
Steinberg, Richard 2006. Economic theories of nonprofit organizations. In *The nonprofit sector: A research handbook*, eds. Walter W. Powell and Richard Steinberg, 117–139. New Haven, CT: Yale University Press.
Thornton, Patricia H, William Ocasio, and Michael Lounsbury. 2012. *The institutional logics perspective: A new approach to culture, structure, and process*. Oxford University Press.
Trägårdh, Lars. 1997. Statist individualism: On the culturality of the Nordic. In *The cultural construction of Norden*, eds. Øystein Sørensen, and Bo Stråth, 253–285. Oslo: Scandinavian University Press.
Trägårdh, Lars. 2008. Det civila samhällets karriär som vetenskapligt och politiskt begrepp i Sverige. *Tidskrift for samfunnsforskning* 49 (4): 575–594.
Tranvik, Tommy, and Per Selle. 2005. State and citizens in Norway: Organisational society and state–municipal relations. *Western European Politics* 28 (4): 852–871.

Author Biography

Håkon Solbu Trætteberg is a senior research fellow at the Institute for Social Research, Oslo, Norway. His main research interest is publicly-funded welfare services in general and the importance of the welfare mix in particular. Trætteberg received his Ph.D. in 2016, partly on work presented in this book.

Open Access This chapter is licensed under the terms of the Creative Commons Attribution 4.0 International License (http://creativecommons.org/licenses/by/4.0/), which permits use, sharing, adaptation, distribution and reproduction in any medium or format, as long as you give appropriate credit to the original author(s) and the source, provide a link to the Creative Commons license and indicate if changes were made.

The images or other third party material in this chapter are included in the chapter's Creative Commons license, unless indicated otherwise in a credit line to the material. If material is not included in the chapter's Creative Commons license and your intended use is not permitted by statutory regulation or exceeds the permitted use, you will need to obtain permission directly from the copyright holder.

7

Does the Type of Service Provider Affect User Satisfaction? Public, For-Profit and Nonprofit Kindergartens, Schools and Nursing Homes in Norway

Tord Skogedal Lindén, Audun Fladmoe
and Dag Arne Christensen

Introduction

Are private welfare services better than those provided by the public sector? One way to address this question is to ask users of public, for-profit, and nonprofit welfare services to evaluate services. User satisfaction is an important topic as it may influence general support for social policy and thus has importance for welfare state legitimacy. However, as social policy research has so far focused more on cash

---

T.S. Lindén (✉)
Uni Research Rokkan Centre, Bergen, Norway
e-mail: tord.linden@uni.no

A. Fladmoe
Institute for Social Research, Oslo, Norway
e-mail: audun.fladmoe@socialresearch.no

D.A. Christensen
Uni Research Rokkan Centre, Bergen, Norway
e-mail: dag.christensen@uni.no

© The Author(s) 2017
K.H. Sivesind and J. Saglie (eds.), *Promoting Active Citizenship*,
DOI 10.1007/978-3-319-55381-8_7

benefits than services, we have limited knowledge about how, for example, service providers influence service quality and user satisfaction (e.g. Jensen 2011). Thus, we need more knowledge about user satisfaction. In this chapter, we shed light on this important yet little studied topic, based on recently collected survey data from Norway within childcare, education and elderly care (DIFI 2011 2013a, b, 2015a, b; Kumlin et al. 2016). This supplements the book, which, so far, has discussed changes in the regulation and provision of nursing homes and schools at the national level in Denmark, Sweden and Norway as well as municipal-level case studies. We have included kindergartens as a third service in this chapter because of the high proportion of private suppliers in Norway. Substantively, this service is also relevant as it has increasingly been considered part of the educational pathway in Norway, most explicitly manifested in 2005 when the responsibility for kindergartens was moved from the Ministry of Children and Family Affairs to the Ministry of Education and Research.

It is important to distinguish between two feedback mechanisms when it comes to rating services and providers. One is 'objective', consisting of so-called 'hard indicators' such as resources and outputs. These indicators have traditionally constituted the main, if not the only, sources for monitoring public sector performance (Bouckart and Van de Walle 2003). It is only recently that 'soft indicators' measuring user satisfaction have become more important as a means to evaluate public services. This change of focus has gone hand in hand with an increased interest in accountability (Bouckart and Van de Walle 2003). This approach originated in the United States during the 1990s and has since spread to Europe. In fact, the Norwegian Citizen Survey is based on the American Customer Satisfaction Index (ACSI) (Christensen et al. 2011). This shift from hard to soft indicators has provided a new set of tools for evaluating public services (Van Ryzin 2004). However, the accuracy of these tools has been a source of concern (Van De Walle and Ryzin 2011). First, it appears that questions about specific services yield higher overall satisfaction than questions dealing with the general evaluation of public services. Second, studies from the United States suggest huge variation in user satisfaction across services (Miller and Miller 1991). Third, even citizens who have no experience with certain public services appear to

7 Does the Type of Service Provider Affect User Satisfaction?... 263

have strong opinions about them. Fourth, there is no one-to-one relationship between user satisfaction and the quality of public services (Rolland 2003). In addition to their experiences with the services as such, evaluation is also based on users' predispositions and expectations (James 2009). Thus, citizens' satisfaction with a particular service will depend on a long list of factors, and there is no straightforward relationship between service satisfaction and the quality of the services.

In the introduction to this volume, Sivesind and Trætteberg asked whether public, nonprofit or for-profit providers are most conducive to active citizenship. Active citizenship implies user choice, empowerment, and participation understood as the actual ability for users to express views and argue for change. In this chapter, we contribute to the book's overall topic by discussing user satisfaction. We are mainly concerned with the dimension of active citizenship Sivesind and Trætteberg referred to as *choice*, which includes two empirical indicators: 'Promoting a broader range of services where more users obtain services that cater to their interests' and 'Formal and real exit opportunities give power to users'. Thus, choice could generate higher user satisfaction through at least two mechanisms: (1) improved service quality and (2) empowerment.

The first mechanism—improved service quality—rests on the idea that a well-functioning market, where users can choose freely between different service providers, will lead to higher satisfaction. Welfare systems combining public financing of services with for-profit or nonprofit service providers are referred to as a 'quasi-market' (Le Grand 1997, 151). As will be empirically described below, although public suppliers are dominant in the Norwegian welfare state, nursing homes, kindergartens, and schools resemble quasi-markets to some extent. According to Le Grand (1997, 159), competition could result in efficiency and responsiveness: 'Schools will be more sensitive to parents, for fear that they will otherwise take their child away—or not apply in the first place —and the school budget will suffer. And they too will have an incentive to be more efficient'.

The other mechanism—empowerment—rests on a great corpus of psychological research that has demonstrated that choice is positively related to satisfaction, even if the outcome is incongruent with previously stated preferences (see e.g. Botti and Iyengar 2004). By introducing the possibility of opting out and choosing a different provider, users may feel empowered as active citizens, a feeling which by itself may lead to increased satisfaction irrespective of actual service improvement.

We draw on two strong data sources to illuminate our research questions: the biennial Norwegian Citizen Survey (*Innbyggerundersøkelsen*) conducted by the Norwegian Agency for Public Management and eGovernment (DIFI) in 2011, 2013 and 2015, and a survey on social capital and welfare attitudes (SuppA) conducted by the Institute for Social Research (ISF) in 2014 and 2015 (Kumlin et al. 2016). The DIFI data provide comprehensive information about satisfaction with public and private welfare providers and has one major benefit compared with other data sources: It distinguishes between actual users with service experience and respondents evaluating services based on other sources of information. Unfortunately, the DIFI data does not distinguish nonprofit from for-profit providers. To be able to fully discuss the importance of the service provider for user satisfaction, we thus introduce a second data source. The SuppA survey not only differentiates between users and non-users, but also includes questions for distinguishing between nonprofit, for-profit providers, and public providers.

The rest of the chapter is structured as follows. First, we give a short overview of existing research on welfare services, followed by a brief presentation of characteristics of the kindergarten sector, schools, and nursing homes. We then present our data sources and describe characteristics of users of private and public services in terms of social background, education, and income. Next, we analyse results on user satisfaction from two angles: differences in user satisfaction between public and private providers in general based on the DIFI data, and then we further elaborate on user satisfaction between different groups based on the SuppA survey for distinguishing nonprofit from for-profit providers. We discuss the general high-level of user satisfaction with Norwegian welfare services as well as differences between the three welfare services with respect to the room needed to create distinctive services. The dependent variable is user satisfaction, and the predictor we are mainly interested in is who is delivering the service. The last section concludes our discussion.

Welfare Services and User Choice

Privatisation is a disputed issue in Norway. While the previous centre–left government largely resisted privatisation, the conservative government that took office in 2013 stated explicitly in their political manifesto that they 'will promote private and voluntary initiatives and allow for the participation of a wider range of actors, including in the provision of welfare services'.[1] By focusing on kindergartens, primary and lower secondary schools, and nursing homes, we included three important sectors of the welfare state. As mentioned by Sivesind in Chap. 2, the role of commercial and non-commercial service providers may vary substantially between sectors. While around 50% of Norwegian children attending day care institutions use a private service, some 3% attend a private primary or lower secondary school, and some 10% of nursing home residents live in privately run institutions. The three sectors vary with regard to the room for creating distinctive services, which is relevant for active citizenship. Overall, analysing important welfare services extends the limited existing knowledge on the consequences of welfare providers for user satisfaction and active citizenship.

As described above, in addition to supposedly increased cost-effectiveness, one of the main arguments in favour of the privatisation of public services is that choice and competition enhance service quality. In academic debates, this has been most boldly stated by Julian Le Grand, who argued that if policies are appropriately designed, extending choice and competition among providers will enhance service quality in most areas of public welfare (Le Grand 1997, 2007). Other studies, however, question this claim. A large meta-study on elderly care in the US has, for instance, suggested that public providers in most cases perform better than commercial providers (Comondore et al. 2009). And in 2015, two leading scholars provided a very critical overview of the results of New Public Management reforms in the UK (Hood and Dixon 2015).

Research conducted in Norway and other Nordic countries on the welfare provision of kindergartens, primary and lower secondary schools, and nursing home services is limited and ambiguous. According to

Børhaug and Lotsberg (2012, 30), we have little knowledge of the relationship between competition and quality in general, and with regard to kindergartens in particular. Gulbrandsen and Eliassen (2013) found few differences in quality between public and private providers in Norway. Børhaug and Lotsberg (2012, 31), however, referred to some recent studies which showed that parents with children in private kindergartens are more pleased than parents with children in public institutions. There is also little research on the quality of public and private primary and lower secondary schools in Norway. Swedish research (e.g. Hartman 2011; Böhlmark and Lindahl 2012; Skolverket 2012) has provided both positive and negative lessons which, however, are not necessarily directly transferable, as conditions vary (e.g. with respect to school profiles and opportunities to yield a profit). Moreover, as many as 27% of Danish and 14% of Swedish pupils attend a non-public lower secondary school, compared to 3% in Norway (Udir 2015b, 32; see Chap. 2 in this volume and Sivesind 2016 for more information). Research on quality in public and private nursing homes is also scarce and inconclusive, and as Trætteberg and Sivesind (2015, 16) have stated, this literature is mostly concerned with differences between public and private providers and hardly distinguishes between for-profit and nonprofit. Vabø et al. (2013) gave an overview of existing research on elderly care and concluded that there is no clear answer to the question of whether privatisation improves quality. Bogen (2011), Gautun et al. (2013), and Petersen et al. (2014) reached similar conclusions. A large Swedish study of nursing homes summarised the mixed nature in this research field by suggesting that commercial and public suppliers outperform each other on different quality indicators. Commercial suppliers perform better on certain service indicators, such as user participation in the formulation of care plans, while public suppliers perform better on structural quality (hard indicators), such as the number of employees per resident (Stolt, Blomqvist and Winblad 2011). As this short overview of existing research reveals, it is difficult to develop clear expectations on user satisfaction with public and private providers based on findings from the Norwegian and Nordic context.

Scope and Characteristics of Public and Private Kindergartens, Schools and Nursing Homes in Norway

Table 7.1 displays the level of public, nonprofit and for-profit private providers in kindergartens, schools, and nursing homes in Norway.[2] Within childcare, Norway has a substantial level of private providers: 53% of kindergartens are private (Statistics Norway 2015). Unfortunately, this statistic does not distinguish between for-profit and nonprofit providers. Even though kindergarten coverage is now more or less universal, the choice of provider is not an option for everyone as private kindergartens are not available everywhere. Moreover, there is a fixed maximum fee irrespective of the service provider, and public demand for kindergartens may in some areas exceed the supply, forcing parents to choose the first available offer. Nevertheless, when it comes to the room for creating distinctive services, private providers do have flexibility (Børhaug et al. 2011, 183; Børhaug and Lotsberg 2012). There are many minimum requirements, but the provider decides, for instance, priority areas, admission requirements, opening hours, and the number of staff beyond minimum requirements of pedagogical leaders (NOU 2012; Kindergarten Act 2005).

Approximately 6% of primary and lower secondary schools are private, and as few as 3% of Norwegian pupils attend a private primary and lower secondary school (Udir 2013, 2015a). Private schools in Norway

Table 7.1 Share of public, nonprofit and for-profit providers (institutions)

	Kindergartens (2014)[a] (%)	Primary and lower secondary schools (2015)[b] (%)	Nursing homes (2011)[c] (%)
Public	47	94	91
Nonprofit	53	6	5
For-profit	0	0	4

Sources [a]Statistics Norway (2015). [b]Udir (2015a). [c]St. Meld (2012–2013, 71)
Note Statistics Norway distinguishes only between public and private providers of kindergartens. The entry (53%) is thus the sum of nonprofit and for-profit providers

receiving public subsidies can only be nonprofit. With a few exceptions, they have to offer a 'religious or pedagogic alternative' to be approved—the Montessori schools being one example. Of the 208 private schools in Norway in 2014–2015, 74 were approved on a religious basis and 99 as a pedagogic alternative (Udir 2015b, 35). Private schools often have few pupils. Sixty percent of new private schools are established after a public school has been closed, typically in remote areas. However, this does not suggest that this happens very often: only 10% of the closed public schools are replaced by new, private schools (Udir 2013, 3). We find most of the private schools in or around large cities (Udir 2015b, 36). This means that private schools in Norway often have clear alternative profiles, but they also sometimes serve as substitutes for public schools that have been closed.

In contrast to the school sector, living in private or public nursing homes is usually not a conscious choice, as demand is much larger than available institutions can offer. However, in some large cities, Oslo for example, private nursing homes constitute a large share of the total number of institutions, allowing some degree of choice. Nationally, around 90% of nursing homes are run by public providers, while private for-profit and nonprofit homes are responsible for some 5% each (St. Meld 2012–2013, 71). Providers' scope of action is limited due to tight municipal regulations (see Feltenius' chapter), but while it is illegal for service providers to distribute profits from primary and lower secondary schools, it is allowed in private kindergartens and nursing home services.

As the literature review in the previous section suggested, it is difficult to establish clear hypotheses concerning variations in user satisfaction between different providers. Nevertheless, as this overview of the present state of the scope and characteristics of kindergartens, schools and nursing homes in Norway has shown, we may propose some expectations. First, based on the observation that real user choice is most evident in the school sector, we expect higher levels of user satisfaction among those intentionally choosing a private (nonprofit) school. This may be the result of quality differences between providers; through well-functioning quasi-markets, private providers have strong incentives to enhance service quality. Alternatively, satisfaction with private alternatives may increase by the act of choosing, which itself can generate feelings of empowerment. Second, as nursing homes are a scarce commodity which barely meets the demands of the public, we expect the least variation in user satisfaction in this sector. The case studies presented in Chaps. 4 and 6 in this volume have shown that there are few differences between nursing homes across the municipalities, implying that variation in user satisfaction should also be limited. Following this logic, we expect the level of variation in satisfaction among users of kindergartens to be located somewhere in between the other two.

Data and Measurement

The data originate from two sources: The first is the Norwegian Citizen survey, consisting of over 30,000 answers from individuals who received the survey in 2010, 2013 and 2015 (response rates were around 42%). The survey was conducted by the Norwegian Agency for Public Management and eGovernment (DIFI) by means of postal questionnaires and with the option to answer online. The survey was introduced in 2010 and was intended to assess citizens' satisfaction not only with public services, but also included several questions about political participation and attitudes towards politicians. In each of the surveys, respondents were asked whether they had used the services they were asked to evaluate. Respondents answering 'yes' to this question received a second (and much shorter) questionnaire that focused on various aspects of that service. These are the datasets used in this study, and the final analysis includes 1998 kindergarten users, 2264 primary and lower secondary school users, and 1622 nursing home users.

The dependent variable in the citizen survey was derived from a single item (here exemplified in the kindergarten survey): 'Think back on the experiences you have had with your child's kindergarten. Overall, how satisfied or dissatisfied are you with this kindergarten?' The items had (in addition to 'Do not know') seven response categories ranging from very dissatisfied (-3) to very satisfied ($+3$). In addition, the three user surveys also asked respondents if the institutions they used were public or private. Hence, the citizen survey does not allow us to differentiate between for-profit and nonprofit welfare institutions. Because of the limited number of private schools and nursing homes, we are left with few users of private institutions in those policy fields (3.3% in primary and lower secondary schools and 4.1% in nursing homes); but when it comes to kindergartens, 40% had their child in a private institution. Thus, the analysis is exploratory in nature.

The second dataset comes from a survey on trust and welfare attitudes carried out in Norway in two waves (2014 and 2015) as part of the project 'Support for the affluent welfare state' (SuppA), financed by the Norwegian Research Council (Kumlin et al. 2016). The data were collected by means of a web survey. Most respondents were recruited from TNS Gallup's access panel, which is a pre-recruited, web-based pool of respondents who have been randomly sampled from the Norwegian population (recruited by means of telephone). As people with an immigrant background are underrepresented in the panel, additional respondents were recruited to the panel from the National Register. Both samples were stratified with an overrepresentation of respondents from the four largest cities. A total of more than 10,000 interviews were carried out in 2014 and 2015, of which about one half of the respondents answered the survey in both waves. In the data analysed for this chapter, we included all respondents who participated in 2014 (n = 5420) and all newly recruited respondents in 2015 (n = 2161), for a total of 7581 respondents. Response rates from the pre-recruited panel were 50–60% (Kumlin et al. 2016).

The advantage of the SuppA dataset is that it allows us to differentiate between public, for-profit and nonprofit providers of kindergartens and nursing homes, in addition to distinguishing between public and private (nonprofit) providers of primary and lower secondary schools. To the best of our knowledge, this is the first Norwegian survey to differentiate between for-profit and nonprofit providers. The dependent variable relies on a single item: 'How satisfied or dissatisfied are you with the following services in your municipality/country?' followed by a list of different services (e.g. a kindergarten operated by a nonprofit organisation or as a family cooperative). Responses were given on a 5-point scale, from 'Very dissatisfied' to 'Very satisfied' (in addition to 'Do not know'). The number of respondents reporting experience with the different services varied between 166 (nonprofit kindergartens) and 1905 (public primary and lower secondary schools).

In both surveys, it is important to emphasise that 'users' typically refer to relatives; parents usually answered the survey for kindergartens and schools, while both residents and relatives may have completed the surveys for nursing homes. Thus, the actual users of the two services aimed at children were their parents, while users of nursing homes may have been either residents or their relatives. This warrants caution, as earlier research has shown that relatives are often more critical than actual users (cf. Christensen and Midtbø 2016). However, all respondents had some kind of user experience, either personally or as relatives, which is different from many other surveys where some respondents have had no experience at all.

The two surveys operated with somewhat different structures. In the citizen survey, each respondent only evaluated one service provider within a maximum of five welfare sectors. If respondents had experience with more than one provider, they were instructed to evaluate only one of them based on a fixed criterion (e.g. respondents evaluating kindergartens were asked to only think of experiences with their oldest child). In the SuppA survey, no such criterion was stated, and respondents could evaluate every service provider they had some sort of experience with.

We will first look at the results from the citizen survey. We specify two models for each dependent variable—with and without control variables—but since the two datasets have different structures, the empirical strategy is somewhat different. In the analysis based on the citizen survey, we analysed user satisfaction with the three welfare services, controlling for the provider (public/private). Public welfare institutions are the reference category in the regression. In the analysis based on the SuppA dataset, we analysed user satisfaction independently for each service/provider. In order to evaluate the difference between each provider, we reported 95% confidence intervals for the constant in each regression model.

It is important to mention that differences in user satisfaction can be related to characteristics of those who choose alternatives to public services and not just qualities of the services as such. Still, in the second regression models, we controlled for some indicators associated with the use of different types of institutions. In the analysis, we included two social background variables that may be associated with the use of different service providers or service satisfaction: Education (1 = University/College) and gender (1 = Male). Education is important as an indicator of social resources. One expectation is that the more social resources people have, the more likely they are to take advantage of the possibility to make active user choices. We also included the respondents' political party choice in the previous parliamentary election (1 = Right-wing parties [Conservative Party/Progress Party] and 1 = Christian People's Party). The latter was included because nonprofit welfare institutions in Norway can be attached to different religions, ideologies or alternative ways of life. Finally, we controlled for the time trend in service satisfaction using 2010 (citizen survey) and 2014 (SuppA) as reference categories. Since respondents from the four largest cities were overrepresented in the SuppA survey, in the analysis based on this dataset, we also included a control variable indicating whether the respondent lived in one of the four largest cities in Norway (1 = Large city).

Results

Are users of private welfare institutions more satisfied with the services than users of public services? We start by presenting the results from the three citizen surveys (Table 7.2). We present two models—one with only the private/public indicator (Model I) and one with controls (Model II).

Starting with the relationship between service satisfaction and service provider, the table illustrates that using a private welfare institution is associated with higher satisfaction (see Model I for all three services). This goes for all three services, but the effect is weak and not statistically distinguishable from zero when it comes to nursing homes. This is in line with the expectation that due to a supply shortage of nursing homes, we would find less variation in user satisfaction in this sector. The two services oriented towards children, kindergartens, and primary and lower secondary schools, have more satisfied users among those using private service providers compared to those using public sector institutions. Also in line with our expectation based on the possibility of real user choice,

Table 7.2 User satisfaction by public or private service providers: Kindergartens, primary and secondary schools, and nursing homes. Unstandardised coefficients (OLS)

	Kindergartens		Primary and lower secondary schools		Nursing homes	
	Model I	Model II	Model I	Model II	Model I	Model II
Constant	5.98	5.98	5.49	5.44	5.45	5.55
Private	0.236***	0.238*	0.802***	0.759***	0.062	0.105
Male		−0.080		−0.136***		−0.141*
University		0.009		0.082		−0.342***
Right-wing		0.013		−0.083		−0.178**
CPP		0.043		0.146		0.437***
2013		0.023		0.110		0.236***
2015		0.068		0.211***		0.218**
Adj. R^2	0.01	0.01	0.01	0.02	0.00	0.03
N	1,998	1,998	2,264	2,264	1,622	1,622

Source DIFI Norwegian Citizen Survey 2010, 2013, 2015. *$P < 0.1$ **$P < 0.05$ ***$P < 0.01$
Note Right-wing (Conservative Party and Progress Party) and CPP (Christian People's Party) denote voter intention

the difference is biggest among the few respondents in private schools (0.76). Having children in a private school increases satisfaction by 0.80 points on the 7-point scale. The corresponding increase in satisfaction among users of private kindergartens is 0.24 on the 7-point scale. For both kindergartens and primary and lower secondary schools, the coefficients are significant at the 0.01 level.

Adding controls does not change the results substantially (Model II for all three services). The coefficients measuring the type of service provider are more or less identical after adding control variables. Note also that none of the controls turns out to be significant when it comes to satisfaction with kindergartens, but male respondents are less satisfied with schools than female respondents. Regarding schools, it is also worth noting that satisfaction increases over time. Compared to 2010, satisfaction with primary and lower secondary schools among actual users increased by 0.21 on the 7-point scale by 2015. Turning to nursing homes, our controls have substantial influence over service satisfaction. Male respondents, those with a university education, and respondents voting for right-wing parties are significantly less satisfied with the services provided by nursing homes. Respondents voting for the Christian People's Party are significantly more satisfied with nursing homes, and satisfaction increased over time compared to the first survey conducted in 2010.

In addition, we carried out supplementary analyses (not shown), including variables such as income, type of user experience, and age, and the coefficients for the type of service provider remained unchanged (but the number of missing values increased). It should be noted that general service satisfaction with services related to children (kindergartens and schools) is high compared to services for the elderly (as nursing homes). Still, users with experience with private kindergartens and schools seem to be significantly more satisfied with these institutions compared to users with experience with public kindergartens and schools. It should also be noted that the explanatory power of the different models is weak. For example, Model II (nursing homes) in Table 7.1 explains 3% of the variation in the data.

What does it look like when we include data which allow us to separate between for-profit and nonprofit service providers? Table 7.3 reports regression results based on the SuppA dataset. As in the citizen survey, these results also suggest that the service provider is irrelevant when it comes to nursing homes. The constants reported in columns 7–9 (Model I and Model II) are virtually identical (4.13–4.20). Contrary to the citizen survey and our initial expectations, the SuppA survey does not suggest any differences in satisfaction levels between users of public and private (nonprofit) providers of primary and lower secondary schools, neither in Model I nor in Model II. The level of satisfaction is somewhat higher among users of private schools, but the difference is small and far from statistically significant.

However, turning to kindergartens, we do find some differences. Looking first at Model I, users of for-profit kindergartens report higher satisfaction than users of both public and nonprofit kindergartens. The difference between users of for-profit kindergartens and users of public/nonprofit kindergartens is 0.22 and 0.37, respectively. Interestingly, users of nonprofit kindergartens report lower levels of satisfaction than users of public kindergartens; however, this difference is not significant. These results

Table 7.3 User satisfaction by public, for-profit and nonprofit service providers: Kindergartens, primary and lower secondary schools, and nursing homes. Unstandardised coefficients (OLS)

	Kindergartens			Primary and lower secondary schools		Nursing homes		
	Public	For-profit	Nonprofit	Public	Nonprofit	Public	For-profit	Nonprofit
Model I								
Constant	3.92	4.14	3.77	3.77	3.87	4.18	4.18	4.19
(95% CI)	(3.86–3.98)	(4.06–4.21)	(3.61–3.92)	(3.73–3.81)	(3.72–4.03)	(4.16–4.21)	(4.13–4.22)	(4.15–4.24)
Model II								
Constant	3.87	4.13	3.79	3.68	3.88	4.13	4.14	4.20
(95% CI)	(3.72–4.01)	(3.95–4.31)	(3.43–4.15)	(3.58–3.77)	(3.46–4.30)	(4.07–4.18)	(4.02–4.27)	(4.08–4.32)
Male	−0.08	−0.23***	−0.34**	−0.01	−0.36**	0.04	−0.01	−0.04
University	0.23***	0.11	0.25	0.15***	0.37**	−0.01	0.03	0.05
Right-wing	−0.18***	0.17**	0.14	−0.09**	0.10	0.05**	0.02	−0.03
CPP	0.12	0.31*	1.04***	−0.02	−0.03	0.05	0.00	−0.01
Large city	−0.01	−0.09	−0.07	0.03	−0.06	0.00	−0.01	−0.02
2015	0.01	−0.01	−0.24	0.09*	−0.08	0.07***	0.12*	0.04
Adj. R2	0.02	0.02	0.07	0.01	0.02	0.01	0.00	0.00
n	980	573	166	1,905	182	1,105	304	330

Source Support for the Affluent Welfare State 2014, 2015. $^*P < 0.1$ $^{**}P < 0.05$ $^{***}P < 0.01$

Note Right-wing (Conservative Party and Progress Party) and CPP (Christian People's Party) denote voter intention suggest that the differences between public and private kindergartens as reported in the citizen survey in reality reflect differences between public and for-profit providers. However, in contrast to the analysis of the citizen survey, these differences do not hold when adding controls (Model II). The constants do not change substantially, but the differences between them become insignificant. This may indicate either that the results are driven by self-selection bias, i.e. that those choosing for-profit kindergartens are different from those choosing public or nonprofit kindergartens, or that the number of observations (n = 573–980) is too small to yield significant differences between public/nonprofit and for-profit providers.

Among the different control variables, we see that supporters of right-wing parties report higher satisfaction with for-profit kindergartens, and that supporters of the Christian People's Party report as much as a scale point higher satisfaction with nonprofit kindergartens. This is not surprising and suggests that some of the selection bias is related to political ideology. Right-wing parties have traditionally been the strongest proponents of private/commercial providers, while the Christian People's Party (together with other centrist parties) has traditionally been the strongest proponent of nonprofit providers. Finally, as in the citizen survey, we also see a somewhat higher level of satisfaction with public nursing homes over time (2014–2015).

Based on our empirical analysis of these two data sources, the overall findings are first that the provider is unrelated to user satisfaction with nursing homes; and second, that user satisfaction is higher among users of for-profit kindergartens than among users of public and nonprofit kindergartens. Third, the results are more mixed when it comes to satisfaction with primary and lower secondary schools. In both surveys, users of private schools report higher satisfaction than users of public schools; however, in the SuppA survey, this difference is small and insignificant. This may be explained by selection bias or too few observations in the SuppA dataset. However, it may also be explained by the methodological differences between the two surveys described above. In contrast to the citizen survey, in the SuppA survey, users were not restricted to evaluating only one service provider. We cannot rule out the possibility that variations are reduced when respondents evaluate more than one service provider in a single question battery.

Concluding Discussion

One of the core ideas behind offering users alternative suppliers of welfare services is to improve service quality. The argument is that quasi-markets combined with user choice empower citizens, increase participation, adapt services to the individuals actually using them, and improve service delivery. With respect to these assumptions, our results do not show a substantial for-profit or nonprofit premium over public services. Rather, the results suggest a mixed picture, where there is a weak tendency for users of for-profit kindergartens and private (nonprofit) primary and lower secondary schools to be somewhat more satisfied than users of public providers, but there was no difference when it came to nursing homes. These results must be interpreted against the backdrop of the generally high level of satisfaction with Norwegians welfare services.

The main reason why differences in user satisfaction between service providers are small in Norway is simply that the overall level of satisfaction with public welfare services is high across services and providers. The majority of respondents place themselves on the positive side of the satisfaction scale irrespective of the type of welfare services rated (see also Christensen and Midtbø 2016). For instance, in the SuppA survey, satisfaction levels for the different services and providers examined here are all close to 4 on a 5-point scale. Consequently, we are analysing variations between generally satisfied users of welfare services. In effect, the significant differences in satisfaction levels we found between service providers are indeed relatively small—the largest being 0.7 on a 7-point scale (primary and lower secondary schools in the citizen survey).

Looking more substantially at the variations we do find in our data, different mechanisms may be more or less relevant in explaining differences between welfare services. Regarding primary and lower secondary schools, private alternatives are scarce, and since such alternatives can only be approved if they provide either a religious or a pedagogic alternative, intentionally choosing either of them is a very active choice by parents compared to sending their children to a public school. It is easy to imagine, as the analysis of the data from the citizen survey indicates, that such an active choice is justified in terms of high user satisfaction.

Added to this, several alternative pedagogical schools in Norway have recently been established based on parent initiatives to compensate for the closing of a public school. The latter should also result in satisfied users of such schools. As such, the observed differences in user satisfaction between private and public schools may be the result of both well-functioning quasi-markets where private initiatives improve service quality (cf. Le Grand 1997) and also the act of choosing. By being empowered to choose, some citizens may respond with higher user satisfaction. This latter mechanism cannot be ruled out because our data are vulnerable to self-selection: users were not randomly assigned to different schools, and those choosing a private alternative are different from those choosing the standard public option. Nevertheless, we only found significant differences in satisfaction levels in one of the datasets.

Kindergartens are a somewhat different story. Private providers are widespread and there is little regulation of the field, with the exception of some minimum requirements for staff. Moreover, as the overall supply of kindergartens barely meets public demands, parents rarely have the opportunity to make an intentional choice between different suppliers. As such, the differences we saw between public and for-profit kindergartens are more likely to be explained by differences in service quality. Although real choice is limited in this sector, the observed differences may be the effect of quasi-markets where different suppliers have incentives to improve quality (cf. Le Grand 1997, 2007). Again, we are hesitant about these interpretations. This is partly because the observed differences are very small: 0.2–0.4 points on either a 5- or 7-point scale, and partly because in the SuppA dataset, the differences are no longer statistically significant when including control variables. A cautious conclusion is therefore that users of for-profit kindergartens are somewhat more satisfied than users of public and nonprofit kindergartens, but that this difference is very small. This is in line with some previous studies (Børhaug and Lotsberg 2012, 31).

Finally, regarding nursing homes, the lack of variation in user satisfaction supports the findings in the case study by Feltenius (see Chap. 4). As with kindergartens, the supply of nursing homes is scarce; but in contrast to kindergartens, municipal regulation of nursing homes is tight. Through standardised quality indicators and contracts, different providers have limited options to develop distinct profiles, and users receive more or less the same service irrespective of provider. In sum, the main finding in our data is that users of the three sectors generally report a high level of satisfaction, producing limited variations between different service providers. We also found indications that users of private kindergartens and schools are somewhat more satisfied with the services compared to users of public services. This finding does not apply to nursing homes. One possible explanation for the variations between services is that real user choice is most present in the school sector and least so in the nursing home sector. Distinguishing further between for-profit and nonprofit services, we still found hardly any differences between different types of nursing homes. With regard to kindergartens, we did, however, find that users of for-profit options are somewhat more satisfied than users of nonprofit options.

In other words, based on our data and other studies from Norway (Christensen and Midtbø 2016), one should be reluctant to use evidence based on soft indicators of service satisfaction as an argument in debates about privatisation. This is partly due to general methodological concerns (cf. Van De Walle and Ryzin 2011; James 2009). The main reason, however, is that the substantial differences in user satisfaction are very small in Norway. As opposed to evidence from the US (Miller and Miller 1991), the vast majority of users are satisfied irrespective of supplier, making user satisfaction a quality indicator with limited value (see also Christensen and Midtbø 2016). This limitation is further underscored by the limited degree of freedom suppliers have in tailoring services. State regulations and user rights often limit the possibility of private as well as public suppliers to offer qualitatively different services. If soft indicators are to have any value in public debates on privatisation, future studies need to develop more accurate indicators that will measure relevant dimensions in a context with limited overall variation at the outset.

To conclude, user choice may result in increased user satisfaction. However, as our analysis shows, Norwegian welfare services already enjoy a high-level of user satisfaction. User choice may thus have more importance for active citizenship by empowering citizens. This quality, though, may have other challenging implications, as in the classical trade-off between equality and freedom to choose. Freedom to choose may increase social inequalities because resourceful citizens are better informed and take advantage of available opportunities to a higher extent than less resourceful citizens. How to balance such values is thus an important political question for a welfare state that increasingly seems to emphasise services over cash benefits.

Notes

1. "Political platform for a government formed by the Conservative Party and the Progress Party". Sundvolden, 7 October 2013. Retrieved from https://www.regjeringen.no/contentassets/ a93b067d9b604c5a82bd3b5590096f74/politisk_platform_eng.pdf.
2. A better statistical measure of the size of each provider/sector would be the number of man-years. Unfortunately, we have not been able to retrieve these numbers from Statistics Norway.

References

Bogen, Hanne. 2011. Privat drift av omsorgstjenester. *Gjennomgang av nyere forskning. Fafo-notat* 2011: 22.

Böhlmark, Anders, and Mikael Lindahl. 2012. Independent schools and long-run educational outcomes—Evidence from Sweden's large scale voucher reform. IZA Discussion Paper no. 6683.

Børhaug, Kjetil, and Dag Øyvind Lotsberg. 2012. Institusjonelle betingelser for konkurranse mellom offentlige og private tjenesteytere i barnehagesektoren. *Nordiske organisasjonsstudier* 14 (2): 27–47.

Børhaug, Kjetil, Ingrid Helgøy, Anne Dåsvatn Homme, Dag Øyvind Lotsberg, and Kari Ludvigsen. 2011. *Styring, organisering og ledelse i barnehagen.* Bergen: Fagbokforlaget.

Botti, Simona, and Sheena S. Iyengar. 2004. The Psychological pleasure and pain of choosing: When people prefer choosing at the cost of subsequent outcome satisfaction. *Journal of Personality and Social Psychology* 87 (3): 312–326.

Bouckaert, Geert, and Steven Van de Walle. 2003. Comparing measures of citizen trust and user satisfaction as indicators of 'good governance':

Difficulties in linking trust and satisfaction indicators. *International Review of Administrative Sciences* 69 (3): 329–343.

Christensen, Dag Arne, Hans-Tore Hansen, and Jacob Aars. 2011. Har utformingen av lokale NAV-avtaler betydning for brukernes tilfredshet? *Nordiske Organisasjonsstudier* 13 (3): 55–80.

Christensen, Dag Arne, and Tor Midtbø. Forthcoming. 2016. Kommuner, kommunestørrelse og tilfredshet med velferdsstatens tjenester. In *Utfallsdemokratiet. Hvordan velferdsstaten omformer måten demokratiet fungerer på*, eds. Dag Arne Christensen, Jacob Aars and Brita Ytre-Arne. Oslo: Universitetsforlaget.

Comondore, Vikram R., P. J. Devereaux, Qi Zhou, Samuel B. Stone, Jason W. Busse, Nikila C. Ravindran, et al. 2009. Quality of care in for-profit and not-for-profit nursing homes: Systematic review and meta-analysis. *British Medical Journal*, 339. doi:10.1136/bmj.b2732.

DIFI (Norwegian Agency for Public Management and eGovernment). 2010. Innbyggerundersøkelsen. Inntrykk av å bo i kommunene og i Norge. DIFI-rapport 2010:01. Oslo: Direktoratet for forvaltning og IKT.

DIFI (Norwegian Agency for Public Management and eGovernment). 2013a. *Innbyggerundersøkelsen 2013: Hva mener innbyggerne? DIFI-rapport 2013:6*. Oslo: Direktoratet for forvaltning og IKT.

DIFI (Norwegian Agency for Public Management and eGovernment). 2013b. *Innbyggerundersøkelsen 2013: Hva mener brukerne? DIFI-rapport 2013:7*. Oslo: Direktoratet for forvaltning og IKT.

DIFI (Norwegian Agency for Public Management and eGovernment). 2015a. Innbyggerundersøkelsen 2015: Hva mener innbyggerne? DIFI-rapport 2015:5. Oslo: Direktoratet for forvaltning og IKT.

DIFI (Norwegian Agency for Public Management and eGovernment). 2015b. Innbyggerundersøkelsen 2015: Hva mener brukerne? DIFI-rapport 2015:6. Oslo: Direktoratet for forvaltning og IKT.

Gautun, Heidi., Hanne Bogen, and Anne Skevik Grødem. 2013. Konsekvenser av konkurranseutsetting. Kvalitet, effektivitet og arbeidsvilkår i sykehjem og hjemmetjenester. Fafo-rapport 2013:24.

Gulbrandsen, Lars, and Erik Eliassen. 2013. Kvalitet i barnehager. Rapport fra en undersøkelse av strukturell kvalitet høsten 2012. NOVA-rapport 1/2013.

Hartman, Laura, ed. 2011. *Konkurrensens konsekvenser. Vad händer med svensk välfärd?*. Stockholm: SNS Förlag.

Hood, Christopher, and Ruth Dixon. 2015. *A Government That Worked Better And Cost Less? Evaluating Three Decades of Reform and Change in UK Central Government*. Oxford: Oxford University Press.

James, Oliver. 2009. Evaluating the Expectations Disconfirmation and Expectations Anchoring Approaches to Citizen Satisfaction with Local Public Services. *Journal of Public Administration Research and Theory* 19 (1): 107–123.

Jensen, Carsten. 2011. Determinants of welfare service provision after the Golden Age. *International Journal of Social Welfare* 20 (2): 125–134.

Kindergarten Act. 2005. Act no. 64 of June 2005 relating to Kindergartens.

Kumlin, Staffan., Audun Fladmoe, Rune Karlsen, Kari Steen-Johnsen, Dag Wollebæk, and Hanna Bugge. 2016. Support for the affluent welfare state (SuppA). A Norwegian panel study on welfare state orientations, social capital, and local context. Unpublished report. Oslo: Institute for Social Research.

Le Grand, Julian. 1997. Knights, knaves or pawns? Human behaviour and social policy. *Journal of Social Policy* 26 (2): 149–169.

Le Grand, Julian. 2007. *The other invisible hand: Delivering public services through choice and competition*. Princeton: Princeton University Press.

Miller, Thomas I., and Michelle A. Miller. 1991. Standards of excellence: US residents' evaluations of local government services. *Public Administration Review* 51 (6): 503–513.

NOU (Official Norwegian Report). (2012: 1): Til barnas beste — Ny lovgivning for barnehagene. Kunnskapsdepartementet, 16. january 2012.

Petersen, Ole Helby., Ulf Hjelmar, Karsten Vrangbæk, and Patricia Thor Larsen. 2014. Effekter ved udlicitering af offentlige opgaver. En forskningsoversigt over danske og internationale studier fra 2011–2014, Roskilde Universitet 2014.

Rolland, Asle. 2003. Brukernes tilfredshet eller tjenestens kvalitet? *Tidsskrift for velferdsforskning* 6 (1): 56–60.

Ryzin, Van, and G. Gregg. 2004. Expectations, performance, and citizen satisfaction with urban services. *Journal of Policy Analysis and Management* 23 (3): 433–448.

Sivesind, Karl Henrik, ed. 2016. *Mot en ny skandinavisk velferdsmodell? Konsekvenser av ideell, kommersiell og offentlig tjenesteyting for aktivt medborgerskap. Rapport (2016:1)*. Oslo: Institutt for samfunnsforskning.

Skolverket, 2012. *En bild av skolmarknaden*. Skolverket: Syntes av Skolverkets skolmarknadsprojekt. Stockholm.

SSB (Statistics Norway). 2015. Barnehager. 2014. endelige tall, available at https://www.ssb.no/utdanning/statistikker/barnehager/aar-endelige/2015-05-04#content.

St. Meld. (Report to the Storting) 29. (2012–2013). Melding til Stortinget. Morgendagens omsorg. Helse- og omsorgsdepartementet.

Stolt, Ragnar, Paula Blomqvist, and Ulrika Winblad. 2011. Privatization of social services: quality differences in Swedish elderly care. *Social Science and Medicine* 72 (4): 560–567.

Trætteberg, Håkon Dalby, and Karl Henrik Sivesind. 2015. Ideelle organisasjoners særtrekk og merverdi på helse- og omsorgsfeltet. Rapport (2015:2). Bergen/Oslo: Senter for forskning på sivilsamfunn og frivillig sektor.

Udir (Norwegian Directorate for Education and Training). 2013. Skolestruktur: Endringer i landskapet de siste ti årene. Statistikknotat 2/2013. Oslo: Udir.

Udir (Norwegian Directorate for Education and Training). 2015a. Tall om grunnskolen 2015/16. Published 11.12.2015, available at http://www.udir.no/Tilstand/Analyser-og-statistikk/Grunnskolen/GSI-tall/Analyse-av-GSI–tall/.

Udir (Norwegian Directorate for Education and Training). 2015b. Utdanningsspeilet. Tall og analyse av barnehager og grunnopplæringen i Norge. Oslo: Udir.

Vabø, Mia, Karen Christensen, Frode F. Jacobsen, and Håkon Dalby Trætteberg. 2013. Marketisation in Norwegian eldercare: Preconditions, trends and resistance. In *Marketisation in Nordic eldercare: A research report on legislation, oversight, extent and consequences*, eds. Marta Szebehely, and Gabrielle Meagher, 163–202. Stockholm: Stockholm University.

Van de Walle, Steven, and Gregg Van Ryzin. 2011. The order of questions in a survey on citizen satisfaction with public services: Lessons from a split-ballot experiment. *Public Administration* 89 (4):1436–1450.

Authors' Biography

Tord Skogedal Lindén is a Senior Researcher and research leader at Uni Research Rokkan Centre, Bergen, Norway. His research has mainly focused on the welfare state, including family policy, ageing, pensions, and social policy recommendations of international organisations. His publications include a coedited volume on the making of ageing policy, and he is currently involved in a book project on welfare services in Norway.

Audun Fladmoe is Senior Research Fellow at the Institute for Social Research, Oslo, Norway. He is also affiliated with the Centre for Research on Civil Society & Voluntary Sector, Norway. His main research interests include different areas in public opinion and political behaviour, such as welfare attitudes, social capital, voluntarism, and participation. He has published articles in *Journal of European Social Policy*, *Scandinavian Journal of Educational Research*, and *Nordicom Review*, among others. He is currently participating in several projects on voluntarism, freedom of speech, and hate speech.

Dag Arne Christensen is Reseach Professor at the Uni Research Rokkan Centre, Bergen, Norway, with experience in managing large projects. His main research interests are political mobilisation, electoral systems, opinion formation, and research methods. Christensen has published in journals such as *Party Politics, Scandinavian Political Studies, West European Politics, Policy & Politics,* and *Local Government Studies*. He has also been an editor of *Scandinavian Political Studies*.

Open Access This chapter is licensed under the terms of the Creative Commons Attribution 4.0 International License (http://creativecommons.org/licenses/by/4.0/), which permits use, sharing, adaptation, distribution and reproduction in any medium or format, as long as you give appropriate credit to the original author(s) and the source, provide a link to the Creative Commons license and indicate if changes were made.

The images or other third party material in this chapter are included in the chapter's Creative Commons license, unless indicated otherwise in a credit line to the material. If material is not included in the chapter's Creative Commons license and your intended use is not permitted by statutory regulation or exceeds the permitted use, you will need to obtain permission directly from the copyright holder.

8

The Future of the Scandinavian Welfare Model: User Choice, Parallel Governance Systems, and Active Citizenship

Karl Henrik Sivesind, Håkon Solbu Trætteberg and Jo Saglie

Introduction

In this concluding chapter, we summarise and discuss the main findings regarding national and EU regulation of welfare services and welfare governance in municipalities and institutions, as well as the impact of these factors on active citizenship. More precisely, we focus on four questions: (1) What are the main similarities and differences between Denmark, Norway, and Sweden? (2) What are the conditions for active citizenship—here defined as choice, empowerment, and participation? (3) Does institutional sector matter for the users? (4) What are the consequences of user choice and other forms of market-emulating

---

K.H. Sivesind (✉) · H.S. Trætteberg · J. Saglie
Institute for Social Research, Oslo, Norway
e-mail: k.h.sivesind@socialresearch.no

H.S. Trætteberg
e-mail: h.s.tratteberg@socialresearch.no

J. Saglie
e-mail: jo.saglie@socialresearch.no

© The Author(s) 2017
K.H. Sivesind and J. Saglie (eds.), *Promoting Active Citizenship*,
DOI 10.1007/978-3-319-55381-8_8

regulation? Finally, we discuss the consequences of recent developments in Scandinavian welfare policies for the so-called Scandinavian welfare model: Where are Scandinavian welfare policies heading?

The Three Countries Compared

When we compare the countries, service areas and economic sectors, we generally find that the users in the Danish school system are more empowered and have access to better systems for participation in decision-making. This has to do with the combination of long traditions of the free school system in Denmark, few legal restrictions on the content of the teaching, and the parents' rights to establish new schools. The users and the administrative system have clear and coherent expectations of 'self-owning institutions' to such an extent that the new type of private kindergartens and 'independent nursing homes', which may take out profit, so far tend to operate in a similar way to the traditional free schools.

Whereas the importance of the nonprofit sector in Denmark constitutes a stable element, Scandinavian welfare provision is also changing. The role of user choice is increasing. In Sweden, this has been combined with increased involvement of for-profit service providers. This has resulted in a strong growth and concentration of ownership in a small number of welfare conglomerates partly owned by international venture capitalists. The large Swedish conglomerates appear to use their financial foundations to gain shares also in the emerging welfare markets in Denmark and Norway (Herning 2015). Moreover, some of them have established businesses also in the UK and other European countries.

The case of Denmark nevertheless illustrates that a relatively strong nonprofit welfare provision is possible within a Scandinavian welfare model, and this has dampened the commercialisation process to some extent. The long-standing tradition for independent nonprofit schools in Denmark points to the importance of path dependency. The strength of the nonprofit sector in Denmark has been conducive to a strong political support across party lines. In contrast, the marginal nonprofit sector in Sweden has not been able to muster much political support. In this respect, Norway occupies a middle position between Denmark and Sweden.

However, none of the Scandinavian countries seem to have a recipe for how to create growth in the nonprofit welfare sector in combination with increasing user choice and other market-emulating tools of governance. Norway has succeeded in keeping up the nonprofit share in a rapidly expanding welfare service sector through prioritising nonprofit in certain service areas, using contracts without termination dates, and invitations to tenders and closed negotiations for nonprofit. This option, however, is now being questioned.

In all three countries, public-sector procurement comes within regulations at the European level. The Norwegian authorities have cast doubt on the possibility of maintaining such exceptions for nonprofit actors after the implementation of the EU's revised Public Procurement Directive in national laws in 2016.[1] However, as Segaard and Saglie argue in Chap. 3, it appears that each individual country still will be able to use discretion to organise its welfare mix, taking its cultural context into consideration. Although the EU regulations constitute an important framework for national policymaking, the intention is not to standardise the welfare mix but, rather, to create competition between providers from different countries where there are potential markets. However, social, health, and educational services are considered by the EU directive to be linked to different cultural traditions and have a limited cross-border dimension. Differences between countries may thus be maintained within regulations at the European level. However, the question is how the Scandinavian countries approach and utilise this latitude. Some Scandinavian politicians and administrators appear to endorse a stronger 'competition fundamentalism' than the EU itself does.

The Conditions for Active Citizenship

We have used the concept of 'active citizenship', defined as choice, empowerment, and participation, in our qualitative case studies, in order to measure aspects of users' experiences with welfare services. This approach emphasises what the citizens can do when they are not satisfied with their current situation. Do they have a real opportunity to choose a welfare provider with a desired profile or to change to another provider if they are not satisfied? Can they influence their own situation at the institution through individual, day-to-day contact with staff or through participation in user boards? Is there participation in municipal decision-making, either through representatives or mediated by civil society organisations? The active citizenship approach focuses on dimensions that enable users to deal with quality problems in relation to the staff, and the administrators, and local politicians at the municipal level. Our findings indicate that administrative systems, real opportunities for choice, and participative structures matter for active citizenship. These are aspects of the welfare system that policymakers may change through normal tools of governance.

The combined insight from the case studies reported in Chaps. 4–6 is that we find the best conditions for active citizenship when there is a real opportunity for users to choose between institutions, and the service providers have room to create distinctive services. This situation typically occurs when there is a right to establish new service institutions, depending on approval on the national level rather than tight regulation at the local level. There must also be some excess capacity in the welfare system to create flexibility between the public and private providers. Active citizenship is less likely to occur when the municipality assigns users to the different institutions, there is insufficient capacity, and public regulation allows little room for distinctiveness. Then the users tend to be more passive both when it comes to seeking adaptation to their particular needs and in participation in decision-making at the institutional level. The power is shifted from the users to the service providers.

These conditions for active citizenship have more to do with regulation, funding, and norms than with whether the providers belong to the public, for-profit, or nonprofit sector. However, the distinctiveness of services and empowerment of users through formal arenas is most prominent in nonprofit service providers, to the extent that they have operative autonomy from public regulation and external owners with privileged steering rights.

The comparative case studies in schools and nursing homes presented in Chaps. 4–6 show that there are considerable differences between the two service areas with regard to active citizenship. As we elaborate below, two key features are decisive for explaining similarities between nursing homes as well as variations between schools: the user choice enjoyed by the citizens and the level of operative autonomy enjoyed by the institutions. The consistency of this finding across countries and service areas suggests that the importance of these mechanisms have a general scope that may apply also to other service areas and welfare contexts.

In no nursing home in this study did users find that they had the power to demand changes based on an opportunity to exit the institution. Moreover, there are no differences between the nursing homes stemming from their institutional sectors. The fragility of some elderly care users makes it difficult to envision that the benefit of user choice is the same for all groups. In a study based on Swedish data, Meinow et al. (2011) concluded that 'those elderly people who are most dependent on care services and who could benefit most from a "good choice", are also those who have the highest prevalence of cognitive and physical limitations associated with the capacity to act as a rational consumer of care services'. This implies that choice mostly benefits the ones who need it the least. Differences in elderly care may thereby increase, since the ones who are weakest and least able to formulate their wishes do not enjoy the benefits from a choice opportunity. To compensate for this and avoid service failures and breaches of human rights that have been documented in elderly care (Norwegian Centre for Human Rights 2014), it is important to involve relatives, institutional boards, and user organisations to play the role of an active citizen on behalf of the frail elderly.

In contrast, we found both a stronger element of user choice and more variation between institutional sectors in schools. All three countries have, in principle, some level of user choice. In all instances, nonprofit schools were distinctive from the public option and thus represented a broadening of the profile of services offered. In Sweden, for-profit schools are to a lesser degree different, and their lack of an alternative vision is explicitly explained through the non-ideological status of the for-profits. However, the for-profits seem to contribute more than the nonprofit in stimulating competition between schools. This is the only place where parents report they can use the possibility to exit as a bargaining chip with the schools. In Denmark, nonprofit schools and public schools do experience competition, but students do not threaten to change schools. This point about for-profit schools must be qualified, however, since for-profit schools are only found in Sweden. There is thus a possibility that specific institutional factors operating in the Swedish context interact with factors related to the institutional sector of the for-profit schools to produce this effect.

Both schools and nursing homes are mainly financed and regulated by the government; and yet, there are differences in terms of how much freedom the providers have. In the school sector, non-public schools are regulated at the national level, while nursing homes are contracted to municipalities. The latter contracts are given after a public tender or are part of long-standing frame arrangements whereby municipalities have ample room to intervene in detailed aspects of their operations. This gives nonprofit schools more room to set their own goals, establish their own unique organisation, and allocate their resources as they wish. This also gives them the opportunity to create distinctive services and involve users in them to a greater extent. The combination of user choice and administrative freedom is important for nonprofit schools, since students who attend non-public schools actively seek to join them, something that makes their distinct operation possible.

Does Institutional Sector Matter?

There is reason to believe that the nonprofit have an advantage in provision of welfare services, because they have less incentive to use the information asymmetry to their own advantage (Hansmann 1987). In addition, in voluntary organisations, that own a major part of the nonprofit providers, member-based democracy has been identified as a mechanism that provides autonomy from public and market forces (Eikås and Selle 2002, 52). In a recent publication, Selle (2016) argued that this mechanism has been weakened, which has in turn also weakened nonprofit distinctiveness. However, distinctiveness may still be secured through alternative mechanisms. Many nonprofit nursing homes and schools are organised as foundations without a membership democracy. The statutes have mechanisms for electing board members that are responsible for realising the mission statement, and not just for economically sustainable operation. There also seem to be an ability and willingness on the part of nonprofit schools to involve users in the governance of the institutions. The distinctiveness of the institutions is the reason why users have chosen them, and they thus look to safeguard this distinctiveness when they are able to influence the operations of the schools. In these cases, users, therefore, function in a comparable manner to members in the above-mentioned studies. At times, users can be both members and users, but by involving stakeholders other than members, nonprofit are able to preserve their distinctiveness. Again, this effect seems dependent on user choice, as user choice is necessary for stakeholders to be sufficiently entrenched in the ideas behind the distinctive profile of the institutions.

These advantages are also recognised by policymakers. For example, an Official Norwegian Report (NOU 2011:11) argued that as society becomes more heterogeneous, welfare sectors will suffer from an increasing lack of labour and more demanding citizens; thus, more diversity in services is needed, especially when it comes to the institutional sector of the providers. The report goes so far as to suggest that by 2025, nonprofit providers should run 25% of the care sector. Although unwilling to support this ambition, the Norwegian government followed up by declaring that user influence, active citizenship, and local democracy will be key features of the future care sector (Report to the Storting (White Paper) nr. 29 2012–2013). In these reports, the connection between service providers, citizenship roles, and services is assumed. However, the mechanisms with the potential to produce the desired outcome received little attention.

The public policy thinking described above reveals faith in the independent importance of institutional sectors. As we have discussed above, the findings in this book suggest that the institutional sector of the provider alone will not produce effects like the ones suggested in the public policy documents. To obtain changes through the strategic use of providers from different institutional sectors, changes in institutional sectors must be combined with other changes to the organisation and governance of the institutions. The substantial differences between service areas demonstrate how looking at the provider alone elucidates only part of the picture. Trætteberg (2015) has documented how detachment from public steering, regulation, and financing is what makes the institutional sectors distinct. It is unclear if this distinctiveness will produce the effects policymakers want, but without distinctiveness, it is difficult to believe that active governance of the welfare mix can achieve anything at all. Providing conditions that enable the distinctive operation of institutions is, therefore, the first step in actively using the welfare mix to obtain societal goals. This has implications for how policymakers approach their steering of the public sector. For a government wishing to reach goals such as social investments in schools (Jenson 2013; Morel et al. 2012) or limiting public expenses in elderly care (Christensen 2012; Brennan et al. 2012) it is natural to increase the level of public steering as a means to reach them. New Public Management may require large administrative resources to make sure that contracts are complied with (Diefenbach 2009). Paradoxically, such public steering undermines the opportunities to develop distinctive services, which is fundamental for reaping some of the benefits of active citizenship.

In addition, Lindén, Fladmoe, and Christensen's analyses in Chap. 7 show that the impact of the institutional sector on user satisfaction is limited. These Norwegian data shows that although there are some differences between the institutional sectors, these differences are very small. In elderly care, there are no differences in user satisfaction in either of the two surveys analysed. In schools, there are some minor differences that disappear after control variables are included. In kindergartens, the users of for-profit institutions are slightly more satisfied after control variables are included. Basically, most users are highly satisfied irrespective of supplier. In elderly care, the finding is consistent with the analysis of Feltenius, showing that the service profiles hardly differ between the sectors because of tight regulation by the municipalities. A high level of satisfaction may be more a result of finally getting a much-needed place than a reflection of the actual quality of the services.

In welfare policymaking, there tends to be a strong focus on measures of user satisfaction but too little analysis of the reasons for satisfaction. User satisfaction is not only related to service quality as such, but may increase with low expectations, lack of alternatives, and even powerlessness. We, therefore, argue that active citizenship dimensions should be brought into research on welfare service quality. By doing so, the results will give clearer advice on which changes are needed to enable users to define and deal with problems in their own situation. This approach is

8 The Future of the Scandinavian Welfare Model: User Choice, ...

also in line with welfare goals set in policy documents with broad political support in all the Scandinavian countries. The concept of active citizenship strengthens the analytic approach to service quality measurement as well as the relevance for policymaking.

In the introductory chapter, we discussed the theory of interdependence. According to this theory, providers from different institutional sectors each have their benefits and drawbacks. The welfare field thus functions best if all providers are present in the welfare mix. This explains why all three institutional sectors appear in most welfare fields and countries (Salamon 1987). The Scandinavian nursing home sector has been an outlier in this sense; up until 25 years ago, there were hardly any for-profit nursing homes, and in Sweden there were also few nonprofit (Meagher and Szebehely 2013). This has changed considerably since then, but it looks as if municipalities have not yet been able to reap the potential benefits of a differentiated provider structure for active citizenship. As Feltenius shows in Chap. 4, the municipalities have arguably made some economic and administrative gains from the use of open tenders. Yet, Trætteberg (Chap. 6) finds no such effects for active citizenship, and consequently, there seems to be an unused potential for active citizenship. Furthermore, Lindén, Fladmoe, and Christensen (Chap. 7) find no important differences in user satisfaction between the institutional sectors. The lack of differences between the different providers may be related to the principle of equivalent service quality that is a basic value in the Scandinavian welfare model, but the downside is that it also reduces the possibility for services to be adapted to a more multifaceted and demanding population. A prerequisite for a successful welfare society is the ability to adapt to changing conditions. The possibility to use the welfare mix to develop distinctive service profiles seems to be underutilised in the context of Scandinavian elderly care.

These findings also indicate that under the present system of governance in Scandinavia, there may be an unused potential for interdependence between the non-public providers and the state (Salamon 1987; Steinberg 2006). The lack of available places in nursing homes is not the result of administrative inability to expand the capacity but, rather, the result of economic considerations in a system where the local governments in the end are responsible for financing the development of new nursing home places within tight budgets. The public administration is also in charge of allocating users to institutions. Under these circumstances, the ability of for-profits to rapidly expand their service is not interesting for the policy makers. The nonprofit ability to cater to niches is also superfluous, as there is no way for users to choose what these niche-oriented providers offer. Competition about public contracts with a focus on costs but with too little emphasis on quality and innovation also gives little room for developing a distinctive profile (Trætteberg and Sivesind 2015). In Sweden and Norway, we have even seen examples of nonprofit organisations that have stopped operating elderly care institutions because they are not able to promote the goals and values set in their mission statements. If nonprofit services do not have room for developing a distinctive character, they cannot fill gaps in the services offered by the public sector (Trætteberg and Sivesind 2015). This underlines the importance of user choice, sufficient capacity, and a minimum of administrative and economic autonomy for distinctive service profiles, which are preconditions for synergies between the institutional sectors. Further empirical research within a Scandinavian context may add robustness to such a conclusion.

Consequences of User Choice and Market Regulation in Scandinavian Welfare Provision

In the introduction to this book, we identify the Scandinavian model with its fundamental ideals, which are public funding and regulation of core welfare services, decentralisation of governance, equal access for all to high-quality services, and adaptation of services to the user's needs and preferences. There is broad political agreement about these goals in all Scandinavian countries, and they appear to be rather stable features. In contrast, there are rapid changes and large differences in how the welfare system is organised between the Scandinavian countries and between the service areas. This is a result of the implementation of different kinds of NPM tools of governance in order to reform the relations between users and public authorities, and between funders (public) and providers (irrespective of the sector) of welfare services. This has been clearly demonstrated through the chapters of this book, comparing changes in welfare mix (Chap. 2), the legal and institutional contexts (Chap. 3), and governance in the municipalities and service institutions in elderly care and schools (Chaps. 4 and 5). However, the regulation of the welfare service provision is also of critical importance for the promotion of active citizenship, defined as choice, empowerment, and participation (Chap. 6). Nonprofit providers have the potential to cater for special interests, ideologies, and faiths that are not interesting business opportunities for private investors and are unsuitable tasks for the state. When nonprofit do not play a sufficiently big role in a welfare field, these niches are in danger of being ignored because of government focus on producing alternatives acceptable to the majority and for-profits' desire to cover large markets, according to economic theories (Salamon 1987; Steinberg 2006). If the nonprofit sector's share of services offered is too small, there will be demands in the population that are not accommodated by the welfare system. How large a share the nonprofit sector should have depends on the heterogeneity of the population (Weisbrod 1977; Sivesind and Selle 2009).

This should be of particular concern for the Scandinavian countries, where the nonprofit sector has much smaller shares of the welfare employment than in other Western European countries (Salamon and Sokolowski 2016). When the Scandinavian welfare states emerged, the populations were rather homogenous with regards to ethnicity, religion, and language, and hence welfare provided by the state was acceptable to a large majority. The primary objective was equal rights to services of high quality given scarce resources (Kuhnle 1983; Seip 1994). With increasing private wealth, and social and cultural diversity, it may not be sufficient to aim for this goal anymore. A dilemma has emerged between providing services of equal quality to all and adaptation to special needs and particular interests. If the latter is ignored, users may opt out of services funded by the government and consequently be less willing to pay taxes. In other words, the legitimacy of the Scandinavian welfare model depends on finding a critical balance between equivalent service quality and a sufficient diversity in service profiles to keep up support for government-funded services. Not all current welfare governance reforms are equally suited for this purpose. Something may have to give: the public funding and regulation, equivalent quality, or adaptation to the users' needs and interests. Failing to find the balance between these sometimes contradictory priorities may result in an inability to reach Scandinavian welfare goals that still have broad political support.

This raises the question of whether we are witnessing an unintended change in welfare goals because of reforms of the governance structures. One of the fundamental changes in the Scandinavian welfare model results from the gradual introduction of user choice in more service areas. In Sweden, this development started in the municipalities in the 90s. Reforms in education were followed by more laws and regulations, which have been gradually imposed on different administrative levels and service areas, most recently the Freedom of Choice Act (LOV 2008:962). In Denmark, there has for a long time been a larger share of nonprofit service employment, which represents a broader spectrum of services to choose from in some service areas. Recently, Denmark has also introduced user choice in several service areas and opened up for new legal categories of independent service institutions in the elderly care and kindergartens, which are disconnected from the municipal governance and funded through a kind of voucher system (Thøgersen 2013, 12 and 16–17). Although they may also take out profits, this has so far not resulted in strong growth in the for-profit share of welfare employment in Denmark in contrast to Sweden (see Chap. 2). This is probably because the Danish population is used to—and therefore still prefers—nonprofit providers similar to the free schools and self-owning institutions at the same time as Denmark has nonprofit providers with the capacity and strength to retain their dominant share of the non-public service provision. In Norway, there has been more emphasis on a supply-side model with competition for contracts mostly within the public welfare system, but also between public, nonprofit, and for-profit providers in some service areas. However, recent legal changes in health, psychiatry, and drug and alcohol addiction treatment imply a shift towards a demand-based model also in Norway (LOV-2016-06-17-48), although on a very limited scale so far. Nonetheless, there is sufficient determination behind these initiatives to potentially produce broad changes over time. In line with global NPM trends, an administrative separation between public purchasers and service providers was introduced in Scandinavia in the 80s and early 90s, creating a supply-based system with tender competition. A logical next step is to develop a demand-based model with user choice, simplified rules for the establishment of private service units, and funding per user.

As a result, more weight is put on individual responsibility for choosing services with the suitable profile and quality and less weight on the government's responsibility for providing equivalent services for all. The consequences could be that the government, also in the Scandinavian countries, assumes a role of 'proactive architect' and coordinator of the welfare provided by the state, the market, the third sector, and by the family and communities (Evers and Guillemard 2013). This emerging citizenship regime relies more on the autonomy of individuals and their capacity to make their own decisions, and it strengthens social rights and responsibilities.

However, to give more power over the profile of welfare services to citizens means reducing the power of public administrators and politicians. When users have increased influence over services, they must also take more responsibility for how the content of welfare functions. Verhoeven and Tonkens (2013) showed that the British government attempts to encourage citizens to take more responsibility for services by emphasising its empowering effects, while in the Netherlands, the emphasis is placed on the duties and responsibilities of citizens. In Chap. 6, Trætteberg takes the perspective of citizens, not governments, and the findings indicate that both experiences exist in the Scandinavian welfare regime. In schools, parents feel empowered and in control when the state reduces its level of control; in nursing homes, users find themselves disempowered. In the first case, users feel they can decide the content of the service; in the second, they feel obliged to take an undue responsibility for the service. In much of the research literature, inequality is regarded as the most likely drawback if power is transferred to individuals (Rothstein 1998, 31–32). Our research does not contradict this point but identifies powerlessness and the burden shift as other possible negative side effects (Trætteberg 2016).

Although user choice gets an increasingly broad implementation in Scandinavia, this is not in principle new to the social democratic regime.

The justification for user choice is and has been to move power from public employees and to the users. This is because frontline service providers need to have room to exercise their professional discretion and decide what measures are suitable in a concrete case for welfare institutions to function. It is then an open question if the outcome that the users experience in fact is related to what has been decided by democratically elected assemblies. This is where the 'black hole of democracy' occurs, according to Blomqvist and Rothstein (2008, 16). The parliament, and regional and local governments, have very limited influence over the shaping of the welfare policy citizens and users in practice meet. The solution, Blomqvist and Rothstein claim, is to let them reject service providers they dislike. There is a potential for improving the democratic rights to fair and equal treatment through user choice.

Recently, the distance between democratic decisions and shaping of services may have increased even further. Provision has to a larger extent been decoupled from the political decision-making through decentralisation and outsourcing, in line with NPM ideals. Instead, citizens and users of welfare services are invited to take part in the evaluation of these services, in consultative arrangements and in limited development projects. Historically, the dominant means for citizen involvement have shifted from popular movements in the formative face of the welfare state, through frontline service providers or street-level bureaucrats (Lipsky 1980), towards participation in 'user democracy' and consultative arrangements. The forms of involvement are to a large extent defined by the operators of decentralised or even subcontracted services. Moreover, the citizen participation is shifting to an ever lower administrative level, from national, through municipal, to the organisational level.

If this is the case, the 'black hole of democracy' has grown wider, and influence through user choice or consultative arrangements may be more important than ever. Will this challenge the Scandinavian welfare model? Not necessarily, Bo Rothstein argues, based on a historical analysis. One of the main intentions of social democratic policies was to give people autonomy and a right to choose how to use the resources made available to them by the welfare system. For example, the preference for universal rights and monetary allowances over means testing and material support is a result of this (Rothstein 1998). The broader implementation of user choice thus does not in itself contradict the ideals behind the social democratic model.

The question is what will happen if the broader implementation of user choice is combined with increased competition for market shares between service providers. For-profit providers have the fastest growth in Sweden, while the changes in Norway and Denmark are more moderate. This is a result of increased use of open tenders and other market-emulating forms of governance, in particular in social services. In Sweden, this development has been much faster because the system of user choice is combined with the free right to the establishment of new service units depending on approval by national agencies enforcing general guidelines. Furthermore, there are no limits on transfer of profit. The purpose of this system is to create competition between the providers of services funded by the government and thereby stimulate quality development. In some service areas, there is also competition on prices, as in elderly care. The tender documents may specify the relative weight that should be put on quality and price. However, studies show that it has been difficult to make these quasi-markets function according to the intentions. There is no clear indication that increased competition has created more efficient services (Hartman 2011; Hood and Dixon 2015; Helby Petersen and Hjelmar 2013; Helby Petersen et al. 2014). The larger differences between high-performing and low-performing students in Swedish results from the PISA tests (Böhlmark and Holmlund 2012), which we discussed in the introduction, may indicate that there are quality issues as well. Such unintended consequences may occur because of double selection effects: Private institutions may prefer to establish themselves in neighbourhoods with a high socio-economic status.[2] In addition, users with more education and cultural capital may be more selective. Furthermore, in many types of services it is, in practice, complicated to change provider if one is not satisfied. The users do not always have the competence to evaluate information that is complex and difficult to measure. They can hardly fulfil their indispensable role of assuring quality and promoting innovation in systems of user choice that expand in the welfare services (Hartman 2011).

In addition, private ownership of Swedish and Norwegian welfare services tends to be concentrated in a few conglomerates. Marketization of

Scandinavian welfare may gradually pull back a public welfare monopoly only to give way to a private oligopoly consisting of a few for-profit conglomerates competing for market shares. According to standard economic models, oligopolies have the potential power to determine prices and to squeeze out smaller competitors and nonprofit with less access to capital (Perloff 2007). Effective markets in such situations may require strong regulation. The reality in Scandinavian welfare services is very different from the theoretical model for quasi-markets, which presupposes easy access to the market for smaller units while those who do not provide good enough service are effectively put out of business (Le Grand 2007). However, the priority of the Scandinavian governments seems to be more on getting the private share up than to establish regulation that structures the ownership in a way that promotes competition.

Competition between providers may have positive effects on service production. As Feltenius shows in Chap. 4, a mix of welfare providers makes it possible to compare providers in terms of costs and quality. Private providers may be useful for benchmarking, seen from the perspective of the municipal administration. From the perspective of the user, competition provides alternatives to choose from. However, these alternatives do not necessarily have distinct profiles, and there is a reason to ask whether a choice between similar alternatives provides the kind of freedom of choice that is necessary to sustain the legitimacy of the Scandinavian welfare model. As we have seen, nonprofit providers seem to have a greater potential to offer distinct alternatives—even though this potential is not always realised under the present administrative regime. A substantial nonprofit sector is not a sufficient condition for distinctive service profiles to choose from, but may be a necessary one.

In current welfare debates, there is not enough consciousness about the consequences of changes in governance for the mix of providers in publicly funded welfare services. The question is whether the services should be operated by the public sector or the private sector. The solution is often to use economic incentives to increase the private share. An underlying assumption, based on economic theories, seems to be that if all providers have equal conditions, the needs in the population will be met in the most efficient manner coordinated through market mechanisms. We find, however, that in the case of the nonprofit welfare providers, this may not be the case. If they are put under too strong pressure by market mechanisms, they may become too similar to the for-profit providers (Salamon 2012). In addition, they may not respond to market opportunities by expanding operations as the for-profit providers do. This is because nonprofit providers have stakeholders that are not interested in growth if it fails to realise the mission statement of the organisation. The specific conditions of the nonprofit providers, therefore, need special attention to ensure a certain share of the welfare employment.

Two fundamental questions are, therefore, how the nonprofit can get resources to expand at a rate comparable to the commercial companies, and how they can do so without losing their distinctive features. If there should be any chance for the nonprofit to have any systemic effects on the welfare provision, the economic and institutional contexts must promote nonprofit welfare entrepreneurs with resources to take risks and expand in several service areas. This will reduce their dependency on single markets and key funding institutions. Unless this happens, the current development towards user choice in more service areas will result in growth only in the for-profit sector. This is a lesson we can learn from the analysis in Chap. 2 of the changes in the employment shares in service areas with open tenders or user choice in Norway and Sweden. There is a clear tendency that when commercial incentives are introduced, it is the for-profit sector that increases. The challenge for the Scandinavian welfare system is how to continue increasing user choice while also regulating the welfare mix. The risk is that the third sector in Scandinavia will not have strength to play its distinctive role by complementing the services of the state and the business sector. The nonprofit sector in the Scandinavian countries has a much weaker institutional foundation than in other countries with advanced welfare systems, as we saw in Chap. 2. Because of the nonprofit welfare sector's small size and weaker historical role, it is also difficult to get political understanding and support for improving frame conditions that will allow it to expand.

In Chap. 3, Segaard and Saglie show that there are parallel systems of governance that may be used to regulate welfare mix in the Scandinavian countries. Service concessions are used in education in Norway and

Denmark with a requirement for getting public funding that there can be no transfer of profit to private owners. This promotes nonprofit alternatives to the public schools in contrast to the development in Sweden. Another example is Danish municipalities that use in-house contracts with self-owning, nonprofit institutions in certain policy areas like nursing homes.[3] This limits their freedom of operation. They get all the users assigned by the municipality and cannot operate in a market at the same time. However, that would be the situation for many of them anyway. It is difficult to develop a distinctive profile when there is too tight steering by the municipality. However, this is no different from what we see in the regulation of non-public welfare provision in general: a certain level of operative autonomy is a precondition for a distinctive service profile.

A third example of parallel governance systems is the Swedish Freedom of Choice Act (LOV 2008:962), which is an alternative to the Public Procurement Act (LOU 2007:1091). However, as we saw in Chap. 2, the LOV-system with built-in economic incentives results in growth only in the for-profit sector, so it is not suited to secure a balanced development of the welfare mix. However, it could be possible to give the nonprofit sector a stronger position within the system for user choice, as suggested in a recent Swedish Government Inquiry (Swedish Government Inquiries SOU 2016:78).

Even the new EU directive for public procurement allows parallel governance systems. It even suggests that the member states establish a separate system for contracting in education, health, and social services. Because services to individuals are highly dependent on the cultural context, there is little potential for cross-border competition. The member states have the opportunity to give funding without using competitive tenders, as long as there are transparency and equal conditions. The EU directive even allows giving contracts to new nonprofit service providers in these service areas for a 3-year period without competition. The UK has already established a Light Touch Regime with guidelines for how to implement these new directives. The Scandinavian countries are now in the process of implementing provisions to their new laws within the framework of the new EU directives for public procurement and service concessions. It is too early to tell how this may affect the composition of welfare service providers. However, these examples illustrate that there are several possibilities for establishing parallel systems of governance that can be used to regulate the welfare mix within a Scandinavian welfare model. The question is whether these opportunities will be used, or if the priority is on promoting competition on equal terms in the welfare services.

Scenarios of the Future for the Scandinavian Welfare Model

Our study shows that different tools of governance have been used in the Scandinavian countries and in the various service areas. We can use this natural experiment to outline some possible future scenarios or at least some development trends. There are lessons to be learnt from the divergent Swedish development of the welfare provider mix, resulting from user choice in combination with open tenders or free rights to establishment—with no restrictions on transfer of profits. When such commercial incentives are implemented and there are no parallel governance systems, there will be growth in the for-profit sector and nonprofit stagnation (See Chap. 2). Some would say that this shows that there is no market for nonprofit services in Sweden. However, our findings indicate that the nonprofit sector needs special conditions to grow, in particular when it is small and has a weak institutional footing as in Sweden. The downside of a too small nonprofit sector is that there will be unmet needs in the population for services with certain distinctive profiles.

Here we see two possible scenarios for the Scandinavian welfare model. One possible development is to let market mechanisms decide which services will be provided. We can call it the 'Swedish model' for simplicity. This means using market-emulating tools of governance such as open tenders or user choice with some kind of voucher system where money follows the users. It is combined with free right to establish new service units pending public approval according to general regulation, and no restrictions on transfer of profit. The users get the critical role of selecting which services will survive. The consequences will be a growing supply of for-profit welfare and decline in the public sector in areas where there are profitable market opportunities, as we saw in Chap. 2. In a Scandinavian context where there is a lack of nonprofit welfare entrepreneurs with a strong economic underpinning, the third sector will not grow under such circumstances. In the USA, the nonprofit sector has increased through market competition; however, the distinctiveness of the sector has suffered under such circumstances (Salamon 2012).

The alternative scenario is to create parallel governance systems. For simplicity, we can call it the 'Danish model'. User choice and market-emulating tools of governance are combined with service concessions and in-house contracts for nonprofit welfare institutions. In addition, the establishment of new nonprofit welfare entrepreneurs is encouraged by reserved service contracts for a limited period as the EU's public procurement directive allows (article 77, Directive 2014/24/EU), or by giving nonprofit organisations public support or loan guarantees to expand service provision in areas where there are increasing demands. In this way, it is possible to compensate for some of the growth disadvantages the nonprofit organisations have because they cannot raise capital from investors by issuing stocks.

How large a share the nonprofit sector should have in different welfare service areas is a political question that depends on striking a balance between different welfare goals. In some areas, the priority may be on equivalent services for all. Some would argue that the government must be able to regulate the school system to promote integration and equal opportunities. However, since parents are legally responsible for the education of their children, they must have some power to decide. In line with basic human rights, the public system cannot be totalitarian. The priorities are different in elderly care, where it is difficult to see that more diverse service profiles would be in contradiction with other political goals. It may be more a question of costs containment, quality assurance, and what is practically possible to arrange for. Many Scandinavian local communities are too small for several alternatives with different profiles that the population can choose from.

We have presented several arguments for promoting the nonprofit sector's role in Scandinavia. The sector already has a very small share of the welfare service employment. This limits its potential to fill niches in areas where there are no interesting market opportunities and no suitable tasks for the public sector. If there is less diversity of services offered to the users, certain demands in the population will be unsatisfied. As Scandinavian societies become more socially and culturally heterogeneous, distinctive alternatives to choose from are also important for the legitimacy of a welfare model funded by taxes. In addition, a small nonprofit sector also limits its potential as a corrective to the for-profit services in areas with information asymmetry between users and service providers. It also limits the potential for innovation in reducing inequality and solving common problems in society, promoted by stakeholders that are dedicated to a mission statement and the common good and have other priorities than profits. Finally, our case studies indicate that the nonprofit welfare providers may promote active citizenship when given adequate frame conditions and government regulations. A certain share of nonprofit sector welfare employment would therefore be important for balancing the Scandinavian welfare goals within an increasing system of user choice. However, this is not what is happening in Sweden, with growth only in the for-profit sector. The Danish case shows that with parallel governance systems it has been possible to regulate the share of nonprofit and for-profit providers under such conditions. These choices are important for the ability to reach the defining welfare goals within a system where core services are funded by the government and, consequently, for the existence of a Scandinavian welfare model in the future.

Notes

1. Directive 2014/24/EU, 114 http://eur-lex.europa.eu/legal-content/EN/TXT/?uri=CELEX%3A32014L0024.
2. See data regarding the location of private schools in Sweden: https://ekonomistas.se/2014/03/14/var-finns-friskolorna/.
3. According to the EU, this is not public procurement and thus not regulated by the directive for service concessions, see article 17, Directive 2014/23/EU.

References

Blomqvist, Paula, and Bo Rothstein. 2008. *Välfärdsstatens nya ansikte: demokrati och marknadsreformer inom den offentliga sektorn*. Stockholm: Agora.

Brennan, Deborah, Bettina Cass, Susan Himmelweit, and Marta Szebehely. 2012. The marketisation of care: Rationales and consequences in Nordic and liberal care regimes. *Journal of European Social Policy* 22 (4): 377–391. doi:10.1177/0958928712449772.

Böhlmark, Anders, and Helena Holmlund. 2012. *Lika möjligheter? Familjebakgrund och skolprestationer 1988–2010*. Uppsala: Institutet för arbetsmarknads- och utbildningspolitisk utvärdering (IFAU).

Christensen, Karen. 2012. Towards a mixed economy of long-term care in Norway? *Critical Social Policy* 32 (4): 577–596.

Diefenbach, Thomas. 2009. New public management in public sector organizations: the dark sides of managerialistic 'enlightenment'. *Public administration* 87 (4): 892–909.

Eikås, Magne, and Per Selle. 2002. A contract culture even in Scandinavia. In *Dilemmas of the Welfare Mix. The New Structure of Welfare in an Era of Privatization*, eds. Ugo Ascoli and Costanzo Ranci. New York: Kluwer Adademic/Plenum Publishers.

Evers, Adalbert, and Anne-Marie Guillemard. 2013. *Social policy and citizenship: The changing landscape*. New York: Oxford University Press.

Hansmann, Henry. 1987. Economic theories of nonprofit organization. *The nonprofit sector: A research handbook.*, 27–42. New Haven: Yale University Press.

Hartman, Laura, ed. 2011. *Konkurrensens konsekvenser: vad händer med svensk välfärd?* Stockholm: SNS Förlag.

Helby Petersen, Ole, and Ulf Hjelmar. 2013. Marketization of welfare services in Scandinavia: A review of Swedish and Danish experiences. *Scandinavian Journal of Public Administration* 17 (4): 3–20.

Helby Petersen, Ole, Ulf Hjelmar, Karsten Vrangbæk, and Patricia Thor Larsen. 2014. *Effekter ved udlicitering af offentlige opgaver. En forskningsoversigt over danske og internationale studier fra 2011–2014*. Roskilde: Roskilde Universitet.

Herning, Linn. 2015. *Velferdsprofitørene*. Oslo: Manifest forlag.

Hood, Christopher, and Ruth Dixon. 2015. *A government that worked better and cost less? evaluating three decades of reform and change in UK central government*. Oxford: Oxford University Press.

Jenson, Jane. 2013. Changing Persepctives on Social Citizenship: A Cross-time Comparison. In *Social policy and citizenship: The changing landscape*, eds. Adalbert Evers and Anne-Marie Guillemard. New York: Oxford University Press.

Kuhnle, Stein. 1983. *Velferdsstatens utvikling—Norge i komparativt perspektiv*. Oslo: Universitetsforlaget.

Julian, Le Grand. 2007. *The other invisible hand: delivering public services through choice and competition*. Princeton: Princeton University Press.

Lipsky, Michael. 1980. *Street-level bureaucracy: Dilemmas of the individual in public services*. New York: Russell Sage Foundation.

Meagher, Gabrielle, and Marta Szebehely, eds. 2013. *Marketisation in Nordic eldercare: a research report on legislation, oversight, extent and consequences*. Stockholm: Department of Social Work, Stockholm University.

Meinow, Bettina, Marti G. Parker, and Mats Thorslund. 2011. Consumers of eldercare in Sweden: The semblance of choice. *Social science & medicine* 73 (9): 1285–1289.

Morel, Nathalie, Bruno Palier, and Joakim Palme. 2012. *Towards a social investment welfare state?: ideas, policies and challenges*. Bristol: Policy Press.

Norwegian Centre for Human Rights. 2014. *Menneskerettigheter i norske sykehjem [Human rights in Norwegian nursing homes]*. Oslo: The Faculty of Law, University of Oslo.

NOU Official Norwegian Report 2011:11. *Innovation in the Care Services*. Oslo: Ministry of Health and Care Services.

Perloff, J.M. 2007. *Microeconomics–theory and applications with calculus: international edition*. Boston, MA: Pearson Addison Wesley.

Report to the Storting (White Paper) nr. 29. 2012–2013. *Future Care*. Oslo: Helse- og omsorgsdepartementet.

Rothstein, Bo. 1998. *Just institutions matter: the moral and political logic of the universal welfare state*. Cambridge: Cambridge University Press.

Salamon, Lester M. 1987. Of market failure, voluntary failure, and third-party government: Toward a theory of government-nonprofit relations in the modern welfare state. *Nonprofit and Voluntary Sector Quarterly* 16 (1–2): 29–49.

———. 2012. *The state of nonprofit America*. Washington, DC: Brookings Institution Press.

Salamon, Lester M., and S. Wojciech Sokolowski. 2016. *The Size and Scope of the European Third Sector*. Brussels: European Union FP7 (grant agreement 613034). Third Sector Impact.

Seip, Anne-Lise. 1994. *Veiene til velferdsstaten: norsk sosialpolitikk 1920–75*. Oslo: Gyldendal.
Selle, Per. 2016. Frivillighetens marginalisering. *Tidsskrift for velferdsforskning* 1 (01).
Sivesind, Karl Henrik, and Per Selle. 2009. Does public spending "crowd out" nonprofit welfare?. *Comparative Social Research. A Research Annual* no. 26: 105–134. doi:10.1108/S0195-6310(2009)0000026009.
Steinberg, Richard. 2006. Economic Theories of Nonprofit organizations. In *The Nonprofit sector: a research handbook*, eds. Walter W. Powell and Richard Steinberg, 117–139. New Haven, Conn.: Yale University Press.
Swedish Government Inquiries SOU 2016:78. Ordning och reda i välfärden. Stockholm: Ministry of Finance.
Thøgersen, Malene. 2013. *Selvejende institutioner i Danmark. Institutionernes udvikling, udbredelse og karakter på udvalgte samfundsområder*. Aalborg: Netværk for forskning i Civilsamfund og Frivillighed.
Trætteberg, Håkon. 2016. User democracy in schools? Comparing Norwegian schools with nursing homes. *Scandinavian journal of educational research*. doi:10.1080/00313831.2016.1188149.
Trætteberg, Håkon Dalby. 2015. Public, For-Profit, and Nonprofit Welfare Institutions in Norway: Distinctive Goals and Steering Mechanisms or Hybridity in a Dominant State. *VOLUNTAS: International Journal of Voluntary and Nonprofit Organizations* 26 (5): 1620–1638. doi:10.1007/s11266-015-9565-3.
Trætteberg, Håkon Dalby, and Karl Henrik Sivesind. 2015. *Ideelle organisasjoners særtrekk og merverdi på helse- og omsorgsfeltet*. Oslo: Senter for forskning på sivilsamfunn og frivillig sektor.
Verhoeven, Imrat, and Evelien Tonkens. 2013. Talking active citizenship: framing welfare state reform in England and the Netherlands. *Social Policy and Society* 12 (3): 415–426.
Weisbrod, Burton A. 1977. *The Voluntary Nonprofit Sector, an Economic Analysis*. Lexington, MA: D.C. Heath.

Authors' Biography

Karl Henrik Sivesind is Research Professor at the Institute for Social Research, Oslo, Norway. He is currently manager of the project 'Conditions and Impacts of Welfare Mix' funded by the Norwegian Research Council, and he is leader for Work Package 'Elaboration and Testing of Impact Indicators' on the project 'Third Sector Impact—The Contribution of the Third Sector to Europe's Socio-economic Development' funded by the EU's 7th Framework Programme. He has studied changes affecting civil society by analysing data from population surveys and local association surveys as a part of the activities of Centre for Research on Civil Society and Voluntary Sector in Oslo/Bergen. He has also been involved in several comparative research projects about the nonprofit sector and welfare services.

Håkon Solbu Trætteberg is a senior research fellow at the Institute for Social Research, Oslo, Norway. His main research interest is publicly-funded welfare services in general and the importance of the welfare mix in particular. Trætteberg received his Ph.D. in 2016, partly on work presented in this book.

Jo Saglie is Research Professor at the Institute for Social Research, Oslo, Norway. His main research interests include party organisations and intra-party democracy, local elections and local democracy, as well as indigenous politics. His publications include the coedited volume *Indigenous Politics: Institutions, Representation, Mobilisation;* as well as articles in *Journal of Elections, Public Opinion & Parties*; *Local Government Studies*; *Regional and Federal Studies*; and *West European Politics*; among others. He is currently directing the Norwegian Local Election Study and the Norwegian Sámi Parliament Election Study, and he participates in several research projects on Norwegian local government and politics.

Open Access This chapter is licensed under the terms of the Creative Commons Attribution 4.0 International License (http://creativecommons.org/licenses/by/4.0/), which permits use, sharing, adaptation, distribution and reproduction in any medium or format, as long as you give appropriate credit to the original author(s) and the source, provide a link to the Creative Commons license and indicate if changes were made.

The images or other third party material in this chapter are included in the chapter's Creative Commons license, unless indicated otherwise in a credit line to the material. If material is not included in the chapter's Creative Commons license and your intended use is not permitted by statutory regulation or exceeds the permitted use, you will need to obtain permission directly from the copyright holder.

Author Index

A
Aars, Jacob, 262
Abramson, A.J., 118, 122
Adcock, Robert, 211
Alber, Jens, 161
Alford, John, 210
Almqvist, Robert, 123
Andersen, Jørgen Goul, 8, 9, 17, 117, 204, 207, 208, 210, 244, 246
Anders, Lindbom, 251
Anheier, Helmut K., 14, 41, 60, 162, 196
Anttonen, Anneli, 123, 205
Arnesen, Anne-Lise, 18, 159
Arts, Wil A., 105
Ascoli, Ugo, 8, 15, 16, 95, 118, 121

B
Baker, Paula C., 210
Baldersheim, Harald, 159
Bang, Henrik P., 210, 213
Bartlett, Will, 209
Béland, Daniel, 117
Ben-Ner, Avner, 243
Bergman, Torbjörn, 117
Bertelsen, Tilde Marie, 127
Blomqvist, Paula, 9, 118, 121, 123, 209, 266, 298
Bogason, Peter, 166
Bogen, Hanne, 54, 56, 58, 266
Böhlmark, Anders, 6, 251, 266, 299
Boje, Thomas P., 40, 44, 207, 208
Børhaug, Kjetil, 266, 267, 278
Boris, Elizabeth T., 15
Boston, Jonathan, 118, 121
Botti, Simona, 263
Bouckaert, Geert, 163, 262
Brennan, Deborah, 292
Bugge, Hanna, 262, 264, 270
Bunar, Nihad, 194
Bundesen, Peter, 43, 61, 163, 196

Author Index

Burau, Viola, 117, 250
Burns, Karen E., 205
Busse, Jason W., 205, 265

C

Cavenago, Dario, 118, 122, 196
Christensen, Dag Arne, 262, 266, 271, 277, 279
Christensen, Karen, 35, 54, 205, 266, 292, 293
Clarke, John, 205
Clemens, Elisabeth S., 12
Collier, David, 211
Comondore, Vikram R., 205, 265
Cook, Deborah J., 205

D

Dahlberg, Matz, 64
Dahler-Larsen, Elizabeth, 118
Dahl, Hanne Marlene, 119, 124, 125
Daly, Mary, 206
Devereaux, P.J., 205, 265
Diefenbach, Thomas, 292
Dixon, Ruth, 205, 209, 265
Dølvik, Jon Erik, T., 118, 162, 194
Domberger, Simon, 205
Donahue, John D., 77–80, 160
Donahue, Johna, 162, 194
Dunleavy, Patric, 118, 121
Dunning, Thad, 23

E

Eikås, Magne, 290
Einarsson, Torbjörn, 38
Einhorn, Eric S., 117

Ejersbo, Niels, 163, 164
Eliassen, Erik, 266
Elinder, Mikael, 64, 121
Engedal, Knut, 127, 218
Eriksen, Erik Oddvar, 205
Erlandsson, Sara, 35, 48, 119, 127
Esping-Andersen, Gøsta, 4, 117, 160
Evers, Adalbert, 13, 162, 208, 297

F

Faaborg-Midtfyn Kommune, 171, 178, 182
Feltenius, David, 118
Ferlie, Ewan, 118, 121
Fladmoe, Audun, 262, 264, 270
Fløtten, Tone, 118
Fridberg, Torben, 2, 75

G

Gautun, Heidi, 127, 240, 266
Gelissen, John, 105
Gerring, John, 20
Gidron, Benjamin, 161
Gjevjon, Edith Roth, 127
Goertz, Gary, 211
Goodin, Robert E., 16
Gregg, G., 262
Greve, Carsten, 163, 164
Grødem, Anne Skevik, 266
Grønbjerg, Kristen A., 12, 163, 196, 209
Grønlie, Tore, 250
Grønningsæter, Arne Backer, 54, 56, 58
Guillemard, Anne-Marie, 208, 297
Gulbrandsen, Lars, 266

Gustafsson, Agne, 126
Gustafsson, Jan-Eric, 195, 196
Gustavsen, Annelin, 208

H
Habermann, Ulla, 194, 196
Haines, Ted, 205
Hansen, Allan Dreyer, 213
Hansen, Hans-Tore, 262
Hansmann, H., 12, 290
Hanushek, Eric A., 205
Hartman, Laura, 118, 266, 299
Hatlebakk, Ingrid Myrset, 56
Haugen, Per Kristian, 127, 218
Haugh, Helen, 16
Haverinen, Riitta, 13
Heikki, Ervasti, 2, 75
Helby Petersen, Ole, 299
Helgøy, Ingrid, 18
Helliwell, John F., 2
Hendriks, Frank, 9, 126
Henrekson, Magnus, 4
Henriksen, Lars Skov, 43, 59, 61, 161, 163, 196, 250
Hermansen, 127, 240
Hernes, Helga M., 9, 204, 250
Herning, kommune, 125
Herning, Linn, 62, 286
Hicks, Timothy, 104
Hinrichs, Karl, 207
Hippe, Fløtten, J.M., 162, 194
Hippe, Jon M., 118
Hirschman, Albert O., 11, 123, 209
Hjelmar, Ulf, 120, 151, 162, 196, 266, 299
Hjerm, Mikael, 2, 75
Hoff, Jens Villiam, 8, 9, 17, 213

Holford, John, 10
Holmlund, Helena, 6, 251, 299
Homme, Anne, 18
Hood, Christopher, 118, 121, 160, 205, 265, 299
Hoskins, Bryony L., 10, 204, 206
Hvid, Helge, 117, 123
Hvinden, Bjørn, 204

I
Ibsen, Bjarne, 194, 196
Isaksson, David, 64
Iyengar, Sheena S., 263

J
Jacobsen, Frode Fadnes, 35, 54, 266
James, Oliver, 263, 279
Janoski, Thomas, 250
Jarl, Maria, 168
Jensen, Carsten, 262
Jensen, Per H., 204, 205
Jenson, Jane, 292
Johansson, Håkan, 4, 64, 204
Johansson, Mairon, 4, 64
Johansson, Ola, 48
Jordahl, Henrik, 4, 64, 121, 127
Jordfald, Bård, 118, 162, 194
Jørgensen, Torben Beck, 163, 164, 170
Julian, Le Grand, 265

K
Kamp, Annette, 117, 123
Kangas, Olli, 75, 207
Karlsen, Rune, 262, 264, 270

Kersting, Norbert, 159
Kiser, Larry, 210
Kitson, Michael, 16
Kjølsrød, Lise, 9, 204, 249
Knudsen, Tim, 60, 61
Kramer, Ralph M., 161
Kristiansen, Mads Bøge, 4
Kröger, Teppo, 9, 204, 205, 250
Kronbøl, Trine, 87
Kuhnle, Stein, 295
Kumlin, Staffan, 262, 264, 270

L

Larsen, Patricia Thor, 266
Laura, Hartman, 48, 118, 266, 299
Layard, Richard, 2
Le Grand, Julian, 122, 209, 263, 265, 278
Leichsenring, Kai, 13
Lewis, Jane, 206
Lidström, Aanders, 9
Lidström, Anders, 126
Lindahl, Mikael, 266
Lindblom, Anders, 64
Link, Susanne, 205
Lipsky, Michael, 298
Logue, John, 117
Lorentzen, Håkon, 26, 38
Lotsberg, Dag Øyvind, 266, 267, 278
Loughlin, John, 9, 126
Lounsbury, Michael, 213
Lundahl, Lisbeth, 18, 159
Lundbäck, Mattias, 15
Lundberg, Anders, 15
Lundström, Tommy, 2, 38, 194

Lyttkens, Carl Hampus, 48

M

Mariani, Laura, 118, 122, 196
Marshall, T.H., 204
Meagher, Gabrielle, 7, 13, 95, 205, 251, 293
Meinow, Bettina, 289
Meuleman, Louis, 163
Midtbø, Tor, 271, 277, 279
Miller, Michelle A., 262, 279
Miller, Thomas I., 262, 279
Morel, Nathalie, 292
Moria-erklæringen, Soria, 49

N

Nasi, Greta, 210
Newman, Janet E., 5, 10, 205
Norsk senter for menneskerettigheter, 205
Nyberg, Linda, 100
Nye, Joseph, 160
Nyhlén, Jon, 159, 164, 170

O

Oakerson, Ronald, 210
Ocasio, William, 213
Ødegård, Anne Mette, 84
Öhrvall, Richard, 64, 127
Olsen, Johan P., 204
Osborne, Stephen P., 118, 122, 210
Östersunds kommun, 130, 131
Ostrom, Elinor, 210

Ostrom, Vincent, 210

P

Palier, Bruno, 208, 292
Palme, Joakim, 117, 292
Parker, Marti G., 289
Parks, Roger B., 210
Percy, Stephen L., 210
Perloff, J.M., 300
Pestoff, Victor A., 162
Petersen, Ole Helby, 120, 162, 196, 266
Petersson, Olof, 8
Pfau-Effinger, Birgit, 204
Phillips, Susan D., 78–80, 102, 162, 208
Pierre, Jon, 118, 120, 208
Pierson, Paul, 49, 120
Politt, Christopher, 163
Potucek, Martin, 207, 208
Powell, Martin A., 162

R

Radnor, Zoe, 210
Ranci, Costanzo, 8, 15, 16, 95, 118, 121
Rasmussen, Bente, 119, 124, 125
Ravindran, Nikila C., 205, 265
Ringdal, Kristen, 2, 75
Røiseland, Asbjørn, 208
Rokkan, Stein, 61
Rolland, Asle, 263
Romøren, Tor Inge, 127
Rönnberg, Linda, 18, 168
Rose, Lawrence E., 87, 159, 210, 250
Rostgaard, Tine, 8, 127, 204, 250

Rothstein, Bo, 2, 9, 60, 61, 204, 205, 207–209, 297, 298
Ryzin, Van, 262

S

Sachs, Jeffrey D., 2
Salamon, Lester M., 4, 12–15, 36, 38, 40, 41, 60, 118, 122, 161, 163, 293, 295, 301, 304
Seeleib-Kaiser, Martin, 161
Segaard, Signe Bock, 17, 76, 84, 90, 107, 160, 169, 194
Seip, Anne-Lise, 295
Sejersted, Francis, 9
Sejersted, Fredri, 84
Selle, Per, 26, 38, 60, 250, 290, 295
Sivesind, Karl Henrik, 2, 17, 18, 35, 38, 40, 44, 50, 56, 60, 61, 95, 105, 118, 121, 160, 169, 263, 265, 266, 294, 295
Smith, Nick, 205
Smith, Steven Rathgeb, 12, 162, 163, 196, 208, 209, 250
Söderström, Lars, 48
Sokolowski, S. Wojciech, 36, 40, 41, 60, 295
Sollentuna kommun, 130, 173, 174, 181, 183, 187–189
Sørensen, Eva, 79, 93, 210
Sörlin, Sverker, 195, 196
St. Meld, 267, 268
Steen-Johnsen, Kari, 262, 264, 270
Steinberg, Richard, 12, 14, 15, 57, 163, 251, 293, 295
Steuerle, C. Eugine, 15
Stolt, Ragnar, 121, 127, 266
Stone, Samuel B., 205, 265

Storm, Palle, 35, 48
Strantz, Anneli, 35, 48
Stringer, Bernadette, 205
Strøm, Kaare, 117
Szebehely, Marta, 7, 13, 35, 48, 95, 107, 119, 251, 293

T

Taylor-Gooby, Peter, 34
Thelen, Kathleen, 163
Thøgersen, Malene, 45, 46, 67, 93, 107, 165, 296
Thornton, Patricia H., 213
Thorslund, Mats, 289
Thuen, Harald, 194, 196
Toepler, Stefan, 12, 13, 15, 163
Tonkens, Evelien, 297
Torfing, Jacob, 79, 93
Traetteberg, Håkon Dalby, 35, 54, 56, 60, 118, 121, 263, 266, 291, 293, 294, 297
Trætteberg, Håkon, 297
Trägårdh, Lars, 3, 61, 63, 207, 251
Tranvik, Tommy, 250
Trydegård, Gunn-Britt, 35, 48
Tveit, Knut, 194, 196

U

Ulrika Winblad, 127

V

Vabø, Mia, 35, 54, 55, 62, 123, 128, 266
Vabo, Signy Irene, 18, 96, 98, 117
van der Veen, Ruud, 10
Van de Walle, Steven, 262, 279

Vandivort, Martha B., 210
Van Ryzin, Gregg, 262, 279
Verhoeven, Imrat, 297
Vetter, Angelika, 159
Vidler, Elizabeth, 205
Vlachos, Jonas, 47
Vlacos, Jonas, 195, 196
Voitto, Helander, 44
Vrangbæk, Karsten, 163, 164, 170, 266

W

Waddan, Alex, 117
Walsh, Kieron, 123, 124
Weigård, Jarle, 205
Weisbrod, Burton Allen., 12, 13, 57, 64, 118, 121, 122, 195, 295
Westmarland, Louise, 205
Whitaker, Gordon P., 210
Wide, Jessika, 118
Wijkström, Filip, 2, 38, 194
Wiklund, Stefan, 48
Wilson, Rick, 210
Winblad, Ulrika, 64, 266
Wintersberger, Helmut, 162
Wistow, Gerald, 13
Woessmann, Ludger, 205
Wollebæk, Dag, 26, 38, 262, 264, 270

Z

Zeckhauser, Richard J., 77–80, 162, 194
Zhou, Qi, 205, 265
Zimmer, Annette, 161, 250
Zweifel, Peter, 48

Subject Index

A

Active citizenship, 5, 7–11, 17–19, 76, 97, 99, 102, 118, 148, 160, 204–214, 224, 225, 237, 238, 247, 249–253, 263, 265, 279, 285, 287, 288, 292, 293, 305

Asker (municipality in Norway), 214

B

Black hole of democracy (Blomqvist and Rothstein), 298

Bourgeoisie, 61

Burden shift, 297

Business sector, 301

By-law, 91, 186

C

Centre-right government, 62, 104

Certification agency, 15

Child and family protection, 56, 59–61

Child and juvenile welfare, 42, 50

Choice, 2, 4–6, 11, 48, 61, 88, 93, 95, 96, 98, 101, 118, 119, 121, 122, 124, 129, 131, 132, 142, 145, 147–149, 165, 192, 194, 204, 209, 211, 212, 215, 225, 226, 228, 230, 237, 238, 240, 241, 251, 252, 263, 265, 267, 278, 279, 285, 287, 289, 295, 300, 305

Citizenship, 118, 148, 204, 291

Civil society, 3, 10, 61, 128, 129, 160, 204, 208, 288

Civil society organization, 49

Closed negotiations, 59, 287

Closed tenders, 49, 60

Collaborative steering, 164, 194

Commercial firm/company, 49, 301

Commercial incentive, 57, 59, 301, 303
Commercialisation, 16, 286
The common good, 305
Compact (between the Government and nonprofit sector), 65
Competition, 7, 8, 35, 49, 54, 56, 62, 66, 79, 96, 104, 121, 122, 140, 164, 165, 170, 178, 182–184, 192, 193, 216, 228–230, 235, 239, 248, 265, 287, 294, 296, 299, 300, 302
Competitive dialogue, 82
Competitive steering, 164
Compulsory education, 52, 165, 166
Conservative coalition government, 65
Conservative government, 3, 53, 265
Consultation, 82, 219, 231, 242
Consultative arrangements, 298
Contracting, 15, 34, 35, 50, 54, 55, 62, 77, 78, 80, 86, 99, 119, 121, 123, 124, 128, 132, 134, 149, 302
Contracting agency, 55, 60, 66
Contracting authority, 83–85, 87
Control-based steering, 164
Co-operative, 48
Core welfare services, 4, 34, 37, 60, 294
Corporative model, 95
Cost control, 56
Counter-cultural popular movement, 61
Curriculum, 6, 169, 184, 195
Customer choice/user choice, 8, 17, 35, 50, 55, 56, 66, 80, 96, 101, 105, 123, 168, 172, 215, 216, 218, 224, 237, 242, 247, 248, 251, 252, 265, 272, 279, 286, 289, 290, 294, 296–299, 301, 302, 304

D

Day-care for children, 42, 45, 83–85. *See also* Kindergarten
Decentralization, 50
Demand-based model (Ascoli and Ranci), 8, 16
Dementia, 127, 129, 138, 146, 218
Denmark, 7, 8, 17, 19, 20, 24, 25, 35, 36, 38, 40–45, 57–61, 65, 75, 81, 85, 86, 89–92, 94, 95, 99, 100, 105, 118, 120, 125, 127, 141, 145, 147, 165, 166, 168, 172, 176–178, 180, 184, 187, 189–191, 193–195, 214, 215, 218, 219, 223–228, 230, 231, 236, 238–240, 246, 248, 262, 286, 289, 296, 299
Diaconal college, 53
Diaconal hospital, 53
Direct government, 77, 78, 98
Disconnected government, 76, 79, 90, 93, 100, 101
Distinctiveness, 15, 60, 64, 184, 190, 191, 194–197, 217, 226–229, 242, 248, 253, 288, 290, 291
Distinctive role, 35, 301
Distinctive service profile, 7, 293, 294, 300, 302

E

Economic nonprofit theory, 57

Subject Index

Economic sector, 38, 51, 286
The Economist, 2, 6
Elderly care, 5, 7, 8, 17–19, 45, 50, 55, 62, 66, 75, 77, 81, 94–98, 100, 102–104, 118, 119, 123, 126, 129, 131, 132, 134, 139, 140, 144–146, 151, 205, 240, 247, 262, 266, 289, 292–294, 296, 299, 304
Empowerment, 17, 76, 98, 122, 204, 209–212, 214, 218, 220, 224, 230, 231, 237, 238, 240, 242, 244, 246–248, 263, 269, 285, 287, 288, 295
Equivalent service quality, 5, 19, 293, 295
Equivalent services, 297, 304
EU-directive, 19, 81, 83, 85–88, 100, 302
EU Directive on the award of concession contracts (Directive 2014/23/EU), 88
EU-regulation, 86, 287
European Economic Area (EEA treaty), 59
Exit (Hirschman), 11, 209

F

Faaborg-Midtfyn (municipality in Denmark), 21, 24, 125, 141, 144, 178, 182
Financial control, 171, 174, 177, 178, 191
Foundation, 7, 48, 175, 290, 301
Frame-conditions, 301, 305
Framework agreement, 7, 54, 55, 60, 62, 96

Freedom of Choice Act (LOV 2008:962) (Sweden), 63, 119, 149, 296, 302
Free establishment (right to), 48, 58, 64, 166, 286, 288, 299, 303
Free school, 6, 43, 60, 61, 286, 296
Full-time equivalent employees (FTE), 51

G

Governance, 5, 7, 8, 10, 11, 15, 18, 19, 34, 35, 38, 42, 59, 62, 66, 79, 93, 94, 97, 101, 103, 118, 131, 137, 140, 147, 150, 163–165, 194, 205, 252, 285, 288, 291–294, 296, 300, 301, 303
Governing through contracts, 123, 124, 132
Government regulations, 305

H

Herning (municipality in Denmark), 21, 24, 286
Higher education, 53
Home-based care, 42, 45, 55
Hospitals, 44, 48, 53
Human rights, 205, 252, 289, 304

I

Independent nursing home, 95, 99, 101, 103, 286
Independent school, 61, 95, 101, 105, 166, 195, 286

Indirect government, 77, 79, 91, 94, 96, 98, 101
In-house, 14, 62
In-house (case) law, 66, 86, 87, 96, 98
In-house contracts, 302, 304
In-house system, 58
Inpatient medical care, 48
Inspections, 91, 123, 134, 144, 164, 170, 177
Institutional context, 20, 295, 301
Institutional sector, 11, 12, 15, 17, 20, 37, 65, 160, 169, 203, 205, 208, 214, 218, 221, 224, 225, 230, 237, 239, 240, 242, 247, 285, 289, 291–294
Interdependence theory (Salamon), 12
International Classification of Non-Profit Institutions (ICNPO), 42
Invisible hand, 148
Involvement, 94, 98, 162, 195, 208, 210, 218, 233, 286, 298

K

Kindergarten, 45, 56, 61, 65, 66, 262, 263, 265–271, 273–276, 278, 286, 296. *See also* Day-care for children

L

Layered government, 80, 98
Liberal model, 8, 40
Light Touch Regime (UK), 302
Limited company, 47, 53

Long-term care, 61, 131, 219
Long-term contract, 66
Løten (municipality in Norway), 23, 172
Lower secondary education, 75, 81, 83, 90–92, 94, 99, 103

M

Management by contract, 123
Market competition, 132, 304
Market-emulating forms of governance, 5, 299
Market-emulating tools of governance, 58, 287, 303, 304
Marketization/marketized, 299
Market share, 37, 56, 299, 300
Mental health care, 50, 53
Migrant, 54
Mission statement, 290, 294, 301, 305
Mixed economy, 11, 205
Monopoly, 63, 78, 300
Montessori school, 52, 172, 180, 268

N

National agencies, 35, 299
Neo-liberal, 2
New public management (NPM), 33, 35, 59, 118, 120, 121, 160, 162, 265, 292
Non-commercial, 49, 52, 103, 265
Non-priority services, 84, 85
Nonprofit employment, 44, 50, 54–56, 58, 65, 68
Nonprofit institution, 43, 45, 50, 56, 63, 91, 213, 240, 244, 248

Subject Index

Nonprofit organisation, 84, 85, 127, 162, 163, 167, 196
Nonprofit provider, 35, 50, 57, 59, 61, 62, 66, 76, 84, 88, 96, 118, 122, 160, 165, 166, 174, 192, 194, 203, 204, 247, 250, 252
Nonprofits, 41, 54, 57, 64, 66, 179, 186, 235, 236, 240, 243, 247
Nonprofit sector, 38, 40, 41, 43, 49, 50, 53, 54, 57, 60, 61, 64–66, 68, 95, 105, 195
Nonpublic provider, 15, 79, 216, 221, 250
The Nordic countries, 2
Nordic welfare model, 59
Norway, 7, 8, 14, 19, 22, 25, 35, 38, 40, 41, 49, 51–53, 55–61, 65, 66, 76, 83, 85, 87, 90–92, 94, 96, 99, 100, 104, 105, 118, 125, 127, 135, 140, 147, 150, 160, 165, 166, 168, 171, 175, 178, 185, 187, 188, 190–196, 214, 215, 218, 219, 221, 222, 224–226, 229–231, 234, 235, 238–241, 248, 262, 265, 266, 268, 277, 279, 285, 287, 296, 299
NPM tools, 7, 60, 66, 294
Nursing homes, 7, 9, 19, 25, 42, 54, 56, 95, 97, 101, 118–120, 125, 127–130, 132, 133, 135–139, 141–146, 215–220, 222, 223, 230, 240–242, 244, 246, 247, 249, 252, 264, 266, 268, 271, 273–275, 278, 289, 290, 293, 297

O

Oligopoly, 300
Open tenders, 7, 35, 56, 59, 299, 301, 303
Operating agreement, 45
Operating contract, 45, 54, 68
Östersund (municipality in Sweden), 21, 24, 173, 175, 180, 181, 187, 189
Out-contracting, 55, 124, 128, 132, 134, 149
Outpatient health and medical treatment, 48
Överenskommelsen (Sweden), 4

P

Paid employment, 37, 38, 43, 44, 51
Parallel government, 102
Participation, 1, 8, 10, 11, 97, 99, 128, 204, 206, 209–211, 214, 218, 221, 224, 227, 234, 239, 245–248, 263, 265, 266, 269, 277, 285–288
Payoff discretion, 78, 103
Pedagogies, 6, 61, 166
Performance measurement, 78
Programme for International Student Assessment (PISA), 6, 299
Popular movement, 2, 298
Powerlessness, 205, 292, 297
Practical user-steered assistance (Norway), 55
Preference discretion, 78
Primary education, 91
Primary health care, 48, 64

322 Subject Index

Private actor, 76, 78, 160, 167, 191
Private schools, 6, 22, 43, 47, 49, 53, 90–93, 100, 101, 103, 159, 161, 164, 166–168, 177, 193–195, 261, 268, 270, 274, 276
Privatization, 49, 61, 64, 65
Production discretion, 78
Professional discretion, 298
Professionals, 62, 124, 139, 186
For-profit, 14, 34, 36, 44, 46, 54, 56–58, 64, 118, 121, 125–127, 135, 138, 247, 251, 289, 294, 295
For-profit employment, 40, 45, 50, 62, 69
For-profit organisation, 3, 40
Profit-oriented companies, 56, 66
For-profit sector, 5, 7, 40, 42, 45, 47, 49, 50, 58, 64–66, 76, 95, 104, 301–303, 305
Psychiatric hospital/clinic, 53
Public certification, 8
Public employment, 2, 36, 38, 41, 44, 50, 57, 61, 62, 68
Publicly funded service, 11, 37, 50, 57
Public procurement, 3, 34, 53, 54, 59, 75, 81–87, 89, 96, 100, 302
Public Procurement Act, 84
Public procurement directive (EU) (Directive 2004/18/EC) replaced by (Directive 2014/24/EU), 67
Public procurement law, 3, 287

Public schools, 2, 6, 21, 22, 43, 61, 92, 104, 159, 161, 164, 165, 167, 168, 171, 172
Public sector, 3, 5, 7, 8, 12, 14–18, 33, 34, 43, 44, 46, 50, 51, 53, 58, 59, 61, 62, 65, 90, 92, 94, 102, 162, 203, 244, 253, 261, 272, 292, 294, 300, 304

Q

Quality control, 55, 177, 178, 191
Quasi-market, 3, 4, 7, 10, 16, 35, 36, 56, 57, 59, 62, 63, 101

R

Red–green government, 49, 53
Regulation, 1, 4, 13, 16, 18, 33, 34, 36, 49, 59, 66–68, 79, 83–85, 93, 97, 100, 103, 159, 162, 167, 169, 172, 174, 176, 178, 190, 194, 196, 203, 225, 244, 251, 252, 262, 278, 279, 285, 287, 288, 291, 292, 296, 300, 302, 303
Rehabilitation (medical), 50, 53, 61
Religion, 12, 63, 228, 272, 295
Religious school, 16

S

Satellite account for non-profit institutions, 45, 51
Scandinavia, 76, 83, 94, 95, 104, 161, 163, 168, 182, 192, 196, 204, 215, 234, 251, 252, 286,

Subject Index

293, 294, 296, 297, 300, 302, 303, 305
Scandinavian welfare goals, 296, 305
Scandinavian welfare model, 6, 8, 18, 33, 59, 249–251, 286, 293, 295, 298, 300, 303, 305
Self-owning institution, 7, 43, 45, 58, 60, 61, 66, 68, 86, 96, 296
Semi-autonomous agency, 35, 50
Service area, 1, 3, 5, 7, 8, 12, 18, 19, 25, 33, 34, 36, 40, 43, 46, 47, 50, 57, 60, 65, 66, 205, 214, 237, 244, 245, 247, 286, 288, 291
Service concession, 53, 58, 66, 83, 84, 87, 91, 96, 301, 302, 304
Service contract, 49, 54, 65, 67
Social democratic model, 41, 207, 299
Social democratic party, 62, 180
Social democratic regime, 297
Social insurances, 60
Social movement, 61, 63
Social origins theory (Salamon and Anheier), 41
Sollentuna (municipality in Sweden), 174, 181
Somatic hospital/clinic, 54
Specialist health system, 58
Stakeholder, 65, 231, 243, 291, 301, 305
State funding, 43, 185
Statistics Denmark, 51, 68
Statistics Norway, 51, 53, 54, 68, 267
Statistics Sweden, 69
Steinkjer (municipality in Norway), 179

Street-level bureaucrats, 250, 298
Subcontractor, 55
Substance abuse treatment, 42, 48, 50, 56, 58, 61
Supply-side model (Ascoli and Ranci), 296
Sweden, 2, 3, 6, 7, 14, 17, 19–21, 35, 36, 38, 40–42, 46, 48, 49, 57, 58, 60–62, 65

T

Tender document, 56, 247, 299
Third sector, 11, 60, 162, 301, 304
Tools of governance, 8, 42, 58, 62, 66, 101, 287, 303, 304
Transfer of profit, 4, 66, 167, 299, 302, 303
Treatment of drug and alcohol addiction, 296

U

Universalism, 250
Universal rights, 76, 298
Universal welfare state, 4, 207
Upper secondary education, 6
User-choice, 6
User democracy, 298

V

Venture capitalist, 63, 286
Voice (Hirschman), 11, 209
Voluntary organisation, 290
Volunteer, 11, 242
Voucher, 6, 7, 14, 35, 63, 296, 303

W

Waldorf school, 183
Welfare area, 37, 49, 62, 65, 68, 170
Welfare conglomerate, 3, 64, 286
Welfare employees, 3, 38, 40, 47, 64
Welfare employment, 38, 40, 41, 49, 50, 57, 61, 62, 296, 301, 305
Welfare mix, 11, 13, 18, 67, 75, 77, 80, 84, 88, 89, 94, 98–100, 102, 103, 161, 167, 195, 203, 205, 253, 287, 292, 293, 295, 302
Welfare municipalities, 9, 204, 250
Welfare provider mix, 15, 38, 43, 46, 49, 62, 66, 303
Welfare reform, 3, 5, 50, 60
Welfare state, 1–4, 11, 36, 46, 47, 63, 75, 80, 94, 104, 105, 159, 163, 194, 197, 204, 207, 208, 261, 263, 265, 270, 295, 298

Subject Index   **325**

© The Editor(s) (if applicable) and The Author(s) 2017. This book is an open access publication.

Open Access This book is licensed under the terms of the Creative Commons Attribution 4.0 International License (http://creativecommons.org/licenses/by/4.0/), which permits use, sharing, adaptation, distribution and reproduction in any medium or format, as long as you give appropriate credit to the original author(s) and the source, provide a link to the Creative Commons license and indicate if changes were made.

    The images or other third party material in this book are included in the book's Creative Commons license, unless indicated otherwise in a credit line to the material. If material is not included in the book's Creative Commons license and your intended use is not permitted by statutory regulation or exceeds the permitted use, you will need to obtain permission directly from the copyright holder.

The manufacturer's authorised representative in the EU is Springer Nature Customer Service Centre GmbH, Europaplatz 3, 69115 Heidelberg, Germany. If you have any concerns regarding our products, please contact ProductSafety@springernature.com

Printed and bound by CPI Group (UK) Ltd, Croydon, CR0 4YY
23/03/2026
02076670-0006